ADVANCED DUNGEONS & DRAGONS™

SPECIAL REFERENCE WORK

MONSTER MANUAL

4th Edition, August, 1979

AN ALPHABETICAL COMPENDIUM OF ALL OF THE MONSTERS FOUND IN
ADVANCED DUNGEONS & DRAGONS, INCLUDING ATTACKS, DAMAGE,
SPECIAL ABILITIES, AND DESCRIPTIONS.

by Gary Gygax

Illustrations by

David C. Sutherland III   Tom Wham
D.A. Trampier   Jean Wells

Cover by Jeff Easley

TSR, Inc.
P.O. Box 756
Lake Geneva,
WI 53147

TSR (UK) Ltd.
The Mill, Rathmore Rd.
Cambridge CB1 4AD
United Kingdom

Distributed to the book trade in the United States by Random House, Inc. and in Canada by Random House of Canada, Ltd.

Inquiries regarding this work should be accompanied by a stamped envelope and sent to:
TSR Hobbies, Inc., POB 756, Lake Geneva, WI 53147

printed in the u.s.a.

FOREWORD

It is with a certain measure of pride that we at TSR bring you this second part of the new DUNGEONS & DRAGONS releases, the long-awaited MONSTER MANUAL for ADVANCED D & D. We are doubly proud of the format of this book — i.e., its special hard cover, a "first" in the gaming world and another step in our continuing quest for top quality products.

As time goes on, the D & D phenomenon shows no sign of subsiding — indeed, the popularity of DUNGEONS & DRAGONS continues to grow and grow. This trend is very gratifying to us at TSR, and encourages us to devote even more time and attention to D & D (witness this series of ADVANCED DUNGEONS & DRAGONS) and related materials — playing aids, accessories, etc. Our aim is to provide a top-quality family of products for use with the DUNGEONS & DRAGONS game system, items that we hope you will find useful, innovative, and enjoyable.

With the outstanding growth of DUNGEONS & DRAGONS has come the growth of TSR Hobbies, since it is no secret that the fantastic response to D & D has allowed TSR to expand and explore many new directions in the gaming hobby. Therefore, we owe our thanks to you — the many devoted gamers — who have supported TSR through your enthusiasm, your encouragement, and finally, your purchases. Our livelihood depends upon your continued support, and we intend to keep earning it by continuing to bring you innovative products in the future. We appreciate the widespread audience that our games (and especially D & D) have achieved, and we look forward to increasing the exposure of our games and rules. Without such an enthusiastic and loyal following, this would not be possible. So, we thank you!

The success of DUNGEONS & DRAGONS has spawned a considerable number of imitations and spin-off products, perhaps inevitably. Some of these have merit; many, however, do not — and although we may concede their right to exist (however dependent they may be on D & D's audience), we would caution the prospective buyer to consider their true value and not to be confused with those items which bear the DUNGEONS & DRAGONS or ADVANCED DUNGEONS & DRAGONS name and constitute the official D & D family of products. As for value, let the others be measured against the standard of quality we have striven for — a hardbound encyclopedia of monsters, for instance, as opposed to a low quality collection which is poorly assembled and bound.

This present work, as will be apparent from its sheer bulk alone, is the result of a considerable amount of work and preparation by many persons. All this has been undertaken with an eye toward providing a final result which can be regarded as the definitive collection of monsters for ADVANCED DUNGEONS & DRAGONS — an encyclopedic collection of information certain to be of invaluable use to players and Dungeon Masters alike, complete with game specifications, background details and, in many cases, with an illustration in addition! Of course, no work can be truly definitive, for as long as players possess an active imagination, many new and fascinating monsters will continue to arise — and this is only as it should be.

One final note: as valuable as this volume is with its wealth of information, some DM's may wisely wish to forbid their players from referring to the MANUAL in the midst of an encounter, since it will be considerably more challenging to confront a monster without an instant rundown of its strengths and weaknesses — and besides, a D & D player's true mettle (and knowledge) will be put to the test. And as even the most casual D & D player knows, that's what this fascinating game is all about . . .

Read on, and enjoy!

Mike Carr

27 September 1977

ALPHABETICAL TABLE OF CONTENTS

$\mathfrak{V}$ VAMPIRE

$\mathfrak{W}$ WASP, GIANT — WATER WEIRD — WEASEL, GIANT — WHALE — WIGHT — WILL-O-WISP — WIND WALKER — WOLF — WOLVERINE — WRAITH — WYVERN

$\mathfrak{X}$ XORN

$\mathfrak{Y}$ YETI

$\mathfrak{Z}$ ZOMBIE

PREFACE

The various creatures contained herein are for use in **ADVANCED DUNGEONS & DRAGONS**. Parameters have been set for that game. Those monsters drawn from the original work, co-authored with Dave Arneson, have been revised and expanded upon accordingly. Except as noted, all new monsters are strictly of this author's creation — just as all those which appeared in *The Strategic Review* were — and I take the burden of full responsibility for them. It is necessary to acknowledge the contributions of the following persons: Steve Marsh for devising the creatures for undersea encounters which originally appeared in *BLACKMOOR*, as I have radically altered them herein; Erol Otus for doing the preliminary work and illustrations of the *anhkheg* and *remorhaz* which appeared in *The Dragon*; Ernie Gygax for the *water weird* and for his help in solidifying many of the characteristics of the creatures herein; Terry Kuntz, who was never thanked for his prototypical beholder, a revised version of which was included in *GREYHAWK*; to the whole crew at TSR, and to Brian Blume, Tim Kask, and Dave Sutherland in particular, is due thanks for helping me get this whole project into a manuscript; and to my wife, Mary, who has been stuck with the job of typing most of the manuscript, my apologies for mistakes needing correcting and my admiration for staying with it day after day. If I have missed thanking any other person, please pardon the oversight.

Gary Gygax

EXPLANATORY NOTES

The term **"monster"** is used throughout this work in two manners. Its first, and most important, meaning is to designate *any* creature encountered — hostile or otherwise, human, humanoid, or beast. Until the encountering party determines what they have come upon, it is a *monster*. The secondary usage of the term is in the usual sense: a horrible or wicked creature of some sort. Thus, a "monster" is encountered during the course of a dungeon expedition, and it is discovered to be an evil high priest, who just might turn out to be a monster in the other sense as well. Note, however, that despite this terminology, humans (and such kin as dwarves, elves, gnomes, half-elves, and haflings) always use the matrix for humans when attacking, even if such humans were encountered as "monsters" in the course of an adventure.

FREQUENCY refers to the likelihood of a particular creature being encountered in a region or area where it might be an inhabitant. *Very rare* indicates a 4% chance of occurrence, *rare* indicates an 11% chance, *uncommon* indicates a 20% chance, and *common* indicates a 65% chance. These probabilities are considered in the encounter matrices found in **ADVANCED DUNGEONS & DRAGONS, DUNGEON MASTER'S GUIDE.**

NUMBER APPEARING indicates a good average spread. This number is furnished as a guideline only, and it should be altered to suit the circumstances particular to any adventure as the need arises. It is not generally recommended for use in establishing the population of dungeon levels.

ARMOR CLASS describes the general type of protection worn by humans or humanoid creatures, protection inherent to the creature due to its physical structure or magical nature, or the degree of difficulty of hitting a creature due to its speed, reflexes, etc.

MOVE shows the relative speed of a creature on a constant basis. Higher speeds may be possible for short periods, but as this is generally applicable to all sorts of creatures, a constant is shown. It can be scaled to whatever time period is desired by adjusting ground scale accordingly. The number might be double, and this indicates that the creature can travel in two mediums or modes:

/#''	= flying speed
//#''	= swimming speed
(#'')	= burrowing speed
*#''	= speed in web

HIT DICE indicates the parameters of the number of hit points a creature can withstand before being killed. Unless stated otherwise, hit dice are 8-sided (1-8 hit points). The indicated number of dice are rolled, and the numbers shown on each are added together to arrive at a total number of hit points. Some creatures have hit points which are less than a full 8-sided die, and this is shown by stating their hit dice as a point spread. Some creatures have additional points added to their hit dice; this is indicated by a plus sign followed by a number shown after the number of hit dice they have, i.e. *HIT DICE: 4 + 4* (which equals 4-32 hit points +4 hit points, or 8-36 hit points).

% IN LAIR indicates the chance of encountering the monster in question where it domiciles and stores its treasure (if any). If a monster encountered is not in its lair it will not have any treasure unless it carries "individual" treasure or some form of magic. Whether or not an encounter is occurring in the monster's lair might be totally unknown to the person or persons involved until after the outcome of the encounter is resolved.

TREASURE TYPE refers to the table which shows the parameters for various types of valuables which the monster in question might possess. If individual treasure is indicated, each individual monster of that type will carry, or possibly carry, the treasure shown. Otherwise, treasures are only found in the lairs of monsters, as explained above. Note also that although an encounter occurs in a monster's lair, and the monster possesses some treasure type, this does not automatically mean that the adventurers will gain treasure by defeating the monster. Most treasure types show probabilities for various kinds of wealth to occur in the treasure of the monster. If subsequent dice rolls indicate that that form of treasure is not in the monster's trove, then it is not there, and it is quite possible to come up with no wealth (including magical items) of any sort in a monster's lair despite the fact that a treasure type is indicated. Finally, it must be stated that treasure types are based upon the occurrence of a mean number of monsters as indicated by the number appearing and adjustments detailed in the explanatory material particular to the monster in question. Adjustment downwards should always be made for instances where a few monsters are encountered. Similarly, a minor adjustment upwards might be called for if the actual number of monsters encountered is greatly in excess of the mean. The use of treasure type to determine the treasure guarded by a creature in a dungeon is not generally recommended. Larger treasures of a given type are denoted by a multiplier in parentheses (× 10, etc.) — not to be confused with treasure type X.

NUMBER OF ATTACKS shows the number of basic attacks the monster is able to make during a given melee round. This number can be modified by hits which sever members, spells such as haste or slow, and so forth. It does not usually consider unusual or special attack forms. Multiple attacks usually indicate the use of several members such as multiple hea   or two paws raking with claws and a bite from the monster's jaws.

DAMAGE PER ATTACK simply indicates the amount of damage a given attack will cause when it hits expressed as a spread of hit points. If the monster employs weapons the damage can not, of course, be shown, for it depends on the type of weapon employed by a particular monster.

SPECIAL ATTACKS detail such attack modes as dragon breath, magic use, etc. The full explanation of the mode is detailed in the material describing the monster.

SPECIAL DEFENSES are simply what the term implies and are detailed in the same manner as are special attacks.

MAGIC RESISTANCE indicates the percentage chance of any spell absolutely failing in the monster's presence. It is based on the spell being cast by a magic-user of 11th level, and it must be adjusted upwards by 5% for each level below 11th or downwards for each level above 11th of the magic-user casting the spell. Thus a magic resistance of

95% means that a 10th level magic-user has no possibility of affecting the monster with a spell, while a 12th level magic-user has a 10% chance. Even if a spell does take effect on a magic-resistant creature, the creature is entitled to normal saving throws. Note also that the magic resistance of a creature has an effect on certain existing spells such as hold portal, where it indicates the probability of the magic resistance shattering the existing spell.

INTELLIGENCE indicates the basic equivalent of human "IQ." Certain monsters are instinctively, or otherwise, cunning, and such is accordingly noted in the body of the descriptive material. The ratings correspond roughly to the following character intelligence scores:

0	Non-intelligent or not ratable
1	Animal intelligence
2-4	Semi-intelligent
5-7	Low intelligence
8-10	Average (human) intelligence
11-12	Very intelligent
13-14	Highly intelligent

15-16	Exceptionally intelligent
17-18	Genius
19-20	Supra-genius
21+	Godlike intelligence

ALIGNMENT shows the characteristic bent of a monster to law or chaos, good or evil or towards neutral behavior possibly modified by good or evil intent. It is important with regard to the general behavior of the monster when encountered.

SIZE is abbreviated as: "S," smaller than a typical human; "M," approximately man-sized (5' to 7' tall and of approximate build); and "L," larger than man-sized in one way or another and generally having greater mass.

PSIONIC ABILITY, and Attack/Defense Modes, indicate the general capabilities, if any, of a monster in these areas.

Where necessary, a sketch of each monster is shown. Details of information pertaining to a given monster are included immediately after the headings explained above.

AERIAL SERVANT — ANHKHEG — ANT, GIANT — APE — AXEBEAK

AERIAL SERVANT

FREQUENCY: *Very rare*
NO. APPEARING: *1*
ARMOR CLASS: *3*
MOVE: *24"*
HIT DICE: *16*
% IN LAIR: *0*
TREASURE TYPE: *Nil*
NO. OF ATTACKS: *1*
DAMAGE/ATTACK: *8-32*
SPECIAL ATTACKS: *Surprises on 1-4*
SPECIAL DEFENSES: *Can be hit only by magic weapons*
MAGIC RESISTANCE: *Standard*
INTELLIGENCE: *Semi-*
ALIGNMENT: *Neutral*
SIZE: *8' tall*
PSIONIC ABILITY: *Nil*
    Attack/Defense Modes: *Nil*

The aerial servant is a semi-intelligent form of an air elemental. It is typically encountered only due to conjuration by a cleric, although these creatures roam the ethereal and astral planes and when encountered there can be dimly seen. An aerial servant is normally invisible. Aerial servants do not fight *per se*, but they are exceedingly strong and very fast. They can carry weights in excess of 10,000 gold pieces, and if they grasp any creature it requires an 18 strength to have *any* chance of breaking free. For each percentage point score the creature has, there is a like chance to escape the grasp of the aerial servant, i.e. a human with an 18/50% strength has a 50% chance of breaking free of the grasp, and a 00% or 19 indicates automatic breaking of the grasp. They travel at twice the speed of an invisible stalker, and when on the physical plane they are able to achieve surprise on a die roll of 1-4 (out of 6). If the aerial servant is frustrated from completion of its assigned mission it becomes insane, returns to the cleric which sent it forth, and attacks as a double strength invisible stalker. Likewise, if it is encountered ethereally or astrally the aerial servant will typically attack in the same fashion. For further details regarding aerial servants consult the volume detailing clerical spells.

ANHKHEG

FREQUENCY: *Rare*
NO. APPEARING: *1-6*
ARMOR CLASS: *Overall 2;*
    Underside 4
MOVE: *12" (6")*
HIT DICE: *3-8*
% IN LAIR: *15%*
TREASURE TYPE: *C*
NO. OF ATTACKS: *1*
DAMAGE/ATTACK: *3-18 (+1-4)*
SPECIAL ATTACKS: *Squirt acid*
SPECIAL DEFENSES: *Nil*
MAGIC RESISTANCE: *Standard*
INTELLIGENCE: *Non*
ALIGNMENT: *Neutral*
SIZE: *L (10' to 20' long)*
PSIONIC ABILITY: *Nil*
    Attack/Defense Modes: *Nil*

The anhkheg burrows through the earth like an earthworm preferring soil rich in minerals and organic matter. Thus it will usually be found in forests and choice agricultural land. This causes farmers great consternation, since the anhkheg likes to supplement its earthly diet of soil with a bit of fresh meat, human or otherwise. Since its mouth is not designed to rip and tear meat, its mandibles crush its prey and secrete a digestive enzyme causing an additional 1-4 points per turn until the prey is completely dissolved. If sorely pressed in battle it is able to squirt its digestive acids 30 feet once per six hours. However when it does this it cannot digest anything for the same length of time, so it usually will bite. A squirt of digestive acid causes 8-32 hit points of damage to the creature struck, half the amount if the creature makes its saving throw. The anhkheg's favorite method of attacking is lying 5-10 feet underneath the ground until its antenna detects a likely victim passing overhead. Then it burrows out directly underneath the prey and grabs it.

Description: The anhkheg has a chitinous shell which is brownish in color. Its underside is pinkish. The creature's eyes are glistening black.

ANT, Giant

FREQUENCY: *Rare*
NO. APPEARING: *1-100*
ARMOR CLASS: *3*
MOVE: *18"*
HIT DICE: *2*
% IN LAIR: *10%*
TREASURE TYPE: *Q (×3), S*
NO. OF ATTACKS: *1*
DAMAGE/ATTACK: *1-6*
SPECIAL ATTACKS: *Warriors have
    poison sting*
SPECIAL DEFENSES: *Nil*
MAGIC RESISTANCE: *Standard*
INTELLIGENCE: *Animal*
ALIGNMENT: *Neutral*
SIZE: *S (2' long)*
PSIONIC ABILITY: *Nil*
    Attack/Defense Modes: *Nil*

When giant ants are encountered it is 90% likely that they will simply be workers. If found in their lair (nest) there will be double the number rolled plus 1 warrior ant for every 5 workers. The warrior ant has 3 hit dice, does 2-8 hit points of damage with its mandibles, and if it hits with them it will also attempt to sting for 3-12 points of damage. If a sting hits, a saving throw versus poison must be made; if successful the victim takes only 1-4 hit points of damage. The queen ant has 10 hit dice, but she neither moves nor attacks. If she is killed the other ants will become confused (as if they were under the influence of that spell) for six melee rounds and then leave the nest. Treasure held by ants will be found in the chamber of the queen ant. The egg chamber will be guarded by 5-50 workers and 5 warriors. Giant ant eggs have no normal market value.

APE, (Gorilla)

FREQUENCY: *Very rare*
NO. APPEARING: *1-4*
ARMOR CLASS: *6*
MOVE: *12"*
HIT DICE: *4 + 1*
% IN LAIR: *Nil*
TREASURE TYPE: *Nil*
NO. OF ATTACKS: *3*
DAMAGE/ATTACK: *1-3/1-3/1-6*
SPECIAL ATTACKS: *Rending*
SPECIAL DEFENSES: *Nil*
MAGIC RESISTANCE: *Standard*
INTELLIGENCE: *Low*
ALIGNMENT: *Neutral*
SIZE: *M (6' tall, broad)*
PSIONIC ABILITY: *Nil*
    Attack/Defense Modes: *Nil*

The typical ape is found only in lonely tropical forest regions. It is non-aggressive and shy, but if threatened or cornered will fight fiercely. If it scores hits with both of its hands it does an additional 1-6 points grabbing and rending its opponent.

APE, Carnivorous

FREQUENCY: *Rare*
NO. APPEARING: *2-8*
ARMOR CLASS: *6*
MOVE: *12"*
HIT DICE: *5*
% IN LAIR: *10%*
TREASURE TYPE: *C*
NO. OF ATTACKS: *3*
DAMAGE/ATTACK: *1-4/1-4/1-8*
SPECIAL ATTACKS: *Rending*
SPECIAL DEFENSES: *Nil*
MAGIC RESISTANCE: *Standard*
INTELLIGENCE: *Low (upper)*
ALIGNMENT: *Neutral*
SIZE: *L (7' +, very broad)*
PSIONIC ABILITY: *Nil*
    Attack/Defense Modes: *Nil*

The carnivorous ape is a larger, stronger and very aggressive relative of the gorilla. This beast has fair intelligence (IQ 70+) and is very cunning. It hungers particularly for human flesh. The eyesight of the ape is keen, as is its hearing and sense of smell, so it is surprised only on a roll of 1. If it strikes its opponent with both hands the ape does an additional 1-8 hit points of rending damage.

AXE BEAK

FREQUENCY: *Uncommon*
NO. APPEARING: *1-6*
ARMOR CLASS: *6*
MOVE: *18"*
HIT DICE: *3*
% IN LAIR: *Nil*
TREASURE TYPE: *Nil*
NO. OF ATTACKS: *3*
DAMAGE/ATTACK: *1-3/1-3/2-8*
SPECIAL ATTACKS: *Nil*
SPECIAL DEFENSES: *Nil*
MAGIC RESISTANCE: *Standard*
INTELLIGENCE: *Animal*
ALIGNMENT: *Neutral*
SIZE: *L (7'+ tall)*
PSIONIC ABILITY: *Nil*
    Attack/Defense Modes: *Nil*

Axe beaks are prehistoric carnivorous flightless birds. They are very fast runners and aggressively hunt during daylight. An axe beak resembles an ostrich in its lower portions, with a strong neck and a heavy, sharp beak.

BABOON — BADGER — BALUCHITHERIUM — BARRACUDA — BASILISK — BEAR — BEAVER, GIANT — BEETLE, GIANT — BEHOLDER — BLACK PUDDING — BLINK DOG — BOAR — BRAIN MOLE — BROWNIE — BUFFALO — BUGBEAR — BULETTE — BULL

BABOON

FREQUENCY: *Common*
NO. APPEARING: *10-40*
ARMOR CLASS: *7*
MOVE: *12"*
HIT DICE: *1 + 1*
% IN LAIR: *Nil*
TREASURE TYPE: *Nil*
NO. OF ATTACKS: *1*
DAMAGE/ATTACK: *1-4*
SPECIAL ATTACKS: *Nil*
SPECIAL DEFENSES: *Climbing*
MAGIC RESISTANCE: *Standard*
INTELLIGENCE: *Low*
ALIGNMENT: *Neutral*
SIZE: *S (4' + tall)*
PSIONIC ABILITY: *Nil*
    Attack/Defense Modes: *Nil*

Baboons are basically herbivorous, group animals. The tribe will be led by 2-8 large males (+1 hit point damage on attacks). Half of the tribe will be young which will not attack. If the home territory of a tribe is invaded the baboons will attempt to drive the invaders off, but it is 90% likely that the tribe will flee if faced by determined resistance.

BADGER

FREQUENCY: *Uncommon*
NO. APPEARING: *2-5*
ARMOR CLASS: *4*
MOVE: *6" (3")*
HIT DICE: *1 + 2*
% IN LAIR: *Nil*
TREASURE TYPE: *Nil*
NO. OF ATTACKS: *3*
DAMAGE/ATTACK: *1-2/1-2/1-3*
SPECIAL ATTACKS: *Nil*
SPECIAL DEFENSES: *Nil*
MAGIC RESISTANCE: *Standard*
INTELLIGENCE: *Semi-*
ALIGNMENT: *Neutral*
SIZE: *S*
PSIONIC ABILITY: *Nil*
    Attack/Defense Modes: *Nil*

These burrowing animals are typically solitary. Their speed accounts for their high armor class rating. They are fierce fighters and will staunchly defend their territory. If more than 1 is encountered it will be a mated pair (and young). The pelt of the badger is typically sold for from 10-30 gold pieces.

Giant Badger: There is a very rare variety of badger which grow to twice the size of the normal sort: Hit dice: 3; 1-3/1-3/1-6; Size: M. They are otherwise identical.

BALUCHITHERIUM

FREQUENCY: *Rare*
NO. APPEARING: *1-3*
ARMOR CLASS: *5*
MOVE: *12"*
HIT DICE: *14*
% IN LAIR: *Nil*
TREASURE TYPE: *Nil*
NO. OF ATTACKS: *2*
DAMAGE/ATTACK: *5-20*
SPECIAL ATTACKS: *Nil*
SPECIAL DEFENSES: *Nil*
MAGIC RESISTANCE: *Standard*
INTELLIGENCE: *Semi-*

ALIGNMENT: *Neutral*
SIZE: *L (20' tall)*
PSIONIC ABILITY: *Nil*
    Attack/Defense Modes: *Nil*

This creature is a prehistoric ancestor of the rhinoceros. It is a huge herbivorous mammal with a tendency to charge at anything nearby in order to trample it. If two are encountered they will be a mated pair, if three are encountered the third will be a young baluchitherium (roll percentile dice to determine size).

BARRACUDA

FREQUENCY: *Uncommon*
NO. APPEARING: *2-12*
ARMOR CLASS: *6*
MOVE: *30"*
HIT DICE: *1-3*
% IN LAIR: *Nil*
TREASURE TYPE: *Nil*
NO. OF ATTACKS: *1*
DAMAGE/ATTACK: *2-8*
SPECIAL ATTACKS: *Nil*
SPECIAL DEFENSES: *Nil*
MAGIC RESISTANCE: *Standard*
INTELLIGENCE: *Non-*
ALIGNMENT: *Neutral*
SIZE: *S to L*
PSIONIC ABILITY: *Nil*
    Attack/Defense Modes: *Nil*

Barracuda inhabit warm salt waters. These predatory fish are lightning quick, going from a motionless state to full speed in a single melee round. They attack any prey which is injured, appears helpless, or is relatively small.

BASILISK

FREQUENCY: *Uncommon*
NO. APPEARING: *1-4*
ARMOR CLASS: *4*
MOVE: *6"*
HIT DICE: *6 + 1*
% IN LAIR: *40%*
TREASURE TYPE: *F*
NO. OF ATTACKS: *1*
DAMAGE/ATTACK: *1-10*
SPECIAL ATTACKS: *Gaze turns to stone*
SPECIAL DEFENSES: *Nil*
MAGIC RESISTANCE: *Standard*
INTELLIGENCE: *Animal*
ALIGNMENT: *Neutral*
SIZE: *M (7' long)*
PSIONIC ABILITY: *Nil*
    Attack/Defense Modes: *Nil*

The basilisk is a reptilian monster. Although it has eight legs, its slow metabolic process allows it only slow movement. While it has strong, toothy jaws, the basilisk's major weapon is its gaze by means of which it is able to turn to stone any fleshly creature which meets its glance. However, if its gaze is reflected so that the basilisk sees its own eyes, it will itself be petrified, but this requires light at least equal to bright torchlight and a good, smooth reflector. Basilisks are usually dull brown with yellowish underbellies. Their eyes are glowing pale green. The basilisk is able to see in both the astral and ethereal planes. In the former plane its gaze kills, while in the latter it turns victims to ethereal stone which can only be seen by those who are in that plane or can see ethereal objects.

BEAR

	Black	Brown	Cave
FREQUENCY:	Common	Uncommon	Uncommon
NO. APPEARING:	1-3	1-6	1-2
ARMOR CLASS:	7	6	6
MOVE:	12″	12″	12″
HIT DICE:	3 + 3	5 + 5	6 + 6
% IN LAIR:	Nil	Nil	Nil
TREASURE TYPE:	Nil	Nil	Nil
NO. OF ATTACKS:	3	3	3
DAMAGE/ATTACK:	1-3/1-3/1-6	1-6/1-6/1-8	1-8/1-8/1-12
SPECIAL ATTACKS:	Hugs: 2-8	Hugs: 2-12	Hugs: 2-16
SPECIAL DEFENSES:	Nil	Nil	Nil
MAGIC RESISTANCE:	Standard	Standard	Standard
INTELLIGENCE:	Semi-	Semi-	Semi-
ALIGNMENT:	Neutral	Neutral	Neutral
SIZE:	M (6′ + tall)	L (9′ + tall)	L (12′ + tall)
PSIONIC ABILITY:	Nil	Nil	Nil
Attack/Defense Modes:	Nil	Nil	Nil

All of these ursoids are omnivorous, although the gigantic cave bear tends towards a diet of meat. All have excellent hearing and smell but rather poor eyesight. Size shown is average for the variety, and larger individuals will be correspondingly more powerful. The grizzly bear is a brown bear of very aggressive disposition. Black bears are usually not aggressive, brown bears are, and cave bears are quite aggressive. If a bear scores a paw hit with an 18 or better it also hugs for additional damage as indicated. The brown and cave bears will continue to fight for 1-4 melee rounds after reaching 0 to -8 hit points. At -9 or greater damage, they are killed immediately.

BEAVER, Giant

FREQUENCY: Very rare
NO. APPEARING: 10-40
ARMOR CLASS: 6
MOVE: 6″//12″
HIT DICE: 4
% IN LAIR: 80%
TREASURE TYPE: C
NO. OF ATTACKS: 1
DAMAGE/ATTACK: 4-16
SPECIAL ATTACKS: Nil
SPECIAL DEFENSES: Nil
MAGIC RESISTANCE: Standard
INTELLIGENCE: Low to average
ALIGNMENT: Neutral
SIZE: M (6′ long)
PSIONIC ABILITY: Nil
    Attack/Defense Modes: Nil

These intelligent but docile creatures will flee any attack if at all possible, but if cornered, or if their huge lodge is threatened, they will fight fiercely. Their habitat is a lake created by their vast dam, and in the middle of the body of water thus created, they build a veritable castle of mud and logs with walls not less than 5′ thick. The entire community lives in this single dwelling, and if an alarm (tail slap on the water) is sounded, all beavers rush to this place to defend it and their young. For every adult beaver there will be a young one (roll percentile dice for size determination). Giant beavers sometimes trade, and if coins or other valuables are offered they can sometimes be persuaded to undertake the building of dam-like constructions if there is water near the building site, for they use such water to work in/from. They prize highly certain barks and tender twigs, notably birch, aspen, and willow. Their hides are worth from 500 to 2,000 gold pieces each. Giant beaver kits of under 8 hit points can be subdued, captured, and sold in the market for from 100 to 200 gold pieces per hit point.

BEETLE, Giant

	Bombardier	Boring	Fire
FREQUENCY:	Common	Common	Common
NO. APPEARING:	3-12	3-18	3-12
ARMOR CLASS:	4	3	4
MOVE:	9″	6″	12″
HIT DICE:	2 + 2	5	1 + 2
% IN LAIR:	Nil	40%	Nil
TREASURE TYPE:	Nil	C, R, S, T	Nil
NO. OF ATTACKS:	1	1	1
DAMAGE/ATTACK:	2-12	5-20	2-8
SPECIAL ATTACKS:	Acid Cloud	Nil	Nil
SPECIAL DEFENSES:	Firing Cloud	Nil	Nil
MAGIC RESISTANCE:	Standard	Standard	Standard
INTELLIGENCE:	Non-	Animal	Non-
ALIGNMENT:	Neutral	Neutral	Neutral
SIZE:	M(4′long)	L(9′ long)	S (2½′ long)
PSIONIC ABILITY:	Nil	Nil	Nil
Attack/Defense Modes:	Nil	Nil	Nil

	Rhinoceros	Stag	Water
FREQUENCY:	Uncommon	Common	Common
NO. APPEARING:	1-6	2-12	1-12
ARMOR CLASS:	2	3	3
MOVE:	6″	6″	3″/12″
HIT DICE:	12	7	4
% IN LAIR:	Nil	Nil	Nil
TREASURE TYPE:	Nil	Nil	Nil
NO. OF ATTACKS:	2	3	1
DAMAGE/ATTACK:	3-18/2-16	4-16/1-10/1-10	3-18
SPECIAL ATTACKS:	Nil	Nil	Nil
SPECIAL DEFENSES:	Nil	Nil	Nil
MAGIC RESISTANCE:	Standard	Standard	Standard
INTELLIGENCE:	Non-	Non-	Non-
ALIGNMENT:	Neutral	Neutral	Neutral
SIZE:	L (12′ long plus horn)	L (10′ long)	L (6′ long)
PSIONIC ABILITY:	Nil	Nil	Nil
Attack/Defense Modes:	Nil	Nil	Nil

General: All beetles are basically unintelligent and always hungry. They feed on virtually any form of organic material, including other sorts of beetles. They taste by means of their antennae or feelers; if the substance is organic, the beetle then proceeds to grasp it with its mandibles, crush it up, and eat it. Because of this thorough grinding, nothing actually eaten by giant beetles can be revived in any manner short of a wish. Beetles do not hear or see well, relying primarily on taste and feel.

Bombardier Beetle: This beetle is usually found in wooded areas above ground. It feeds on offal and carrion primarily, gathering huge heaps of such material in which to lay its eggs. If this beetle is attacked or disturbed there is a 50% chance each melee round that it will turn its rear towards its attacker(s) and fire off an 8′ X 8′ X 8′ cloud of reeking, reddish acidic vapor from its abdomen. This cloud causes 3-12 hit points of damage to any creature within it. Furthermore, the sound caused by the release of the vapor has a 20% chance of stunning any creature with a sense of hearing within 16′ radius, and a like chance for deafening any creature within the 16′ radius which was not stunned. Stunning lasts for 2-8 melee rounds, plus an additional 2-8 melee rounds of deafness after stunning. Deafening lasts 2-12 melee rounds. The giant bombardier can fire its vapor cloud every third melee round, but not more often than twice in eight hours.

Boring Beetle: These beetles favor rotting wood and similar organic material upon which to feed, so they are usually found inside huge trees or in unused tunnel complexes underground. In the latter areas they will grow molds, slimes and fungi substances for food, starting such cultures on various forms of decaying vegetable and animal matter and wastes. These creatures are individually not of much greater intelligence than others of their kind, but it is rumored that groups develop a communal intelligence which generates a level of consciousness and reasoning ability approximating that of the human brain.

Fire Beetle: The smallest of the giant beetles, fire beetles, nevertheless are capable of delivering serious damage with their powerful mandibles. They are found both above and below ground, being primarily nocturnal. Fire beetles have two glands above their eyes and one near the back of their abdomen which give off a red glow. For this reason they are highly prized by miners and adventurers, as this luminosity will persist for from 1-6 days after the glands are removed from the beetle. The light shed illuminates a 10' radius.

Rhinoceros Beetle: This uncommon monster inhabits tropical and subtropical jungles. They roam these regions searching for fruits and vegetation, crushing anything in their paths. The horn of a giant rhinoceros beetle extends about 6'.

Stag Beetle: These woodland dwelling beetles are very fond of grains and similar growing crops, so they will sometimes become highly pestiferous and raid cultivated lands. Like other beetles, they have poor sight and hearing, but they will fight if attacked or attack if they encounter organic material they consider food. The giant stag beetle's two horns are usually not less than 8' long.

Water Beetle: The giant water beetle is found only in fresh water of not less than 30' deep. As they are voracious eaters, they prey upon virtually any form of animal but will eat almost anything. Slow and ponderous on land, they move very quickly in water. Giant water beetles hunt food by scent and vibration.

BEHOLDER

FREQUENCY: *Very rare*
NO. APPEARING: *1*
ARMOR CLASS: *0/2/7*
MOVE: *3"*
HIT DICE: *45-75 hit points*
% IN LAIR: *80%*
TREASURE TYPE: *I, S, T*
NO. OF ATTACKS: *1*
DAMAGE/ATTACK: *2-8*
SPECIAL ATTACKS: *Magic*
SPECIAL DEFENSES: *Anti-magic ray*
MAGIC RESISTANCE: *Special*
INTELLIGENCE: *Exceptional*
ALIGNMENT: *Lawful evil*
SIZE: *L (4'-6' dia.)*
PSIONIC ABILITY: *Nil*
    Attack/Defense Modes: *Nil*

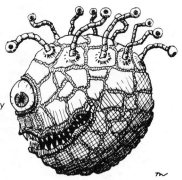

The beholder (eye tyrant, sphere of many eyes) is most frequently found underground, although it infrequently will lair in desolate wildernesses. The globular body of this monster is supported by levitation, and it floats slowly about as it wills. Atop the sphere are 10 eyestalks, while in its central area are a great eleventh eye and a large mouth filled with pointed teeth. The body is protected by a hard chitinous covering. The creature's eyestalks and eyes are also protected, although less well (thus the armor classes of 2 and 7 respectively). Because of its particular nature the beholder is able to withstand the loss of its eyestalks, these members are not computed as part of its hit point damage potential, and lost eyestalks will eventually grow back (1 week per lost member). The body of the monster can withstand two-thirds of its total damage potential, while the great central eye can withstand one-third this total, i.e. a beholder with 45 hit points can withstand 30 hit points of damage to its body before being killed; the eleventh eye can withstand 15 points before ceasing to function. Eyestalks take from 8 to 12 hit points each before being lost. The body of a beholder represents 75% of potential hit area, the central eye and the eyestalks 10% each, and the 10 small eyes 5%.

Eyes: The various eyes of a beholder each have a different function. Typically only the central eye, plus 1-4 of those on stalks are able to function considering that the attack is coming from an arc 90° before the monster. If attacks come from 180° double the number of eyestalks able to function, and for 270° or 360° triple or quadruple the number. Attacks from above enable all 10 eyestalks to function, but the central eye cannot. Functions of the eyes are:

1	Charm person spell	6	Disintegrate ray (2" range)
2	Charm monster spell	7	Fear (as a wand)
3	Sleep spell	8	Slow spell
4	Telekinese 2,500 GP wt.	9	Cause serious wound (5" range)
5	Flesh-stone ray (3" range)	10	Death ray (4" range)
	11 Anti-magic ray (14" range)		

Nature: The beholder is hateful, aggressive, and avaricious. They will usually attack immediately. If confronted by a particularly powerful party there is a 50% chance they will listen to negotiations — either to be bribed

not to attack or to pay a ransom to not be attacked, depending on the strength of the opposing party. They can speak their own language as well as that tongue known to lawful evil creatures.

BLACK PUDDING

FREQUENCY: *Uncommon*
NO. APPEARING: *1 to 1-4*
ARMOR CLASS: *6*
MOVE: *6"*
HIT DICE: *10*
% IN LAIR: *Nil*
TREASURE TYPE: *Nil*
NO. OF ATTACKS: *1*
DAMAGE/ATTACK: *3-24*
SPECIAL ATTACKS: *Dissolve wood and metal*
SPECIAL DEFENSES: *Blows, cold and lightning do not harm*
MAGIC RESISTANCE: *Standard*
INTELLIGENCE: *Non-*
ALIGNMENT: *Neutral*
SIZE: *S to L (5' dia. to 8' dia.)*
PSIONIC ABILITY: *Nil*
    Attack/Defense Modes: *Nil*

The black pudding is a monster composed of groups of single cells. It is a scavenger/hunter found only in underground areas normally. The body structure of a black pudding is such that it can pass (flow) through narrow openings (such as a 1" crack under a door). The monster travels equally well on walls or ceilings as well as floors. Its tiny mouths and saliva do 3-24 hit points of damage per melee round to exposed flesh. If the monster needs to dissolve wood in order to obtain food, it can eat away about a two inch thickness of wood equal in area to its diameter in 1 melee round. Black puddings also eat away metal with their corrosive saliva: Chainmail in 1 melee round, plate mail in 2, and an additional melee round for magical armor at a rate of 1 melee round for each plus of armor. Thus, +1 magic (plate) armor would have to be in contact with a black pudding for 3 melee rounds before it dissolved. If chopped or struck, the monster is broken into two or more parts, each able to attack. The same is true if it is attacked by lightning. Cold does not affect it. Fire causes normal damage to this monster, and they avoid flames. Black puddings sometimes have color variation, grey, brown, and white being not uncommon.

Black puddings with 10-20 hit points are about 5' diameter, those of 21-40 hit points 6', 41-60 are 7', and 61-80 are 8'. Note that even those of the smallest size (or those as small as 1' diameter) are able to deliver normal damage. This is due to the fact that larger puddings simply do not use all of their mouth openings as they are not exposed.

BLINK DOG

FREQUENCY: *Rare*
NO. APPEARING: *4-16*
ARMOR CLASS: *5*
MOVE: *12"*
HIT DICE: *4*
% IN LAIR: *20%*
TREASURE TYPE: *C*
NO. OF ATTACKS: *1*
DAMAGE/ATTACK: *1-6*
SPECIAL ATTACKS: *From rear 75% of time*
SPECIAL DEFENSES: *Teleporting*
MAGIC RESISTANCE: *Standard*
INTELLIGENCE: *Average*
ALIGNMENT: *Lawful, good*
SIZE: *M (3' at shoulder)*
PSIONIC ABILITY: *Nil*
    Attack/Defense Modes: *Nil*

These brown and yellowish creatures are as intelligent as normal humans and have a fairly complex language consisting of barks, yaps, whines, and growls. They are also able to use a limited form of teleportation (the blink). In attack, pack members will blink in and out in a random fashion at random intervals, teleporting individuals having a 75% chance of appearing behind the opponent. An individual will teleport on a score of 7 or better on a 12-sided die. Roll again to determine where the blink dog teleporting reappears: 1 = in front of opponent, 2 = shielded (or left) front flank, 3 = unshielded (or right) front flank, 4-12 = behind. When blinking in, the creature will be from 1' to 3' from the opponent and immediately able to attack. Blinking is an inborn instinct, and it never allows the animal to reappear in a space already occupied by a solid object. If seriously threatened (or if 25% or greater loss has been sustained) the entire pack will blink out and not return. There is a great enmity between blink dogs and displacer beasts (qv) and the two creatures will always attack each other. If encountered in their lair there is a 50% chance that there will be from 3-12 pups (1-2 hit dice, 1-2/1-3 hit points damage/attack). These young are worth from 1,000 to 2,000 gold pieces on the market as they can be tamed and trained.

BOAR

	Boar, Wild	Giant Boar	Warthog
FREQUENCY:	Common	Uncommon	Common
NO. APPEARING:	1-12	2-8	1-6
ARMOR CLASS:	7	6	7
MOVE:	15''	12''	12''
HIT DICE:	3 + 3	7	3
% IN LAIR:	Nil	Nil	Nil
TREASURE TYPE:	Nil	Nil	Nil
NO. OF ATTACKS:	1	1	2
DAMAGE/ATTACK:	3-12	3-18	2-8/2-8
SPECIAL ATTACKS:	Nil	Nil	Nil
SPECIAL DEFENSES:	Nil	Nil	Nil
MAGIC RESISTANCE:	Standard	Standard	Standard
INTELLIGENCE:	Semi-	Animal	Animal
ALIGNMENT:	Neutral	Neutral	Neutral
SIZE:	M (3' at shoulder)	L (5' at shoulder)	M (2½' at shoulder)
PSIONIC ABILITY:	Nil	Nil	Nil
Attack/Defense Modes:	Nil	Nil	Nil

These creatures are typically pig-like omnivores. Only the warthog has a range restricted to warmer climes.

Boar, Wild: If more than 1 is encountered the others will be sows (3 hit dice, 2-8 hit points damage/attack), on a 1:4, sows: sounders, ratio. Thus if 12 are encountered there will be 1 boar, 3 sows, and 8 young. The boar will fight for 2-5 melee rounds after reaching 0 to -6 hit points but dies immediately at -7 or greater damage.

Giant Boar *(Elothere):* This prehistoric forerunner of the wild boar is also very aggressive. If 3 or more are encountered there is only a 25% chance that there will be young (2-6 hit dice, 1-4/2-5/2-7/2-8/3-12 hit points damage/attack) numbering from 1-4 of the total herd. The boars and sows fight equally, and either will fight for 1-4 melee rounds after reaching 0 to -10 hit points but die immediately upon reaching -11 or more hit points.

Warthog: These tropical beasts are aggressive only if their territory is threatened or if cornered or threatened. They make two slashing attacks with their large tusks. Male and female fight equally. If 3-6 are encountered the balance will be young (1-2 hit dice, 1-3/2-5 hit points damage/attack). The warthog will continue to fight for 1-2 melee rounds after reaching 0 to -5 hit points but at -6 or greater damage dies immediately.

BRAIN MOLE

FREQUENCY: *Very rare*
NO. APPEARING: *1-3*
ARMOR CLASS: *9*
MOVE: *1''*
HIT DICE: *1 hit point*
% IN LAIR: *Nil*
TREASURE TYPE: *Nil*
NO. OF ATTACKS: *Nil*
DAMAGE/ATTACK: *Nil*
SPECIAL ATTACKS: *Psionic only*
SPECIAL DEFENSES: *Nil*
MAGIC RESISTANCE: *Standard*
INTELLIGENCE: *Animal*
ALIGNMENT: *Neutral*
SIZE: *S (3'' long)*

PSIONIC ABILITY: *121 point attack*
    Attack/Defense Modes: *B/Nil*

Small mole-like animals which inhabit most places above and below ground, brain moles are attracted by psionic activity of any sort — including magic spells which duplicate psionic effects. When a brain mole is within 30' of any creature exercising such psionic activity, it will seek to feed upon the energy being used by psionically "burrowing" into the mind. This has the effect of attacking the mind with a 121 point strength mind thrust upon the creature using psionic energy. This burrowing will have a 20% chance per melee round of causing permanent insanity in non-psionically endowed creatures employing psionic energy through spells or magical items. Cessation of the spell or abandoning the use of the magic item will immediately relieve the attack. A psionic under attack must escape the range of the brain mole or kill it to halt its burrowing.

BROWNIE

FREQUENCY: *Rare*
NO. APPEARING: *4-16*
ARMOR CLASS: *3*
MOVE: *12''*
HIT DICE: *½*
% IN LAIR: *20%*
TREASURE TYPE: *O, P, Q*
NO. OF ATTACKS: *1*
DAMAGE/ATTACK: *1-3*
SPECIAL ATTACKS: *Spells*
SPECIAL DEFENSES: *Save as 9th level cleric*
MAGIC RESISTANCE: *As above*
INTELLIGENCE: *High*
ALIGNMENT: *Lawful good*
SIZE: *S (1½' tall)*
PSIONIC ABILITY: *Nil*
    Attack/Defense Modes: *Nil*

Brownies are distant relatives of halflings, (perhaps half halfling, half pixie) but they are smaller and far less common. They are basically friendly to humans and their ilk (dwarves, elves, and halflings), but because they are shy, they are seldom seen and favor quiet, pastoral areas in which to dwell. If encountered on friendly terms, brownies can often (50%) be convinced to help lawful good characters. They are able to make or repair items of wood, leather, metal, etc. with ease. They are also good guides. Brownies can use the following spells once per day: *protection from evil, ventriloquism, dancing lights, continual light, mirror image* (3 images), *confusion,* and *dimension door.* Brownies do not usually carry weapons other than short swords. They have exceptional senses in general, are never surprised, and have 18 dexterity. Brownies are capable of blending into the landscape very quickly, in effect using natural cover and speed to become invisible (and escape if desired).

Besides their own language and the alignment tongue, brownies speak elvish, pixieish, and the language of sprites and halflings.

BUFFALO

FREQUENCY: *Uncommon*
NO. APPEARING: *4-24*
ARMOR CLASS: *7*
MOVE: *15''*
HIT DICE: *5*
% IN LAIR: *Nil*
TREASURE TYPE: *Nil*
NO. OF ATTACKS: *2*
DAMAGE/ATTACK: *1-8/1-8*
SPECIAL ATTACKS: *Charge*
SPECIAL DEFENSES: *Head is armor class 3*
MAGIC RESISTANCE: *Standard*
INTELLIGENCE: *Semi-*
ALIGNMENT: *Neutral*
SIZE: *L (5' at shoulder)*
PSIONIC ABILITY: *Nil*
    Attack/Defense Modes: *Nil*

These dangerous herd animals of tropical and subtropical plains will usually attack if approached too closely (6'' or less). When attacking, the whole herd is likely to charge. A charging buffalo does 3-18 hit points of damage impacting and 1-4 points trampling. A charge must cover at least 40'. Some species of buffalo (50% chance) are non-aggressive and will flee if threatened.

BUGBEAR

FREQUENCY: *Uncommon*
NO. APPEARING: *6-36*
ARMOR CLASS: *5*
MOVE: *9"*
HIT DICE: *3 + 1*
% IN LAIR: *25%*
TREASURE TYPE: *Individuals J, K, L, M. B in lair*
NO. OF ATTACKS: *1*
DAMAGE/ATTACK: *2-8 or by weapon*
SPECIAL ATTACKS: *Surprise on a 1-3*
SPECIAL DEFENSES: *Nil*
MAGIC RESISTANCE: *Standard*
INTELLIGENCE: *Low to Average (low)*
ALIGNMENT: *Chaotic evil*
SIZE: *L (7'+ tall)*
PSIONIC ABILITY: *Nil*
    Attack/Defense Modes: *Nil*

Bugbears live in loose bands, and are typically found in the same areas as are goblins. Unlike their smaller cousins, however, these hairy giant goblins operate equally well in bright daylight or great darkness (as they have infravision to 60'), so they are as likely to choose a habitation above ground as they are to select a subterranean abode.

If 12 or more bugbears are encountered there will be a leader with 22-25 hit points (armor class 4, attacks as a 4 hit dice monster, gets +1 on damage caused). If 24 or more are encountered there will be the following additional bugbears: a chief (armor class 3, 28-30 hit points, attacking as 4 hit dice monster, and doing +2 damage) and a sub-chief (as per leader-type above). If encountered in their lair there will always be a chief and sub-chief, and there will be females and young equal to 50% each of the number of males. Neither of the latter types of bugbears will fight unless in a life or death situation. In the latter case the females fight as hobgoblins and the young will fight as kobolds.

The arms carried by bugbears range the gamut of available weapons — from swords to wooden clubs with spikes set in them (morning stars). A fair number of spears are carried by these monsters, and they tend to use them, along with axes, maces, and hammers, as missile weapons. As bugbears are strong they can throw these weapons up to 4", anything under 2" being treated as medium range.

Although bugbears are clumsy looking and walk with a shambling gait, they are actually able to move very quickly and with great stealth, thus surprising opponents 50% of the time.

Bugbears speak goblin and hobgoblin in addition to their racial and alignment tongues.

Description: The skin of bugbears is light yellow to yellow brown — typically dull yellow. Their hair ranges in color from lusterless tannish brown to brick red. Their eyes are greenish white with red pupils. The odds and ends of armor they wear, as well as whatever cloth, skins, or hides they drape themselves in, tends to be ill-kept, dirty, and dingy. They live for approximately 75 years.

BULETTE

FREQUENCY: *Very rare*
NO. APPEARING: *1-2 (10% chance)*
ARMOR CLASS: *-2/4/6*
MOVE: *14" (3")*
HIT DICE: *9*
% IN LAIR: *Nil*
TREASURE TYPE: *Nil*
NO. OF ATTACKS: *3*
DAMAGE/ATTACK: *4-48/3-18/3-18*
SPECIAL ATTACKS: *8' jump*
SPECIAL DEFENSES: *Nil*
MAGIC RESISTANCE: *Standard*
INTELLIGENCE: *Animal*
ALIGNMENT: *Neutral*
SIZE: *L (9½' tall, 12'+ long)*
PSIONIC ABILITY: *Nil*
    Attack/Defense Modes: *Nil*

The bulette (or landshark) was thought to be extinct until recently when this horror reappeared. It was the result of a mad wizard's experimental cross breeding of a snapping turtle and armadillo with infusions of demons' ichor. They range temperate climates feeding on horses, men, and most other flesh — although they dislike dwarf and shun elf of any sort. They love halfling and will hungrily dig them from their burrows. The stupid bulette is irascible and always hungry, and they fear nothing, so a bulette will attack a large, powerful party just to eat a horse or two. Sometimes the crest of a burrowing landshark will break the ground — thus the name "landshark." When fighting they usually employ their front feet and gaping maw, but when cornered or seriously wounded they can jump up to 8' in the air with blinding speed and strike with all four feet (3-18 points damage for each of the rear feet as well). The shell under the bulette's crest, an area about a foot and one-half square, is only AC 6, and in a fierce fight the monster tends to raise its crest and expose this vulnerable area. Its eyes are armor class 4, but they are relatively small (8" oval).

The bulette is solitary. Only a mated pair will share the same territory. No young have ever been seen, but smaller (as few as 6 hit dice) specimens have been killed. No one is certain how or where the young are born or hatched. Very large bulette have been reported, one being no less than 11 hit dice and over 11' tall at the shoulder. The great plates behind the bulette's head are highly prized for use in shield making, for a skilled dwarven craftsman can fashion them into a shield of +1 to +3 value.

Description: Typical specimens have blue-brown heads and hind portions, with plates and scales of gray-blue to blue-green. Nails and teeth are dull ivory. The area around the eyes is brown-black, the eyeballs are yellowish, and the pupils of the eyes are dark-green.

BULL

FREQUENCY: *Common*
NO. APPEARING: *1-20*
ARMOR CLASS: *7*
MOVE: *15"*
HIT DICE: *4*
% IN LAIR: *Nil*
TREASURE TYPE: *Nil*
NO. OF ATTACKS: *2*
DAMAGE/ATTACK: *1-6/1-6*
SPECIAL ATTACKS: *Charge*
SPECIAL DEFENSES: *Nil*
MAGIC RESISTANCE: *Standard*
INTELLIGENCE: *Semi-*
ALIGNMENT: *Neutral*
SIZE: *L (5' at shoulder)*
PSIONIC ABILITY: *Nil*
    Attack/Defense Modes: *Nil*

The bull is a dangerous opponent, being aggressive and easily aroused to anger. There is a 75% chance that if approached within 8" it will attack. A charging bull will do 3-12 points of damage upon impact with an additional 1-4 points of trampling damage. A charge must cover at least 30'. Such animals as the wild ox and the aurochs fall under this general class. When a herd is present there will be several bulls which will defend the rest.

CAMEL, WILD — CARRION CRAWLER — CATOBLEPAS — CATTLE, WILD — CENTAUR — CENTIPEDE, GIANT — CEREBRAL PARASITE — CHIMERA — COCKATRICE — COUATL — CRAB, GIANT — CRAYFISH, GIANT — CROCODILE

CAMEL, Wild

FREQUENCY: *Common*
NO. APPEARING: *1-12*
ARMOR CLASS: *7*
MOVE: *21"*
HIT DICE: *3*
% IN LAIR: *Nil*
TREASURE TYPE: *Nil*
NO. OF ATTACKS: *1*
DAMAGE/ATTACK: *1-4*
SPECIAL ATTACKS: *Spitting*
SPECIAL DEFENSES: *Nil*
MAGIC RESISTANCE: *Standard*
INTELLIGENCE: *Animal to Semi-*
ALIGNMENT: *Neutral*
SIZE: *L*
PSIONIC ABILITY: *Nil*
    Attack/Defense Modes: *Nil*

Single humped camels (*dromedaries*) are found only in very warm desert areas. The double humped (*bactrian*) sort are able to abide cold and even non-desert regions. All camels are able to go for up to two weeks without food or water. They can carry loads up to 6,000 gold pieces weight, although this reduces their speed to 9"; if loaded between 4,000 and 5,000 gold pieces, their speed is 15" maximum. (The bactrian camel is 3" slower than the dromedary, so reduce its movement accordingly).

Camels can attack by biting (they can kick, but do not typically do so). They tend to be nasty tempered and may spit at persons coming to ride or use them similarly — 50% chance to do so, 25% chance of blinding for 1-3 melee rounds if they do spit.

Horses tend to dislike the odor of camels.

CARRION CRAWLER

FREQUENCY: *Uncommon*
NO. APPEARING: *1-6*
ARMOR CLASS: *3/7*
MOVE: *12"*
HIT DICE: *3 + 1*
% IN LAIR: *50%*
TREASURE TYPE: *B*
NO. OF ATTACKS: *8*
DAMAGE/ATTACK: *Paralysis*
SPECIAL ATTACKS: *As above*
SPECIAL DEFENSES: *Nil*
MAGIC RESISTANCE: *Standard*
INTELLIGENCE: *Non-*
ALIGNMENT: *Neutral*
SIZE: *L (9' long)*
PSIONIC ABILITY: *Nil*
    Attack/Defense Modes: *Nil*

Carrion crawlers strongly resemble a cross between a giant green cutworm and a huge cephalopod. They are usually found only in subterranean areas. The carrion crawler is, as its name implies, a scavenger, but this does not preclude aggressive attacks upon living creatures, for that insures a constant supply of corpses upon which to feed or for deposit of eggs. The head of the monster is well protected, but its body is only armor class 7. A carrion crawler moves quite rapidly on its multiple legs despite its bulk, and a wall or ceiling is as easily traveled as a floor, for each of the beast's feet are equipped with sharp claws which hold it fast. The head is equipped with 8 tentacles which flail at prey; each 2' long tentacle exudes a gummy secretion which when fresh, will paralyze opponents (save versus paralyzation or it takes effect). As there are so many tentacles with which to hit, and thus multiple chances of being paralyzed, these monsters are greatly feared.

CATOBLEPAS

FREQUENCY: *Very rare*
NO. APPEARING: *1-3*
ARMOR CLASS: *7*
MOVE: *6"*
HIT DICE: *6 + 2*
% IN LAIR: *60%*
TREASURE TYPE: *C*
NO. OF ATTACKS: *1*
DAMAGE/ATTACK: *1-6 + stun*
SPECIAL ATTACKS: *Gaze causes death*
SPECIAL DEFENSES: *Nil*
MAGIC RESISTANCE: *Standard*
INTELLIGENCE: *Semi-*
ALIGNMENT: *Neutral*
SIZE: *L (6' at shoulder)*
PSIONIC ABILITY: *Nil*
    Attack/Defense Modes: *Nil*

This nightmare creature is loathsome beyond description and has no redeeming features. Its body resembles that of a huge, bloated buffalo and gives off an offensive odor. The catoblepas' neck is long and thin, and perched atop it is a big head uglier than that of a warthog. Its legs are thick and stumpy, much like a hippopotamus. The creature's tail is strong and snakey, however, and moves with amazing swiftness to strike enemies. Any creature so struck has a base 75% chance of being stunned for 1-10 melee rounds; the base chance being modified by adjustment downward by 5% for every level (or hit die for monsters) above 1. Thus, if an 11th level character is struck by the tail there is only a 25% chance of stunning. Perhaps its habitat — fetid swamps and miasmal marshes — caused the bizarre combination of genetic characteristics in this monster, or perhaps it was due to some ghastly tinkering with life by a demented godling. In any case, the most horrid aspect of the catoblepas is its bloodshot eyes.

The gaze of the catoblepas is equal to a *death ray*, extending 6" from the eyes (even into the astral and ethereal planes). Any creature which meets this gaze dies without any chance to save itself. Complete surprise (a 2 on 6-sided die) means one of the party encountering the monster has met its gaze. Otherwise the very weak neck of the catoblepas has only a 25% chance of raising the head high enough to use its eyes. If both parties are still this chance increases by 15% per melee round. If the monster must follow quick movements, or if it is shambling along in pursuit of prey, there is only a 10% chance per melee round of the neck raising the head sufficiently high to fix its gaze. A fleeing victim, even with eyes averted, is subject to the deadly effect of the catoblepas' eyes, although there is a saving throw.

CATTLE, Wild

FREQUENCY: *Common*
NO. APPEARING: *20-200*
ARMOR CLASS: *7*
MOVE: *15"*
HIT DICE: *1-4*
% IN LAIR: *Nil*
TREASURE TYPE: *Nil*
NO. OF ATTACKS: *1*
DAMAGE/ATTACK: *1-4*
SPECIAL ATTACKS: *Stampede*
SPECIAL DEFENSES: *Nil*
MAGIC RESISTANCE: *Standard*
INTELLIGENCE: *Semi-*
ALIGNMENT: *Neutral*
SIZE: *L*
PSIONIC ABILITY: *Nil*
    Attack/Defense Modes: *Nil*

Wild cattle roam many wilderness areas, and they are frequently encountered. They are likely to flee any threat, although the males of the herd are likely (75%) to attack if the intruders come upon the herd before it has a chance to run away (see *BULL*). There is also a 25% chance that a herd of wild cattle will stampede directly at the party. If cattle stampede and there is no cover (rocks, trees, logs, a wall, etc.) then roll two 4-sided dice for each member of the party in the path of the stampede in order to find how many cattle trample each party member. Trampling causes 1-4 hit points of damage per creature trampling.

CENTAUR

FREQUENCY: *Rare*
NO. APPEARING: *4-24*
ARMOR CLASS: *5 (4)*
MOVE: *18"*
HIT DICE: *4*
% IN LAIR: *5%*
TREASURE TYPE: *M, Q, with each;*
  D, I, T in lair
NO. OF ATTACKS: *2*
DAMAGE/ATTACK: *1-6/1-6*
SPECIAL ATTACKS: *Human*
  weapon
SPECIAL DEFENSES: *Nil*
MAGIC RESISTANCE: *Standard*
INTELLIGENCE: *Low-Average*
ALIGNMENT: *Neutral-Chaotic*
  good
SIZE: *L*
PSIONIC ABILITY: *Nil*
  Attack/Defense Modes: *Nil*

Centaurs dwell in secluded pastures, far from human habitation. Roving bands of these creatures always carry weapons, and leaders will carry shields. Half of the centaurs in a band will be armed with oaken clubs (equal to morning stars, 1-8 or 1-6 hit points damage/attack), one-quarter will have composite long bows and 10-30 arrows (24" range, 1-6 hit points damage/attack), and the remaining quarter will be leaders (AC 4) with shield and lance (1-8 or 2-24 hit points damage/attack). Leaders will have double treasure. In melee each centaur attacks two times, once with his weapon and then as a horse with his two fore hooves.

If centaurs are encountered in their lair it will be a hidden glen with rich grass and running water. Here, there will be found 1-6 additional males, females equal to twice the number of males, and young from 5-30 in number. Females (3 hit dice) and young (1-3 hit dice) do not use weapons and will only fight with their hooves in a life and death situation. If the females and young are threatened, the centaurs will be 90% likely to ransom them with their main treasure. They speak their own language and that of their alignment.

Centaurs are not generally friendly with humans or dwarves; they tolerate gnomes and halflings; they are friendly with elves and like wood elves.

CENTIPEDE, Giant

FREQUENCY: *Common*
NO. APPEARING: *2-24*
ARMOR CLASS: *9*
MOVE: *15"*
HIT DICE: *¼*
% IN LAIR: *Nil*
TREASURE TYPE: *Nil*
NO. OF ATTACKS: *1*
DAMAGE/ATTACK: *Nil*
SPECIAL ATTACKS: *Poison*
SPECIAL DEFENSES: *Nil*
MAGIC RESISTANCE: *Standard*
INTELLIGENCE: *Non-*
ALIGNMENT: *Neutral*
SIZE: *S (1'+ long)*
PSIONIC ABILITY: *Nil*
  Attack/Defense Modes: *Nil*

These nasty creatures are found nearly everywhere. They are aggressive and rush forth to bite their prey, injecting poison into the wound, but in many cases this poison is weak and not fatal (add +4 to saving throw die roll). Also, as the centipede is small, it is less likely to resist attacks which allow it a saving throw (-1 on die).

Centipedes come in many colors — pale gray to black, red to brown.

CEREBRAL PARASITE

FREQUENCY: *Rare*
NO. APPEARING: *3-12*
ARMOR CLASS: *n/a*
MOVE: *n/a*
HIT DICE: *n/a*
% IN LAIR: *Nil*
TREASURE TYPE: *Nil*
NO. OF ATTACKS: *0*
DAMAGE/ATTACK: *0*
SPECIAL ATTACKS: *Infestation*
SPECIAL DEFENSES: *Not harmed*
  except by cure disease
MAGIC RESISTANCE: *Standard*
INTELLIGENCE: *Non-*
ALIGNMENT: *Neutral*
SIZE: *S (flea-sized)*
PSIONIC ABILITY: *Nil*
  Attack/Defense Modes: *Nil*

These creatures are not visible to the human eye and can only be detected psionically by means of careful examination of a person's aura. They can be removed only by a *cure disease* spell. If a psionically endowed creature comes within 1" of cerebral parasites they will attack but the attack will be completely unnoted. Thereafter, whenever psionic abilities, including attacks/defenses, are used, the parasites will drain additional psionic energy to feed upon. Each parasite will drain one energy point. Furthermore, after one has fed upon six psionic energy points it will reproduce another parasite, and thereafter continue to drain energy, as will its offspring. They cannot be psionically attacked.

Cerebral parasites inhabit the astral and ethereal planes as well as the material plane.

CHIMERA

FREQUENCY: *Rare*
NO. APPEARING: *1-4*
ARMOR CLASS: *6/5/2*
MOVE: *9"/18"*
HIT DICE: *9*
% IN LAIR: *40%*
TREASURE TYPE: *F*
NO. OF ATTACKS: *6*
DAMAGE/ATTACK: *1-3/1-3/1-4/*
  1-4/2-8/3-12
SPECIAL ATTACKS: *Breath weapon*
SPECIAL DEFENSES: *Nil*
MAGIC RESISTANCE: *Standard*
INTELLIGENCE: *Semi-*
ALIGNMENT: *Chaotic evil*
SIZE: *L (4' at shoulder)*
PSIONIC ABILITY: *Nil*
  Attack/Defense Modes: *Nil*

The chimera combines features of three creatures in a monstrous manner. Its hind quarters are those of a huge goat, its foreparts are those of a lion, its body sports dragon wings, and it has three large heads. It can claw with its fore legs, its goat head is armed with two long horns, its lion head has powerful jaws and sharp teeth, and its dragon head is likewise equipped. If a chimera desires (50% chance) its dragon head can breathe fire with a range of 5" and causing 3-24 points damage (saving throw applicable). Chimerae speak a very limited form of red dragon language.

Description: The goatish body parts are black with amber eyes and yellowish horns. The lion-like parts are tawny yellow with a dark brown mane, green eyes, and red maw. The dragon wings are brownish-black, the dragon head orange, and the eyes and mouth black.

COCKATRICE

FREQUENCY: *Uncommon*
NO. APPEARING: *1-6*
ARMOR CLASS: *6*
MOVE: *6''/18''*
HIT DICE: *5*
% IN LAIR: *30%*
TREASURE TYPE: *D*
NO. OF ATTACKS: *1*
DAMAGE/ATTACK: *1-3*
SPECIAL ATTACKS: *Touch turns to stone*
SPECIAL DEFENSES: *Nil*
MAGIC RESISTANCE: *Standard*
INTELLIGENCE: *Animal*
ALIGNMENT: *Neutral*
SIZE: *S*
PSIONIC ABILITY: *Nil*
    Attack/Defense Modes: *Nil*

Cockatrices are found in temperate to tropical regions, both above and below ground. They can inflict only minor wounds with their beaks, but their touch will turn *flesh to stone* (save versus stone or petrified). Note that the petrification aura of this monster extends into both the astral and ethereal planes and can thus affect creatures in these planes as well (cf. *BASILISK*).

Description: The serpentine tail of the cockatrice is yellow green, its feet and beak yellow, its wings are gray, its feathers are golden brown, and its wattles, comb, eyes, and tongue are red.

COUATL

FREQUENCY: *Very rare*
NO. APPEARING: *1-4*
ARMOR CLASS: *5*
MOVE: *6''/18''*
HIT DICE: *9*
% IN LAIR: *10%*
TREASURE TYPE: *B, I*
NO. OF ATTACKS: *2*
DAMAGE/ATTACK: *1-3/2-8*
SPECIAL ATTACKS: *Poison, magic use*
SPECIAL DEFENSES: *Become ethereal*
MAGIC RESISTANCE: *Standard*
INTELLIGENCE: *Genius*
ALIGNMENT: *Lawful good*
SIZE: *M (12' long)*
PSIONIC ABILITY: *60-110*
    Attack/Defense Modes: *vary*

These winged, feathered serpents are rarely found anywhere except in warm, jungle-like regions or flying through the ether. Due to their intelligence and powers they are regarded with awe by the inhabitants of their homelands and considered to be divine. Couatl rarely interfere in human affairs. They are able to polymorph themselves and they use magic — as a 5th level magic-user and/or 7th level cleric (45% use magic-user spells, 35% clerical spells, 20% use both). In melee they attack both by poisonous bite (saving throw applicable) and constriction; if a constriction attack succeeds, the victim takes 2-8 hit points of damage that melee round and each round thereafter until one or the other is killed.

Couatl are psionically aware and have 2 major and 4 minor disciplines, with commensurate attack and defense modes. Couatl speak several human languages and most serpent and avian languages as well.

CRAB, Giant

FREQUENCY: *Rare*
NO. APPEARING: *2-12*
ARMOR CLASS: *3*
MOVE: *9''*
HIT DICE: *3*

% IN LAIR: *Nil*
TREASURE TYPE: *Nil*
NO. OF ATTACKS: *2*
DAMAGE/ATTACK: *2-8/2-8*
SPECIAL ATTACKS: *Nil*
SPECIAL DEFENSES: *Nil*
MAGIC RESISTANCE: *Standard*
INTELLIGENCE: *Non-*
ALIGNMENT: *Neutral*
SIZE: *L (4'+ dia.)*
PSIONIC ABILITY: *Nil*
    Attack/Defense Modes: *Nil*

Giant crabs are found in any area near water of any sort. They operate equally well on land or in water, always seeking to find something to eat. Their eyes, being on stalks, can peek over ledges or around corners with ease. They tend to hide and rush forth to seize their prey (surprise on a 1-4 on a 6-sided die).

CRAYFISH, Giant

FREQUENCY: *Uncommon*
NO. APPEARING: *1-4*
ARMOR CLASS: *4*
MOVE: *6'' // 12''*
HIT DICE: *4 + 4*
% IN LAIR: *Nil*
TREASURE TYPE: *Nil*
NO. OF ATTACKS: *2*
DAMAGE/ATTACK: *2-12/2-12*
SPECIAL ATTACKS: *Nil*
SPECIAL DEFENSES: *Nil*
MAGIC RESISTANCE: *Standard*
INTELLIGENCE: *Non-*
ALIGNMENT: *Neutral*
SIZE: *L (8'+ long)*
PSIONIC ABILITY: *Nil*
    Attack/Defense Modes: *Nil*

These strange monsters are found only in fresh water. They move slowly when walking, but they can swim with great rapidity for short periods. Like giant crabs, giant crayfish hide in order to rush out and seize their prey (surprise on a 1-3 on a 6-sided die).

CROCODILE

	Normal	Giant
FREQUENCY:	Common	Very rare to common
NO. APPEARING:	3-24	1 to 2-12
ARMOR CLASS:	5	4
MOVE:	6''//12''	6''//12''
HIT DICE:	3	7
% IN LAIR:	Nil	Nil
TREASURE TYPE:	Nil	Nil
NO. OF ATTACKS:	2	2
DAMAGE/ATTACK:	2-8/1-12	3-18/2-20
SPECIAL ATTACKS:	Nil	Nil
SPECIAL DEFENSES:	Nil	Nil
MAGIC RESISTANCE:	Standard	Standard
INTELLIGENCE:	Animal	Animal
ALIGNMENT:	Neutral	Neutral
SIZE:	L (8'-15' long)	L (21'-30' long)
PSIONIC ABILITY:	Nil	Nil
Attack/Defense Modes:	Nil	Nil

Although some of these reptiles are of giant-size, such monsters are typically found only in salt water or in prehistoric settings. All crocodiles are stupid and voracious eaters. They are sluggish in cold weather (cut movement 50%). They typically lie in concealment in order to surprise prey (surprise on 1-3 on a 6-sided die).

DEMON — DEVIL — DINOSAUR — DISPLACER BEAST — DJINNI — DOG — DOLPHIN — DOPPLEGANGER — DRAGON — DRAGONNE — DRAGON TURTLE — DRYAD — DWARF

DEMON

Each type of demon, and especially the high-level demon lords and princes, have many unusual characteristics and extraordinary abilities. Characteristics and abilities which are common to all demons are covered here. See the individual treatment of each demon for specific information.

Demons are able to move from their own plane into those of *Tarterus, Hades,* or *Pandemonium* or roam the astral plane. However, they cannot enter the material plane without aid (conjuration, gate, or by name speaking or similar means).

Demons are chaotic and evil; the smarter and stronger rule those of their kind who are weaker and less intelligent. The less intelligent will attack without question and fight until slain. Demons of type V and above are not actually slain when their material form is killed in combat; their material form being removed from their use, the demon in question is thereby forced back to the plane from whence it originally came, there to remain until a century has passed or until another aids it to go forth again. However, if demons are encountered on their own plane, they can be slain. No demon can ever be subdued. All are able to divide their attacks amongst two or even three opponents if their means allow.

Demons will never willingly serve anyone or anything. If forced to serve through magic or threat they will continually seek a way to slay their master/captor. Those to whom demons show a liking are typically carried off to the demons' plane to become a slave (although a favored one). Note that demons can be summoned by characters of any alignment, but controlling a demon is another matter entirely. A thaumaturgic circle will serve to keep out demons of types I-V. A special pentacle is required for demons of type VI or greater. The threat or reward which the conjuring party uses to attempt gaining a demon's service must be carefully handled by the dungeon master. Demons are repelled by holy (good) relics or artifacts.

Demons' Amulets: Demon lords and princes maintain their vital essences in small containers — their souls, so to speak, are thus at once protected and yet vulnerable if some enterprising character should gain the amulet. Demons with amulets are able to *magic jar* once per day. Demons' amulets cannot be detected as such by any magical means, and they do not otherwise appear unusual in any way. The device need not be with the most powerful princes, although the lesser demons typically need to carry theirs on or near their persons. Possession of an amulet gives the possessor power over the demon to whom it "belongs" for the space of, for example, one adventure, and never more than a day (24 hours). The amulet must then be returned to the demon — or it can be destroyed and thus condemn the prince to abyssment for a year (and he may return thereafter only if summoned). Use of an amulet is very, very dangerous. Possession of one will double chances of calling the attention of another demon, and any demon not controlled by the device will immediately attack the person possessing such an amulet. If the amulet leaves the hand of the one commanding the demon to whom it belongs, that demon attacks him in its most effective fashion immediately, attempting his utmost to slay and then to carry all that remains to his own domain, i.e. that character is lost and gone forever. On the positive side, however, if the wielder of the amulet carefully repays the demon for aid rendered, adds a considerable sum for having the temerity to dare to command the demon in the first place, and then carefully restores the amulet to the demon, the prince might not bear him a grudge forever afterwards nor seek to hunt him out whenever possible.

Demons frequently roam the astral and ethereal planes. Their attention is also attracted by persons in an ethereal state. If the name of a particularly powerful demon is spoken there is a chance that he will hear and turn his attention to the speaker. A base 5% chance is recommended to the referee. Unless prepared to avoid such attention — or to control the demon — the demon will thereupon immediately kill, by whatever means are most expeditious, the one pronouncing his name.

If demon types I through VI are encountered in lair there will be 1-6 of the same type 75% of the time and 1-6 mixed types I-VI 25% of the time.

In addition to the separate characteristics and abilities of each sort of demon, these monsters have the following in common:

Types I-III are affected by non-magical weapons
Type IV and greater are not affected by non-magical weapons

All demons have these abilities:
Infravision 　　　　　　　　　*Teleportation* (no error)
Darkness (r. varies) 　　　　　*Gate* (specifics vary)

Demons are affected by the listed attack forms as noted below:

Attack	Maximum Damage Will be:
acid	full
cold	half
electricity (lightning)	half
fire (dragon, magical)	half
gas (poisonous, etc.)	half
iron weapon	full
magic missile	full
poison	full
silver weapon	none*

*unless affected by normal weapons in which case damage will be according to the weapon type.

Because they have a special form of telepathy, demons are able to understand every intelligent communication. Demons with average or better intelligence are likewise able to converse.

Demogorgon, (Prince of Demons)

FREQUENCY: *Very rare*
NO. APPEARING: *1*
ARMOR CLASS: *-8*
MOVE: *15"*
HIT DICE: *200 hit points*
% IN LAIR: *50%*
TREASURE TYPE: *R, S, T, V*
NO. OF ATTACKS: *3*
DAMAGE/ATTACK: *All special*
SPECIAL ATTACKS: *See below*
SPECIAL DEFENSES: *+2 or better weapon to hit*
MAGIC RESISTANCE: *95%*
INTELLIGENCE: *Supra-genius*
ALIGNMENT: *Chaotic evil*
SIZE: *L (18' tall)*
PSIONIC ABILITY: *150/head*
　　Attack/Defense Modes: *All/all*

Rivalry between demon lords is great, but the enmity between Demogorgon and Orcus is immense and unending. Demogorgon is a terrible opponent. First, he possesses great powers in his two heads. Should he fix the gaze of both upon his enemies he is able to *hypnotize.* This hyponosis will affect from 10-100 creatures of 1 to 3 hit dice, from 5 to 40 with 4 to 6 hit dice, from 3 to 24 with 7 to 9 hit dice, 2 to 12 with 10 to 12 hit dice, and from 1-4 with 13 or more hit dice. Those over 15 hit dice save versus magic, all others are automatically hypnotized. This hypnosis of the mass sort is limited in that the victims are only under its influence for 1 turn, but during this time will follow most instructions absolutely (self destruction would not be heeded) and for from 1 to 6 turns afterwards will tend to believe or carry out the residual of the hypnosis. Demogorgon's left head has a gaze which has the effect of a *rod of beguiling,* and the gaze of his right head causes *insanity* for from 1 to 6 turns. When used independently in this manner the potential victim or victims save versus magic to determine whether or not they avoid the eyes.

Second, Demogorgon is able to lash his forked tail, striking with it as a whip-like weapon. Its touch causes energy drain from one to four levels, the tail striking as a flail for hit determination.

Third, his tentacles also are deadly weapons, each causing 1-6 hit points of damage to any opponent, but those opponents which are of lesser stature (particularly those hailing from the material plane such as humans, dwarves, elves, etc.) will be subject to *rot* — a limb becomes useless in 6 melee rounds and drops off in another six; the body sustains damage which permanently removes 25% of the person's hit points in 6 melee rounds, cumulative per hit. A *cure disease* made within the 6 melee round limit will save the member so that it will heal in 1 to 4 weeks, and body hits will be restored entirely with the cure if made within the 6 melee rounds after the hit.

Whenever desiring to do so, Demogorgon uses any one of the following powers: Cast *continual darkness, charm person, create illusion* (as an illusion wand), *cause fear* (as a wand of that ilk), *levitate* (as a 16th level magic-user), *detect magic, read magic, read languages, detect invisible objects, ESP, dispel magic, clairvoy,* use *clairaudience, suggest, water breathe, polymorph self, wall of ice, charm monster, telekinese* 7,000 gold piece weight with each of his two heads (or with but one), cast a *feeblemind* spell once per day, *project an image,* use *power word stun* once per day, use *any symbol* once per day, turn *sticks to snakes* and *gate* in other demons, 85% chance of success: 50% chance for a type I-IV, 50% chance of gating in a type V or VI.

Description: It is contended by some that this demon prince is supreme, and in any event he is awesome in his power. This gigantic demon is 18' tall and reptilian. Demogorgon has two heads which bear the visages of evil baboons or perhaps mandrills with the hideous coloration of the latter named beasts. His blue-green skin is plated with snake-like scales, his body and legs are those of a giant lizard, his twin necks resemble snakes, and his thick tail is forked. Rather than having arms, he has great tentacles. His appearance testifies to his command of cold-blooded things such as serpents, reptiles, and octopi.

Juiblex (The Faceless Lord)

FREQUENCY: *Very rare*
NO. APPEARING: *1*
ARMOR CLASS: *-7*
MOVE: *3''*
HIT DICE: *88 hit points*
% IN LAIR: *60%*
TREASURE TYPE: *P (×2), R (×2)*
NO. OF ATTACKS: *1*
DAMAGE/ATTACK: *4-40*
SPECIAL ATTACKS: *See below*
SPECIAL DEFENSES: *+2 or better
    weapon to hit*
MAGIC RESISTANCE: *65%*
INTELLIGENCE: *Genius*
ALIGNMENT: *Chaotic evil*
SIZE: *L (9'+ tall)*
PSIONIC ABILITY: *225*
    Attack/Defense Modes: *All/all*

There is no question that this is the most disgusting and loathsome of all demons. Juiblex is foul and nauseating in the extreme. His dripping form can lash forward in melee to cause terrible damage — both from the force of his blow and the caustic properties of his noisome secretions. Juiblex is reclusive and hates intrusion by any form of normal creature but surrounds his person with slimes, jellies, and puddings. If encountered in his lair there will be from 1-4 green slimes, 2-8 ochre jellies, 1-4 gray oozes, and 1-4 black puddings. He is similarly shunned by other demons and other creatures.

Juiblex is able to shed a *circle of darkness* (15' radius) at will. He can also *cause fear* (as a fear wand), cast a *circle of cold* (10' radius), and regenerate at 2 hit points per melee round. This demon lord is also able to do any one of the following during a melee round: *detect invisible, locate object, ESP, fly, dispel magic, invisibility* (10' radius), *charm monster, hold monster, telekinese* 15,000 gold piece weight, *project image, phase door, putrify food & water, cause disease, speak with monsters,* speak an *unholy word* once per day, and *gate* in 1-4 type II demons (70% chance of success). He is also able to spew forth a jelly-like slime (combining the effects of an ochre jelly and green slime) once per turn (every ten melee rounds) with a 15' range and a blob size of 3 cubic feet.

Description: Juiblex has no set form (he can spread himself into a vast pool of slime or raise up into a towering column of disgusting ordure 18' or more in height) but he usually takes the form of a 9' tall cone-like heap, striated in disgusting blackish greens, foul browns and yellows, and sickly translucent grays and ambers. From this mass protrude several glaring red eyes.

Manes (Sub-Demon)

FREQUENCY: *Rare*
NO. APPEARING: *4-16*
ARMOR CLASS: *7*
MOVE: *3''*
HIT DICE: *1*
% IN LAIR: *Nil*
TREASURE TYPE: *Nil*
NO. OF ATTACKS: *3*
DAMAGE/ATTACK: *1-2/1-2/1-4*
SPECIAL ATTACKS: *Nil*
SPECIAL DEFENSES: *+1 or better
    weapons to hit*
MAGIC RESISTANCE: *Standard*
INTELLIGENCE: *Semi-*
ALIGNMENT: *Chaotic evil*
SIZE: *S (3' tall)*
PSIONIC ABILITY: *Nil*
    Attack/Defense Modes: *Nil*

Those dead which go to the 666 layers of the demonic abyss become *manes.* The most evil of them are confined in the tiers of flames of Gehenna. They are only semi-intelligent and attack any non-demon with nails and teeth. Killing them simply dissipates them into stinking clouds of vapor which reform into manes in one day. Demon lords and princes sometimes feed upon these creatures, destroying them utterly. Treat them as undead with regard to sleep, charm, and similar spells.

Certain manes will be used to form shadows or ghasts, (qqv), depending upon the greatness of their evil in material life. They can also be sent forth by a lord or prince to exist on the material plane for a day. These are typically those from Gehenna.

Orcus (Prince of the Undead)

FREQUENCY: *Very rare*
NO. APPEARING: *1*
ARMOR CLASS: *-6*
MOVE: *9''/18''*
HIT DICE: *120 hit points*
% IN LAIR: *50%*
TREASURE TYPE: *P, S, T, U.*
NO. OF ATTACKS: *2*
DAMAGE/ATTACK: *See below*
SPECIAL ATTACKS: *See below*
SPECIAL DEFENSES: *+3 or better
    weapon to hit*
MAGIC RESISTANCE: *85%*
INTELLIGENCE: *Supra genius*
ALIGNMENT: *Chaotic evil*
SIZE: *L (15' tall)*
PSIONIC ABILITY: *350*
    Attack/Defense Modes: *All/all*

It is probable that this creature is one of the most powerful and strongest of all demons. If he so much as slaps with his open hand the blow causes 1-4 hit points of damage. His terrible fists can deliver blows of 3-13 hit points. If he uses a weapon he strikes with a bonus of +6 to hit and +8 on damage. Additionally his tail has a virulent poison sting (-4 on all saving throws against its poison), and his tail strikes with an 18 dexterity which does 2-8 hit points each time it hits.

Orcus can, at will, use any one of the following powers: Cast *continual darkness, charm person, create illusion* (as a wand of that kind), *cause fear* (as a fear wand), *detect magic, read magic, read languages, detect invisible objects, ESP, cause pyrotechnics, dispel magic, clairvoy,* use *clairaudience,* cast a 12-die *lightning bolt, suggest, polymorph self, create a wall of fire, telekinese* 12,000 gold piece weight, *animate dead* (as a 19th level magic-user), cast a *feeblemind* spell once per day, *project image,* use *any one of the symbols* once per day each, *polymorph any object, shape change, time stop* once per day, and has an 80% chance of *gating* in any demon of type I-V (but only a 50% chance of gating a type V or VI and will never call upon another prince). Orcus can speak with the dead (as 20th level cleric).

Orcus furthermore is able to summon certain of the undead, for he is their prince. If random calling is desired by the referee the following chart is suggested:

1 — 4-48 skeletons
2 — 4-32 zombies
3 — 4-24 shadows
4 — 2-8 vampires

Finally, Orcus holds the wand of death (Orcus' Wand) which is a rod of obsidian topped by a skull. This instrument causes death (or annihilation) to any creature, save those of like status (other princes or devils, saints, godlings, etc.) merely by touching their flesh. Other powers of this device as rumored amongst mortals are dealt with in another book.

Description: Orcus is a grossly fat demon lord, some 15' tall. His huge gray body is covered with goatish hair, and his head is goat-like although his horns are similar to those of a ram. His great legs are also goat-like, but his arms are human. Vast bat wings sprout from his back, and his long, snaky tail is tipped with a poisonous head.

Succubus

FREQUENCY: *Rare*
NO. APPEARING: *1*
ARMOR CLASS: *0*
MOVE: *12"/18"*
HIT DICE: *6*
% IN LAIR: *5%*
TREASURE TYPE: *I, Q*
NO. OF ATTACKS: *2*
DAMAGE/ATTACK: *1-3/1-3*
SPECIAL ATTACKS: *energy drain*
SPECIAL DEFENSES: *+1 or better*
     weapon to hit
MAGIC RESISTANCE: *70%*
INTELLIGENCE: *Exceptional*
ALIGNMENT: *Chaotic evil*
SIZE: *M (6' tall)*
PSIONIC ABILITY: *200*
     Attack/Defense Modes: *D/G, I*

These female demons are usually not found in numbers, for they prefer to act alone. A succubus in its natural form appears very much like a tall and very beautiful human female — although the bat-like wings immediately show the observer its true character. Succubi cannot be harmed by any sort of normal weaponry. Succubus can *cause darkness* in a 5' radius. The kiss of the succubus drains the victim of one energy level, and all succubi are able to perform any one of the following feats at will: Become ethereal (as if using the oil of that name), *charm person, ESP, clairaudience, suggestion* (as the spell), *shape change* (to any humanoid form of approximately their own height and weight only), or *gate* in a type IV (70% chance), type VI (25%), or one of the lords or princes (5% chance) — there is only a 40% chance of such a gate opening, however.

Succubi rule lower demons through wit and threat.

Type I (Vrock)

FREQUENCY: *Common*
NO. APPEARING: *1-3 or 1-6*
ARMOR CLASS: *0*
MOVE: *12"/18"*
HIT DICE: *8*
% IN LAIR: *5%*
TREASURE TYPE: *B*
NO. OF ATTACKS: *5*
DAMAGE/ATTACK: *1-4/1-4/1-8/1-8/1-6*
SPECIAL ATTACKS: *See below*
SPECIAL DEFENSES: *See below*
MAGIC RESISTANCE: *50%*
INTELLIGENCE: *Low*
ALIGNMENT: *Chaotic evil*
SIZE: *L (8½' tall)*
PSIONIC ABILITY: *Nil*
     Attack/Defense Modes: *Nil*

These are among the weakest of their kind; type 1 demons somewhat resemble a cross between a human and a vulture. Strength is standard. They may be struck with normal missiles and by normal weapons. *Darkness* caused by them is the typical 5' radius sort. In addition these demons have the ability to do any one of the following, one at a time, at

will: *Detect invisible objects, telekinese* 2,000 gold piece weight, *gate* in another type I demon (10% chance of success).

These creatures are very fond of the flesh of the human sort, and they also prize precious metals and stones. Because of their stupidity they are not often prone to listen to bribe offers.

Type II (Hezrou)

FREQUENCY: *Common*
NO. APPEARING: *1-3 or 1-6*
ARMOR CLASS: *-2*
MOVE: *6"//12"*
HIT DICE: *9*
% IN LAIR: *10%*
TREASURE TYPE: *C*
NO. OF ATTACKS: *3*
DAMAGE/ATTACK: *1-3/1-3/4-16*
SPECIAL ATTACKS: *See below*
SPECIAL DEFENSES: *See below*
MAGIC RESISTANCE: *55%*
INTELLIGENCE: *Low*
ALIGNMENT: *Chaotic evil*
SIZE: *L (7'+ tall)*
PSIONIC ABILITY: *100*
     Attack/Defense Modes: *E/F, G*

The next most common type of demon, these foul creatures are a foot shorter than the tall type I sort, looking somewhat like a gross toad with arms in place of forelegs. These demons can be struck by normal weapons or missiles. The *darkness* they cause at will is of the variety which covers a 15' radius. These sorts of additional abilities can be performed by these demons, one at a time, at will: *Cause fear* (as a fear wand), *levitate* (as an 8th level magic-user), *detect invisible objects, telekinese* 3,000 gold piece weight, *gate* in another type II demon (20% chance of success).

Type II demons are like type I with regard to their appetites. Note that either sort will gladly fight the other for any reason whatsoever.

Type III (Glabrezu)

FREQUENCY: *Uncommon*
NO. APPEARING: *1-3 or 1-6*
ARMOR CLASS: *-4*
MOVE: *9"*
HIT DICE: *10*
% IN LAIR: *15%*
TREASURE TYPE: *D*
NO. OF ATTACKS: *5*
DAMAGE/ATTACK: *2-12/2-12/1-3/1-3/2-5*
SPECIAL ATTACKS: *See below*
SPECIAL DEFENSES: *See below*
MAGIC RESISTANCE: *60%*
INTELLIGENCE: *Average*
ALIGNMENT: *Chaotic evil*
SIZE: *L (9½' tall)*
PSIONIC ABILITY: *100*
     Attack/Defense Modes: *E/F*

Towering to well over nine feet in height, this not unusual kind of demon has a ghastly appearance, being broad and strong-looking covered with a wrinkled hide, with a head much like a goat-horned dog, pincers instead of normal hands, and a small pair of human arms protruding from its chest. Normal attacks will affect this demon type. It causes *darkness* in a 10' radius when it so wills. Additional abilities, any one of which can be performed at will, are: *Fear* (as a fear wand), *levitate* (as a 10th level magic-user), *cause pyrotechnics, polymorph self, telekinese* 4,000 gold piece weight, *gate* in another demon of types I-III (roll for which type) (30% chance of success).

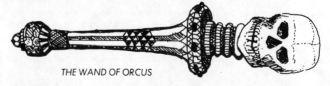

THE WAND OF ORCUS

Type IV (Nalfeshnee, etc.)

FREQUENCY: *Uncommon*
NO. APPEARING: *1-3 or 1-6*
ARMOR CLASS: *-1*
MOVE: *9"/12"*
HIT DICE: *11*
% IN LAIR: *15%*
TREASURE TYPE: *E*
NO. OF ATTACKS: *3*
DAMAGE/ATTACK: *1-4/1-4/2-8*
SPECIAL ATTACKS: *bonus of +2 to hit; also see below*
SPECIAL DEFENSES: *+1 or better weapons to hit*
MAGIC RESISTANCE: *65%*
INTELLIGENCE: *Very*
ALIGNMENT: *Chaotic evil*
SIZE: *L (10½'+ tall)*
PSIONIC ABILITY: *150*
　　Attack/Defense Modes: *A, C, E/F, G, H*

These demons combine the worst features of an ape and a boar, and their small wings appear unable to bear their ponderous ten foot tall bodies. Unlike lower sorts of demons, type IV can be hit only by weapons and missiles of the magical sort. Much as a type III, these demons cause *darkness* in a 10' radius at will. They have these other abilities which can be employed one per melee round: *Create illusion* (similar to that from an illusion wand), *cause fear* (as a fear wand), *levitate* (as a 12th level magic-user), *detect magic, read languages, dispel magic, polymorph self, telekinese* 5,000 gold piece weight, *project image*, use a *symbol* of fear or discord, and *gate* in a demon of type I-IV (dice for which sort) (60% chance).

Some type IV demons have names, and these can be spoken with if the conjuring party knows the proper one to say; this will make it 90% certain the demon will listen to offers of great rewards for some small service. These demons are also fond of human flesh and blood.

Type V (Marilith, etc.)

FREQUENCY: *Rare*
NO. APPEARING: *1-3 or 1-6*
ARMOR CLASS: *-7/-5*
MOVE: *12"*
HIT DICE: *7 + 7*
% IN LAIR: *10%*
TREASURE TYPE: *G*
NO. OF ATTACKS: *7*
DAMAGE/ATTACK: *2-8/& 6 varying*
SPECIAL ATTACKS: *See below*
SPECIAL DEFENSES: *+1 or better weapon to hit*
MAGIC RESISTANCE: *80%*
INTELLIGENCE: *High*
ALIGNMENT: *Chaotic evil*
SIZE: *L (7' tall)*
PSIONIC ABILITY: *130*
　　Attack/Defense Modes: *A, E/F, G, H*

Another of the female demons with a multiarmed female torso atop the body of a great snake. Type V demons are taller than a large man and far more terrible. Their six arms are all able to use weapons. The favored weapons are swords and battle axes. They can constrict a victim with their snakey tails as well. When desiring to do so, they cause *darkness* in a 5' radius. Other extraordinary abilities, any one of which can be performed as desired are: *charm person, levitate* (as an 11th level magic-user), *read languages, detect invisible object, cause pyrotechnics, polymorph self, project image*, and *gate* in a type I (30% chance), type II (25% chance), type III (15% chance), type IV (15% chance), type VI (10% chance), or one of the lords or princes (5%); but the chance of successfully opening such a gate is a mere 50%.

Lower level demons greatly fear the domineering and cruel type V demons. All of these creatures have names which can be used to aid in negotiations. Demons of this type are likely to desire the sacrifice of strong warriors to them.

Type VI (Balor, etc.)

FREQUENCY: *Rare*
NO. APPEARING: *1-3 or 1-6*
ARMOR CLASS: *-2*
MOVE: *6"/15"*
HIT DICE: *8 + 8*
% IN LAIR: *20%*
TREASURE TYPE: *F*
NO. OF ATTACKS: *1*
DAMAGE/ATTACK: *2-13*
SPECIAL ATTACKS: *Whip & flame for 2-12/3-18/4-24*
SPECIAL DEFENSES: *+1 or better weapon to hit*
MAGIC RESISTANCE: *75%*
INTELLIGENCE: *High*
ALIGNMENT: *Chaotic evil*
SIZE: *L (12' tall)*
PSIONIC ABILITY: *180*
　　Attack/Defense Modes: *A, B, C, E/F, G, H*

Each type VI demon has its own name. (Balor is a type VI demon of the largest size.) Six are known to exist. The favored weapons of these monsters are a large +1 sword and a whip with many "tails." The latter weapon is employed to drag the opponent into the flames which the demons are able to create around themselves. During any combat there is a two-thirds chance (1-4 on a 6-sided die) each melee round that any type VI demon will immolate and use its whip. The two largest of these demons do 4-24 hit points of damage when a victim is drawn within their flames, the middle-sized and smallest do 3-18 and 2-12 respectively.

They shed *darkness* in a 10' radius at will. Their other singular abilities are: *Cause fear* (as a fear wand), *detect magic, read magic, read languages, detect invisible objects, cause pyrotechnics, dispel magic, suggestion, telekinese* 6,000 gold piece weight, use a *symbol* of fear, discord, sleep or stunning, and they also have a 70% chance of successfully *gating* in a demon of type III (80%) or type IV (20%). Each of these terrible abilities can be employed as often as desired, but only one may be used at any given time.

With proper invoking, offerings, and promises type VI demons might be convinced to co-operate with a character or group for a time. Naturally, the demon will attempt to assume/usurp command at every opportunity. Most chaotic evil monsters are drawn to the strong evil charisma of this creature, and of all its kind, the type VI demon tends towards a more organized evil (which makes it less than popular with demon lords and princes).

Yeenoghu (Demon Lord of Gnolls)

FREQUENCY: *Very rare*
NO. APPEARING: *1*
ARMOR CLASS: *-5*
MOVE: *18"*
HIT DICE: *100 hit points*
% IN LAIR: *35%*
TREASURE TYPE: *C, G, I*
NO. OF ATTACKS: *1 (special)*
DAMAGE/ATTACK: *3-18 (+ special)*
SPECIAL ATTACKS: *See below*
SPECIAL DEFENSES: *+1 or better weapon to hit*
MAGIC RESISTANCE: *80%*
INTELLIGENCE: *Exceptional*
ALIGNMENT: *Chaotic evil*
SIZE: *L (12' tall)*
PSIONIC ABILITY: *300*
　　Attack/Defense Modes: *All/all*

Amongst the ranks of demon princes, Yeenoghu is one of the most powerful and most feared. There will normally be 66 gnolls of the strongest sort (14-16 hit points each) in attendance upon Yeenoghu, and if he is alone he can summon from 6-66 in one turn. As this demon prince also receives homage from the King of Ghouls, he can similarly summon from 6-16 ghouls if he so desires. He typically carries his dreaded flail, a weapon 7' long, with three chains of adamantite, each bearing a spiked ball. When he strikes with this weapon each of the balls is rolled for to determine if it scored a hit, for each does different things: 1st — scores 3 to 18 points of damage; 2nd — if a hit is scored the saving throw versus *wands* must be made or the victim is *paralyzed*; 3rd — if a hit is scored the saving throw versus *magic* must be made or the victim is *confused* (as per the spell). Yeenoghu speaks all of the "giant class" languages, as well as the common tongue. He can also telepathically project his speech to any single creature, but he cannot thereby influence them other than by the persuasiveness of his speech. He sees into the ethereal and astral planes. Yeenoghu is able to use any of the following magical powers, one per melee round: *darkness* (10' radius); *magic missile* (3/day, 6 missiles/cast), each doing 2-8 points of damage and having a +2 to hit; *detect magic, read magic, read languages, detect invisible objects, invisibility, fly, hold person, dispel magic* (equal to a 20th level magic-user), *suggestion, polymorph self, fear* (as a fear wand), *teleport, telekinese* 10,000 gold piece weight, *transmute rock to mud, mass charm,* and *gate* in type I demons (once/day, 80% chance for from 2-5).

Description: Yeenoghu resembles a human in general form, but only at first glance. His head is that of a hyena, his chest is canine in form, his hands are paw-like, and his feet are pawed. Yeenoghu is thin to the point of being skeletal, and his only body hair is a mangy crest of putrid yellow from his head to his mid-back. Yeenoghu's skin is a dead gray in color, and it is smooth. His eyes are lambent amber and large.

DEVIL

The inhabitants and rulers of the planes of hell are principally devils, the most powerful of lawful evil creatures. They somewhat resemble the demons of chaos in their characteristics and abilities, and general attributes will be dealt with below, while specifics pertaining to each individual type or arch-devil are given in the category or name detail listings.

Devils follow a definite order, a chain of command, which they dare not break for fear of the arch-devils. Still, there is great rivalry, even open antagonism, between the devils of the various planes and between the various arch-devils. While the lesser devils squabble, the dukes of Hell vie to usurp the throne of Asmodeus. But the Archfiend has always succeeded in playing one off against the other, and still rules from his lowest plane.

All devils are able to move about the planes of Hell (although they dare not do so without authorization, save for the dukes). They can move to the planes of *Gehenna, Hades,* and *Acheron* at will. Devils can also move through the astral plane, although they seldom do so. No devil is able to enter the other planes unless the proper ritual is performed, a gate is opened, or the proper name of a devil is spoken (and heard).

It is possible to destroy the material form of a greater devil or duke of Hell, but such creatures can not actually be slain unless encountered and fought in Hell or those lower planes adjacent to it. Devils can never be subdued. The lesser ones will always fight until destroyed; the greater ones will negotiate if seriously threatened. Devils will serve if properly commanded, but it is risky business, for an improper command will break the law which binds them to service. (It also typically requires a contract for the soul of the creature commanding the internal power to obey.) It is possible for other than lawful evil persons to invoke or otherwise treat with devils (but the long spoon, oft spoken of, had better be used when supping with such monsters). Magic circles will keep devils off for a time if they are properly scribed (and ensymboled in the case of a greater and arch-devils). Devils are repelled by holy (good) artifacts or relics.

All devils can direct their attacks against two or more opponents if the means are at hand. If a greater devil has its material form destroyed it is forced to lemure status for nine decades of torment before it resumes its former station. If the material form of a duke is destroyed, that arch-devil is bound to its own particular plane of Hell for a decade (unless again properly called forth prior to the end of the 10 years) and a great loss of face is suffered (and fury in Hell *is* unmatched then).

Devils' Talismans: Each type of lesser devil has a special combination of inscriptions which will bind them to the wielder for the space of nine days, or at least prevent the devils of that type from harming the possessor. Greater devils can likewise be commanded for nine hours or kept at bay. Arch-devils' talismans will cause them to perform a single service, or prevent the bearer from being harmed by a particular duke of Hell, when properly used. The employment of any devil's talisman requires great care and caution. Human sacrifice is required of evil creatures using a talisman. Merely looking at these talismans is dangerous. If not properly protected by spells or a magic circle, study of a charm gives a 10% chance of summoning the kind or specific devil to whom the talisman belongs. Speaking the name on the talisman will *always* call forth the kind or

specific devil. Arch-devils will be aware of improperly protected talismans, and they will send something to slay persons in possession of them if the talismans pertain to them or their planes.

General Characteristics:

Only erinyes, barbed devils, and bone devils can be hit by non-magical weapons. The greater devils (malebranche, ice devils, and pit fiends) can be struck by magical weapons, or weapons of silver, but ordinary arms do them no harm.

All devils have or are able to perform the following:

Charm Person
Suggestion
Illusion
Infravision
Teleportation (no error)
Know Alignment
Cause Fear (effect varies)
Animate Dead

Devils are able to summon their fellows, summoning being similar to a *monster summoning spell.*

Because they have a special form of telepathy, devils are able to understand and converse with any intelligent creature.

Devils are affected by the listed attack forms as noted below:

Attack	Maximum Damage Will be:
acid	full
cold	half
electricity (lightning)	full
fire (dragon, magical)	none
gas (poisonous, etc.)	half
iron weapon	none*
magic missile	full
poison	full
silver weapon	full

*unless affected by normal weapons, in which case damage will be according to the weapon type.

Asmodeus (Arch-devil)

FREQUENCY: *Very rare*
NO. APPEARING: *1*
ARMOR CLASS: *-7*
MOVE: *12"/24"*
HIT DICE: *199 hit points*
% IN LAIR: *90%*
TREASURE TYPE: *I, R, U, V*
NO. OF ATTACKS: *1*
DAMAGE/ATTACK: *4-14*
SPECIAL ATTACKS: *See below*
SPECIAL DEFENSES: *+3 or better weapon to hit*
MAGIC RESISTANCE: *90%*
INTELLIGENCE: *Supra genius*
ALIGNMENT: *Lawful evil*
SIZE: *L (13½' tall)*
PSIONIC ABILITY: *366*
    Attack/Defense Modes: *All/all*

Asmodeus, arch-fiend, the Overlord of all the dukes of Hell rules by both might and wit. He is physically stronger than any other devil (as strong as a storm giant) and the most cunning and artful. His mighty palace rests upon the floor of the lowest rift in Hell's ninth plane. His servitors are *pit-fiends* (q.v.) and whichever of the other lesser and greater devils he commands to service. Once per year he can command the arch-devils to attend his court and pay homage.

The powers possessed by Asmodeus which are usable at will, once per turn or melee round, are: *pyrotechnics, produce flame, wall of fire, ice storm, wall of ice, continual light, read languages, read magic, detect invisible, locate object, invisibility, dispel magic, hold person, hold monster, shape change, beguile, rulership, mass charm, geas, restoration, raise dead fully,* or (fulfill another's) *wish*. Asmodeus can use the following powers once per day: *symbol of pain, symbol of insanity, symbol of hopelessness* (save versus magic or submit to Asmodeus' will), *(un) holy word*. He can always *summon* 2 lesser or 1 greater devil. The gaze of this arch-fiend causes *fear, fear and weakness* or *chill* (slows 50% and -5 on all dice rolls) at his option. Saving throw versus magic applies.

Asmodeus has a glowing rod of pure ruby. It acts as a *rod of absorption*. It also causes *serious wounds* on anyone touched by its opaline tip. Upon command it will shoot forth a cone of frost, a jet of acid, or a bolt of lightning (all according to the appropriate dragon breath weapon). The value of this instrument is 1,000,000 gold pieces considering the gem qualities only!

Description: There can be no question that Asmodeus is the most handsome of all devils as well as being the strongest and most cunning. The ultimate evil he represents can be seen in his beauty only when he so wills or if he forgets himself and flies into a rage.

Baalzebul *(Arch-devil)*

FREQUENCY: *Very rare*
NO. APPEARING: *1*
ARMOR CLASS: *-5*
MOVE: *9''/24''*
HIT DICE: *166 hit points*
% IN LAIR: *80%*
TREASURE TYPE: *E, R, V*
NO. OF ATTACKS: *1 bite*
DAMAGE/ATTACK: *2-12 + poison*
SPECIAL ATTACKS: *See below*
SPECIAL DEFENSES: *+3 or better weapon to hit*
MAGIC RESISTANCE; *85%*
INTELLIGENCE: *Genius*
ALIGNMENT: *Lawful evil*
SIZE: *L (12' tall)*
PSIONIC ABILITY: *313*
　　Attack/Defense Modes: *All/all*

The sixth and seventh planes of Hell, *Malbolge* and *Maladomini* respectively, are ruled by Baalzebul, "Lord of the Flies" ("lies"?) He is an arch-devil of great power, second only to Asmodeus. Malbolge is a black stone plane, filled with stinking vapors, smokes, fire pits, and huge caves and caverns. Maladomini is similar, but there will be found the moated castles of the *malebranche* and the great fortress of Baalzebul.

This arch-devil can employ any of the following powers, one at a time, as desired, during a turn or melee round, as applicable: *pyrotechnics, produce flame, wall of fire, continual light, read languages, read magic, detect invisible, locate object, invisibility, dispel magic, shape change, beguile, rulership* (as a *rod of rulership*), *hold person, charm monster, geas, restoration, raise dead fully,* (fulfill another's) *wish*. Once per day Baalzebul can use: *symbol of pain, symbol of insanity, (un) holy word*. He can always *summon* 1-4 horned devils. His glance causes *fear* and *weakness* (saving throw versus magic or collapse in trembling until 1-4 melee rounds after the gaze is lifted) whenever he directly stares at any person.

Barbed *(Lesser devil)*

FREQUENCY: *Uncommon*
NO. APPEARING: *1-2 or 3-12*
ARMOR CLASS: *0*
MOVE: *12''*
HIT DICE: *8*
% IN LAIR: *50%*
TREASURE TYPE: *Nil*
NO. OF ATTACKS: *3*
DAMAGE/ATTACK: *2-8/2-8/3-12*
SPECIAL ATTACKS: *See below*
SPECIAL DEFENSES: *See below*
MAGIC RESISTANCE: *35%*
INTELLIGENCE: *Very*
ALIGNMENT: *Lawful evil*
SIZE: *M (7' tall)*
PSIONIC ABILITY: *Nil*
　　Attack/Defense Modes: *Nil*

Barbed devils populate the third and fourth planes of Hell. They are excellent guards and alert at all times (never surprised). Unauthorized creatures are immediately cast into one of the many cells to be tormented.

While these monsters carry no weapons, they have sufficient weaponry with their horny, barbed hands and horrid tails. They are able to generate fear (saving throw versus wand is applicable) upon striking an opponent. Barbed devils can perform any of the following, one at a time, per turn or melee round, as applicable: *pyrotechnics, produce flame, hold person,* or *summon* another barbed devil (30% chance of success).

Bone *(Lesser devil)*

FREQUENCY: *Uncommon*
NO. APPEARING: *1-2 or 2-8*
ARMOR CLASS: *-1*
MOVE: *15''*
HIT DICE: *9*
% IN LAIR: *55%*
TREASURE TYPE: *Nil*
NO. OF ATTACKS: *1*
DAMAGE/ATTACK: *3-12*
SPECIAL ATTACKS: *See below*
SPECIAL DEFENSES: *See below*
MAGIC RESISTANCE: *40%*
INTELLIGENCE: *Very*
ALIGNMENT: *Lawful evil*
SIZE: *L (9½' tall)*
PSIONIC ABILITY: *Nil*
　　Attack/Defense Modes: *Nil*

Bone devils populate the lower planes of Hell, particularly the fifth. They are particularly malicious and delight in making less powerful creatures suffer. As they prefer cold to heat, these monsters also have ultravision, seeing light in the ultra-violet spectrum at 60' range.

Bone devils have a great bone hook they employ to snare and wound opponents. Any creature caught (hit) by it has a 50% chance of being stuck fast. The bone devil will then strike such victims with its tail doing 2-8 hit points of damage, plus causing a loss of strength (1-4 points) unless a save versus poison is made; strength loss lasts for 10 melee rounds.

At will, once per turn or melee round, as applicable, bone devils can: generate *fear* in a 5' radius sphere, *create illusion, fly, become invisible, detect invisible, fear* (spell), or *summon* another bone devil (40% chance of success). Once per day it is able to create a *wall of ice*.

Dispater *(Arch-devil)*

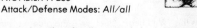

FREQUENCY: *Very rare*
NO. APPEARING: *1*
ARMOR CLASS: *-2*
MOVE: *15''*
HIT DICE: *144 hit points*
% IN LAIR: *80%*
TREASURE TYPE: *Q (×10), S*
NO. OF ATTACKS: *See below*
DAMAGE/ATTACK: *See below*
SPECIAL ATTACKS: *See below*
SPECIAL DEFENSES: *+2 or better weapon to hit*
MAGIC RESISTANCE: *80%*
INTELLIGENCE: *Genius*
ALIGNMENT: *Lawful evil*
SIZE: *M (7' tall)*
PSIONIC ABILITY: *266*
　　Attack/Defense Modes: *All/all*

Dispater is the ruler of Hell's second plane. His capitol is the iron city of Dis, named after the whole of the plane. Dispater's palace there is infernally grand. The city is filled with zombies, erinyes (q.v.), and a sprinkling of barbed devils and malebranche.

The following powers are possible at will for Dispater, one at a time per turn or melee round, as applicable: *pyrotechnics, produce flame, wall of fire, light, read magic, read languages, detect invisible, shape change, beguile, geas, restoration, raise dead fully,* (fulfill another's) *wish*. He can summon 1-3 erinyes (75%) or (25%) a pit fiend (90% chance of success). Once per day Dispater can employ a *symbol* of *pain*; he can also pronounce an *(un)holy word* once per day. His stare causes *fear* or *chill* in all persons who fail their saving throws versus magic.

Description: Dispater is evilly handsome, and only his small horns, tail, and cloven left hoof distinguish him from humanity. He has a rod which has the powers of a *rod of rulership* and a double strength *staff of striking* (4-24 hit points of damage).

Erinyes (Lesser devil)

FREQUENCY: *Uncommon*
NO. APPEARING: *1-3 or 4-16*
ARMOR CLASS: *2*
MOVE: *6"/21"*
HIT DICE: *6 + 6*
% IN LAIR: *20%*
TREASURE TYPE: *R*
NO. OF ATTACKS: *1*
DAMAGE/ATTACK: *2-8*
SPECIAL ATTACKS: *See below*
SPECIAL DEFENSES: *See below*
MAGIC RESISTANCE: *30%*
INTELLIGENCE: *Average*
ALIGNMENT: *Lawful evil*
SIZE: *M (6' tall)*
PSIONIC ABILITY: *Nil*
    Attack/Defense Modes: *Nil*

The erinyes are the devils common to Hell's second plane as well as the kind most commonly sent forth to garner more souls. They are female but can appear as male. They are armed with a magical dagger which drips a caustic venom and causes terribly painful wounds (save versus poison or faint for 1-6 melee rounds). They also carry a *rope of entanglement* with which to bind their victims. Erinyes can be struck with normal weapons. They can, at will, *cause fear* in all who look at them (saving throw versus wand is applicable). In addition, they have the power to do any one of the following during any turn or melee round, as applicable: *detect invisible, locate object, invisibility, polymorph self, produce flame,* or summon another erinyes (25% chance of success).

Erinyes are strong — 18/01, but no hit/damage bonuses are applicable. They will pursue evil persons unceasingly in order to take them alive into Hell. They will sometimes bargain with others, hoping to tempt them into evil doing.

Geryon (Arch-devil)

FREQUENCY: *Very rare*
NO. APPEARING: *1*
ARMOR CLASS: *-3*
MOVE: *3"/18"*
HIT DICE: *133 hit points*
% IN LAIR: *70%*
TREASURE TYPE: *H, R*
NO. OF ATTACKS: *3*
DAMAGE/ATTACK: *3-18/3-18/2-8*
SPECIAL ATTACKS: *See below*
SPECIAL DEFENSES: *+2 or better*
    weapon to hit
MAGIC RESISTANCE: *75%*
INTELLIGENCE: *Exceptional*
ALIGNMENT: *Lawful evil*
SIZE: *L (10' tall, 30' long)*
PSIONIC ABILITY: *213*
    Attack/Defense Modes: *All/all*

Sometimes referred to as the "Wild Beast," Geryon is the gigantic ruler of the fifth plane of Hell. This arch-devil is as powerful as a storm giant, and he loves to grab his opponents and rend them with his claws while stabbing them with his terrible poisonous tail (save versus poison at -4 on die). Geryon dwells in a huge castle in the very middle of the plane, and seldom ventures forth.

Geryon is able to use any of the following powers at will, once per melee round or turn, as applicable: *ice storm, wall of ice, light, read languages, read magic, detect invisible, locate object, dispel magic, invisibility, shape*

change, beguile, geas, raise dead fully, (fulfill another's) wish. Once per day Geryon can use a *symbol* of *pain*; he is likewise able to pronounce an *(un)holy word*. He can summon 1-2 bone devils (60%) or (40%) an ice devil (95% chance of success). Geryon's glare will cause *fear* in all those who he directs it upon (saving throw versus magic applicable).

Geryon has a great bull's horn which he can wind. It brings forth 5-20 minotaurs. These monsters will obey to the death. The horn can be blown but once per week.

Description: A handsome head and torso sit atop Geryon's snakey trunk. This arch-devil has no legs, but travels in a snakelike mode along the ground. He has huge bat wings. His tail is barbed and drips poison. Geryon's arms are strong and hairy, ending in paw-like hands.

Horned (Malebranche) (Greater devil)

FREQUENCY: *Uncommon*
NO. APPEARING: *1-2 or 2-5*
ARMOR CLASS: *-5*
MOVE: *9"/18"*
HIT DICE: *5 + 5*
% IN LAIR: *55%*
TREASURE TYPE: *I*
NO. OF ATTACKS: *4 or 1+*
    weapon
DAMAGE/ATTACK: *1-4/1-4/2-5/1-*
    3 or 1-3 and weapon
SPECIAL ATTACKS: *See below*
SPECIAL DEFENSES: *+1 or better*
    weapon to hit
MAGIC RESISTANCE: *50%*
INTELLIGENCE: *High*
ALIGNMENT: *Lawful evil*
SIZE: *L (9' tall)*
PSIONIC ABILITY: *113*
    Attack/Defense Modes: *B, C/F, G, H*

The "evil horns" (*male branche*) are primarily from Hell's sixth and seventh planes. These are the least of the greater devils, and have such names as "Dogretch," "Evil Tail," and "Bent Wing." They hate anything stronger than themselves and fear stronger devils accordingly.

If armed, they will carry a two-tined fork (75%) which causes 2-12 points of damage, or a barbed whip (25%) which will cause 1-4 points of damage plus a stunning effect for the same number of melee rounds unless a saving throw versus magic is made. An unarmed horned devil attacks with a claw/claw/bite. Armed or unarmed these devils are also able to attack with their tails, causing 1-3 hit points of damage and a wound which will bleed thereafter unless bound up (lose 1 hit point/turn until bound or cured). They exude *fear* in a 5' radius (saving throw versus wand applies).

Horned devils can do any one of the following, at will, once per turn or melee round, as applicable: *pyrotechnics, produce flame, ESP, detect magic, illusion,* or summon another horned devil (50% chance of success). Once per day they can create a *wall of fire* of triple normal strength with regard to the damage it causes (3-24 hit points).

Ice (Greater devil)

FREQUENCY: *Uncommon*
NO. APPEARING: *1 or 1-4*
ARMOR CLASS: *-4*
MOVE: *6"*
HIT DICE: *11*
% IN LAIR: *60%*
TREASURE TYPE: *Q, R*
NO. OF ATTACKS: *4*
DAMAGE/ATTACK: *1-4/1-4/2-8/3-12*
SPECIAL ATTACKS: *See below*
SPECIAL DEFENSES: *+2 or better*
    weapon to hit
MAGIC RESISTANCE: *55%*
INTELLIGENCE: *High*
ALIGNMENT: *Lawful evil*
SIZE: *L (10½' tall)*
PSIONIC ABILITY: *166*
    Attack/Defense Modes: *C, D/F, G, H*

The frigid eighth plane of Hell is populated in the main with ice devils. They are greater devils in every sense of the word, preferring to attack and torment victims by means of their claws, mandibles, and tails. A few (25%) carry great spears which inflict 2-12 hit points damage and numb with *cold* the creature thus struck (slow 50% unless save versus paralyzation is made). Being greater devils, they have personal names.

Ice devils can do any one of the following at will, once per turn or melee round, as applicable: *fly, wall of ice, detect magic, detect invisible, polymorph self,* or *gate* in two bone devils (70%) or another ice devil (30%) (60% chance of success). Once per day an ice devil can cause an *ice storm* (as per that spell).

These creatures have ultravision (60'), are able to regenerate 1 hit point per melee round, and a grasping strength of 18/76. They radiate *fear* in a 10' radius (saving throw vs. wand applies).

Lemure

FREQUENCY: *Common*
NO. APPEARING: *5-30*
ARMOR CLASS: *7*
MOVE: *3"*
HIT DICE: *3*
% IN LAIR: *100%*
TREASURE TYPE: *Nil*
NO. OF ATTACKS: *1*
DAMAGE/ATTACK: *1-3*
SPECIAL ATTACKS. *Nil*
SPECIAL DEFENSES: *See below*
MAGIC RESISTANCE: *Standard*
INTELLIGENCE: *Semi-*
ALIGNMENT: *Lawful evil*
SIZE: *M*
PSIONIC ABILITY: *Nil*
    Attack/Defense Modes: *Nil*

The lemures are the form which the dead whom inhabit the Nine Hells are put in. These vaguely human blobs are then tormented by devils. Their minds are quite gone, and they will attack anything non-devilish which they see. Lemures regenerate at a rate of 1 hit point per melee round, so they are not usually destroyed by the wounds inflicted on them by their environment or by the devils filling it. These wretched things can be destroyed permanently only by blessed things (holy water, holy swords, etc.). They are not subject to any form of sleep, charm, or the like.

After being in hell for a time certain lemures will be chosen to form wraiths or spectres (qqv).

Pit Fiend (Greater devil)

FREQUENCY: *Rare*
NO. APPEARING: *1 or 1-3*
ARMOR CLASS: *-3*
MOVE: *6"/15"*
HIT DICE: *13*
% IN LAIR: *65%*
TREASURE TYPE: *J, R*
NO. OF ATTACKS: *2*
DAMAGE/ATTACK: *5-8/7-12*
SPECIAL ATTACKS: *See below*
SPECIAL DEFENSES: *+2 or better weapon to hit*
MAGIC RESISTANCE: *65%*
INTELLIGENCE: *Exceptional*
ALIGNMENT: *Lawful evil*
SIZE: *L (12' tall)*
PSIONIC ABILITY: *213*
    Attack/Defense Modes: *A, C, E/G, H, I*

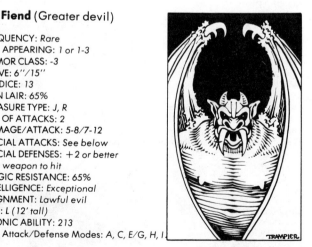

The lowest plane of Hell is the home of the dreaded pit fiend, a devil of great power. They possess a terrible strength and the most evil nature. All pit fiends have personal names. They are the personal servants of Asmodeus. Each typically carries an ancus-like weapon and a jagged-toothed club, and all can strike with both in a melee round.

Pit fiends are able to perform any of the following at will, once per turn or melee round, as applicable: *pyrotechnics, produce flame, wall of fire,*

detect magic, detect invisible, polymorph self, hold person, or *gate* in 1-3 barbed devils (60%) or another pit fiend (70% chance of success). Once per day a pit fiend can use a *symbol* of pain — (save versus magic or suffer -4 on attack dice rolls to hit and a -2 on dexterity for 2-20 melee rounds). They shed *fear* in a 20' radius (save versus magic is applicable).

All pit fiends have a strength of 18/00. They regenerate at 2 hit points per melee round. If they strike with their tail and score a hit the opponent is held with 2-8 hit points of constriction damage per turn.

DINOSAUR

Dinosaurs are reptiles, their name being derived from the Greek "terrible lizard," descended from a variety of the species called thecodonts. The two orders of dinosaurs are saurischians and ornisthischians. All carnivorous dinosaurs fall into the former order. All armored and/or horned dinosaurs fall into the latter order.

Because of the nature of time in planes where magic works, dinosaurs widely separate in time are discussed hereunder, for they can be found intermingled on some alternate world, strange plane, or isolated continent somewhere. Great detail will not be given to any one kind, but all major forms are depicted.

It must be borne in mind that all of these reptiles are extremely stupid. Their motivation is primarily hunger. The predatory types are both ferocious and voracious. The herbivorous dinosaurs are likewise insatiable eaters, but they tend to either ignore all non-eatable things which do not appear to threaten them or flee in panic from anything which they view as dangerous. Certain plant eaters, however, are aggressive in their defense, and these sorts are dangerous, notably stegosaurs, ankylosaurs, and ceratopsians.

Marine dinosaurs might overturn vessels to get at the "food" aboard, or they might snatch unsuspecting creatures from the decks of passing ships. Land carnivores will pursue anything that looks or smells edible, only ceasing pursuit when the prey has obviously moved completely out of their grasp. Herbivorous dinosaur herds might stampede in virtually any direction, as long as it is away from one of the big meat-eaters. Any creature directly in the path of such a stampede will be carried along or killed — the latter if smaller, slower, and weaker.

Anatosaurus (Trachodon)

FREQUENCY: *Common*
NO. APPREARING: *2-12*
ARMOR CLASS: *5*
MOVE: *12"*
HIT DICE: *12*
% IN LAIR: *Nil*
TREASURE TYPE: *Nil*
NO. OF ATTACKS: *1*
DAMAGE/ATTACK: *1-4*
SPECIAL ATTACKS: *Nil*
SPECIAL DEFENSES: *Nil*
MAGIC RESISTANCE: *Standard*
INTELLIGENCE: *Non-*
ALIGNMENT: *Neutral*
SIZE: *L (30'+ long)*
PSIONIC ABILITY: *Nil*
    Attack/Defense Modes: *Nil*

These are duck-billed dinosaurs of the plant eating sort. They run from attack; their only defense is by a lashing tail.

Ankylosaurus

FREQUENCY: *Uncommon*
NO. APPEARING: *2-5*
ARMOR CLASS: *0*
MOVE: *6"*
HIT DICE: *9*
% IN LAIR: *Nil*
TREASURE TYPE: *Nil*
NO. OF ATTACKS: *1*

DAMAGE/ATTACK: 3-18
SPECIAL ATTACKS: *Nil*
SPECIAL DEFENSES: *Nil*
MAGIC RESISTANCE: *Standard*
INTELLIGENCE: *Non-*
ALIGNMENT: *Neutral*
SIZE: *L (15'+ long)*
PSIONIC ABILITY: *Nil*
    Attack/Defense Modes: *Nil*

This armadillo-like ornithischian weighs four or five tons — most of this weight being his armor plating, side spines, and great knobbed tail. If attacked (or threatened) this creature will lash its tail delivering blows of considerable force. They are herbivores of the same family as paleocincus.

Antrodemus (Allosaurus)

FREQUENCY: *Uncommon*
NO. APPEARING: *1-2*
ARMOR CLASS: *5*
MOVE: *15''*
HIT DICE: *15*
% IN LAIR: *Nil*
TREASURE TYPE: *Nil*
NO. OF ATTACKS: *3*
DAMAGE/ATTACK: *1-4/1-4/6-24*
SPECIAL ATTACKS: *Nil*
SPECIAL DEFENSES: *Nil*
MAGIC RESISTANCE: *Standard*
INTELLIGENCE: *Non-*
ALIGNMENT: *Neutral*
SIZE: *L (30' long)*
PSIONIC ABILITY: *Nil*
    Attack/Defense Modes: *Nil*

One of the most vicious of predators, this monster can run across hard ground at great speed.

Apatosaurus (Brontosaurus)

FREQUENCY: *Common*
NO. APPEARING: *1-6*
ARMOR CLASS: *5*
MOVE: *6''*
HIT DICE: *30*
% IN LAIR: *Nil*
TREASURE TYPE: *Nil*
NO. OF ATTACKS: *1*
DAMAGE/ATTACK: *3-18*
SPECIAL ATTACKS: *Nil*
SPECIAL DEFENSES: *Nil*
MAGIC RESISTANCE: *Standard*
INTELLIGENCE: *Non-*
ALIGNMENT: *Neutral*
SIZE: *L (70' long)*
PSIONIC ABILITY: *Nil*
    Attack/Defense Modes: *Nil*

The thunder-lizard is a 40 ton plant-eater found near marshes and lakes. The creature spends much of his time in shallow water to support his bulk. It moves to deep water to avoid carnivores. Apatosaurus ignores small things, but it is prone to step on anything in its way (doing 4-40 points of damage).

Archelon Ischyras

FREQUENCY: *Uncommon*
NO. APPEARING: *1-4*
ARMOR CLASS: *3*
MOVE: *3''//15''*
HIT DICE: *7*
% IN LAIR: *Nil*
TREASURE TYPE: *Nil*
NO. OF ATTACKS: *1*

DAMAGE/ATTACK: 3-12
SPECIAL ATTACKS: *Nil*
SPECIAL DEFENSES: *Nil*
MAGIC RESISTANCE: *Standard*
INTELLIGENCE: *Non-*
ALIGNMENT: *Neutral*
SIZE: *L (12' dia.)*
PSIONIC ABILITY: *Nil*
    Attack/Defense Modes: *Nil*

These are reptiles but not dinosaurs. These marine turtles seldom venture onto dry land. Archelon's shell is not solid, but it is nevertheless very strong.

Brachiosaurus

FREQUENCY: *Uncommon*
NO. APPEARING: *1-6*
ARMOR CLASS: *5*
MOVE: *6''*
HIT DICE: *36*
% IN LAIR: *Nil*
TREASURE TYPE: *Nil*
NO. OF ATTACKS: *1*
DAMAGE/ATTACK: *5-20*
SPECIAL ATTACKS: *Nil*
SPECIAL DEFENSES: *Nil*
MAGIC RESISTANCE: *Standard*
INTELLIGENCE: *Non-*
ALIGNMENT: *Neutral*
SIZE: *L (60' long)*
PSIONIC ABILITY: *Nil*
    Attack/Defense Modes: *Nil*

The heaviest of all dinosaurs, these 85 ton monsters dwell in warm swamps and lakes. Similar to apatosaurs, they might step on something small, causing 8-80 points of damage.

Camarasaurus

FREQUENCY: *Common*
NO. APPEARING: *2-8*
ARMOR CLASS: *6*
MOVE: *6''*
HIT DICE: *20*
% IN LAIR: *Nil*
TREASURE TYPE: *Nil*
NO. OF ATTACKS: *1*
DAMAGE/ATTACK: *3-12*
SPECIAL ATTACKS: *Nil*
SPECIAL DEFENSES: *Nil*
MAGIC RESISTANCE: *Standard*
INTELLIGENCE: *Non-*
ALIGNMENT: *Neutral*
SIZE: *L (50' Long)*
PSIONIC ABILITY: *Nil*
    Attack/Defense Modes: *Nil*

These marsh or swamp dwelling herbivores are smallish for their type. They panic more easily than do apatosaurs, for example. Stepping or trampling damage is 3-30 points.

Ceratosaurus

FREQUENCY: *Uncommon*
NO. APPEARING: *1-4*
ARMOR CLASS: *5*
MOVE: *15''*
HIT DICE: *8*
% IN LAIR: *Nil*
TREASURE TYPE: *Nil*
NO. OF ATTACKS: *3*
DAMAGE/ATTACK: *1-6/1-6/4-16*
SPECIAL ATTACKS: *Nil*

SPECIAL DEFENSES: *Nil*
MAGIC RESISTANCE: *Standard*
INTELLIGENCE: *Non-*
ALIGNMENT: *Neutral*
SIZE: *L (17' long)*
PSIONIC ABILITY: *Nil*
 Attack/Defense Modes: *Nil*

These smallish semi-bipedal monsters are both heavy and fast. This carnivore is unusual in that it has a horn on its nose, but it does not use it for attacking.

Cetiosaurus

FREQUENCY: *Uncommon*
NO. APPEARING: *1-4*
ARMOR CLASS: *6*
MOVE: *6"*
HIT DICE: *24*
% IN LAIR: *Nil*
TREASURE TYPE: *Nil*
NO. OF ATTACKS: *1*
DAMAGE/ATTACK: *3-18*
SPECIAL ATTACKS: *Nil*
SPECIAL DEFENSES: *Nil*
MAGIC RESISTANCE: *Standard*
INTELLIGENCE: *Non-*
ALIGNMENT: *Neutral*
SIZE: *L (60' long)*
PSIONIC ABILITY: *Nil*
 Attack/Defense Modes: *Nil*

These huge plant-eaters dwell in lakes and marshes. Their heads are somewhat larger than similar reptiles (apatosaurus, etc.). If they step on some small things — such as a human for example — they do 4-40 points of damage.

Dinichtys

FREQUENCY: *Common*
NO. APPEARING: *1-4*
ARMOR CLASS: *7*
MOVE: *21"*
HIT DICE: *10*
% IN LAIR: *Nil*
TREASURE TYPE: *Nil*
NO. OF ATTACKS: *1*
DAMAGE/ATTACK: *5-20*
SPECIAL ATTACKS: *Swallow*
SPECIAL DEFENSES: *Nil*
MAGIC RESISTANCE: *Standard*
INTELLIGENCE: *Non-*
ALIGNMENT: *Neutral*
SIZE: *L (25' + long)*
PSIONIC ABILITY: *Nil*
 Attack/Defense Modes: *Nil*

Dinichtys are not actually dinosaurs but huge prehistoric fish ("terrible fish"). Its huge mouth can swallow man-sized prey (on a score of 20).

Diplodocus

FREQUENCY: *Common*
NO. APPEARING: *1-6*
ARMOR CLASS: *6*
MOVE: *6"*
HIT DICE: *24*
% IN LAIR: *Nil*
TREASURE TYPE: *Nil*
NO. OF ATTACKS: *1*
DAMAGE/ATTACK: *3-18*
SPECIAL ATTACKS: *Nil*
SPECIAL DEFENSES: *Nil*
MAGIC RESISTANCE: *Standard*
INTELLIGENCE: *Non-*
ALIGNMENT: *Neutral*

SIZE: *L (80' long)*
PSIONIC ABILITY: *Nil*
 Attack/Defense Modes: *Nil*

This dinosaur is another semi-aquatic type which eats water plants. It is able to submerge its body to a bottom depth of 30' or so and still breathe easily. If it steps on any small object it causes 3-30 points of damage.

Elasmosaurus

FREQUENCY: *Uncommon*
NO. APPEARING: *1-2*
ARMOR CLASS: *7*
MOVE: *15"*
HIT DICE: *15*
% IN LAIR: *Nil*
TREASURE TYPE: *Nil*
NO. OF ATTACKS: *1*
DAMAGE/ATTACK: *4-24*
SPECIAL ATTACKS: *Nil*
SPECIAL DEFENSES: *Nil*
MAGIC RESISTANCE: *Standard*
INTELLIGENCE: *Non-*
ALIGNMENT: *Neutral*
SIZE: *L (50' long)*
PSIONIC ABILITY: *Nil*
 Attack/Defense Modes: *Nil*

These long-necked reptiles are rather fish-like in appearance. They are carnivorous and highly aggressive.

Gorgosaurus

FREQUENCY: *Uncommon*
NO. APPEARING: *1-2*
ARMOR CLASS: *5*
MOVE: *15"*
HIT DICE: *13*
% IN LAIR: *Nil*
TREASURE TYPE: *Nil*
NO. OF ATTACKS: *3*
DAMAGE/ATTACK: *1-3/1-3/7-28*
SPECIAL ATTACKS: *Nil*
SPECIAL DEFENSES: *Nil*
MAGIC RESISTANCE: *Standard*
INTELLIGENCE: *Non-*
ALIGNMENT: *Neutral*
SIZE: *L (30' + long)*
PSIONIC ABILITY: *Nil*
 Attack/Defense Modes: *Nil*

These horrid creatures are probably ancestors of tyrannasaurus rex. The gorgosaurus is a fleet carnivorous dinosaur of very aggressive instincts.

Iguanadon

FREQUENCY: *Common*
NO. APPEARING: *3-18*
ARMOR CLASS: *4*
MOVE: *15"*
HIT DICE: *6*
% IN LAIR: *Nil*
TREASURE TYPE: *Nil*
NO. OF ATTACKS: *3*
DAMAGE/ATTACK: *1-3/1-3/2-8*
SPECIAL ATTACKS: *Nil*
SPECIAL DEFENSES: *Nil*
MAGIC RESISTANCE: *Standard*
INTELLIGENCE: *Non-*
ALIGNMENT: *Neutral*
SIZE: *L (30' long)*
PSIONIC ABILITY: *Nil*
 Attack/Defense Modes: *Nil*

These typically bipedal plant-eaters typically travel in herds. They run from carnivores, but if cornered they will employ their "thumb" spikes and lashing tail to defend themselves.

Lambeosaurus

FREQUENCY: *Common*
NO. APPEARING: *2-16*
ARMOR CLASS: *6*
MOVE: *12"*
HIT DICE: *12*
% IN LAIR: *Nil*
TREASURE TYPE: *Nil*
NO. OF ATTACKS: *1*
DAMAGE/ATTACK: *2-12*
SPECIAL ATTACKS: *Nil*
SPECIAL DEFENSES: *Nil*
MAGIC RESISTANCE: *Standard*
INTELLIGENCE: *Non-*
ALIGNMENT: *Neutral*
SIZE: *L (20'+ long)*
PSIONIC ABILITY: *Nil*
    Attack/Defense Modes: *Nil*

One of the family of crested herbivorous dinosaurs, this creature is able to see, hear, and smell exceptionally well. They are thus able to detect enemies frequently and flee to safety — either outdistancing the predator or hiding in a swampy area. Other crested dinosaurs include corythosaurus, parasaurolophus, prosaurolophus, and saurolophus.

Megalosaurus

FREQUENCY: *Uncommon*
NO. APPEARING: *1-2*
ARMOR CLASS: *5*
MOVE: *12"*
HIT DICE: *12*
% IN LAIR: *Nil*
TREASURE TYPE: *Nil*
NO. OF ATTACKS: *1*
DAMAGE/ATTACK: *3-18*
SPECIAL ATTACKS: *Nil*
SPECIAL DEFENSES: *Nil*
MAGIC RESISTANCE: *Standard*
INTELLIGENCE: *Non-*
ALIGNMENT: *Neutral*
SIZE: *L (25' long)*
PSIONIC ABILITY: *Nil*
    Attack/Defense Modes: *Nil*

Megalosaurus often travels on all fours, although they are able to function bipedally. They have very large jaws and teeth, using them to bring down any unsuspecting victim.

Monoclonius

FREQUENCY: *Common*
NO. APPEARING: *2-12*
ARMOR CLASS: *3/4*
MOVE: *6"*
HIT DICE: *8*
% IN LAIR: *Nil*
TREASURE TYPE: *Nil*
NO. OF ATTACKS: *1*
DAMAGE/ATTACK: *2-16*
SPECIAL ATTACKS: *Nil*
SPECIAL DEFENSES: *Nil*
MAGIC RESISTANCE: *Standard*
INTELLIGENCE: *Non-*
ALIGNMENT: *Neutral*
SIZE: *L (18' long)*
PSIONIC ABILITY: *Nil*
    Attack/Defenses Modes: *Nil*

These reptiles somewhat resemble a single-horned rhinoceros. Their head and neck is protected by a bone shield (armor class 3) while their

skins are very thick — almost plated. They are herbivorous, but they tend to be somewhat aggressive. They will trample smaller creatures in a charge, inflicting 2-16 hit points damage.

Mosasaurus

FREQUENCY: *Uncommon*
NO. APPEARING: *1-3*
ARMOR CLASS: *7*
MOVE: *3"//15"*
HIT DICE: *12*
% IN LAIR: *Nil*
TREASURE TYPE: *Nil*
NO. OF ATTACKS: *1*
DAMAGE/ATTACK: *4-32*
SPECIAL ATTACKS: *Nil*
SPECIAL DEFENSES: *Nil*
MAGIC RESISTANCE: *Standard*
INTELLIGENCE: *Non-*
ALIGNMENT: *Neutral*
SIZE: *L (50' long)*
PSIONIC ABILITY: *Nil*
    Attack/Defense Modes: *Nil*

These typical marine dinosaurs travel on land only very slowly, but their flippers move them with ease and grace in water. They prey on all forms of marine animals.

Paleoscincus

FREQUENCY: *Uncommon*
NO. APPEARING: *1-4*
ARMOR CLASS: *-3*
MOVE: *3"*
HIT DICE: *9*
% IN LAIR: *Nil*
TREASURE TYPE: *Nil*
NO. OF ATTACKS: *1*
DAMAGE/ATTACK: *2-12*
SPECIAL ATTACKS: *Nil*
SPECIAL DEFENSES: *See below*
MAGIC RESISTANCE: *Standard*
INTELLIGENCE: *Non-*
ALIGNMENT: *Neutral*
SIZE: *L (20' long)*
PSIONIC ABILITY: *Nil*
    Attack/Defense Modes: *Nil*

These reptiles are veritable "walking dreadnoughts," for their heavy plated skin, sharp side spines, and spiked tail make them nearly invulnerable to attack. A predator trying to bite one is likely to inflict 3-12 hit points damage upon itself if it scores a hit! Of course, the paleocincus will be lashing its thorny tail to drive off its attacker. These creatures are sometimes aggressive if intruded upon.

Pentaceratops

FREQUENCY: *Common*
NO. APPEARING: *2-12*
ARMOR CLASS: *2/6*
MOVE: *9"*
HIT DICE: *12*
% IN LAIR: *Nil*
TREASURE TYPE: *Nil*
NO. OF ATTACKS: *3*
DAMAGE/ATTACK: *1-6/1-10/1-10*
SPECIAL ATTACKS: *Nil*
SPECIAL DEFENSES: *See below*
MAGIC RESISTANCE: *Standard*
INTELLIGENCE: *Non-*
ALIGNMENT: *Neutral*
SIZE: *L (20'+ long)*
PSIONIC ABILITY: *Nil*
    Attack/Defense Modes: *Nil*

This is another of the quadrupedal dinosaurs of the ornithischian order; it is a relative of monoclonius, styracosaurus, and triceratops. It is an aggressive but plant-eating creature. Its shield and horns give its head armor class 2, while its body is armor class 6. If it charges it will trample smaller creatures for 2-20 hit points.

Although these flying reptiles typically dive for marine prey, they will attack any creature which appears to be vulnerable. They have no teeth but spear victims with their beaks if they are too large to swallow at a gulp. The beak of a typical pteranodon is about 4' long. The creature weighs only 40 or 50 pounds, but they can carry off prey four times their own weight.

Plateosaurus

FREQUENCY: Common
NO. APPEARING: 5-20
ARMOR CLASS: 5
MOVE: 12''
HIT DICE: 8
% IN LAIR: Nil
TREASURE TYPE: Nil
NO. OF ATTACKS: Nil
DAMAGE/ATTACK: Nil
SPECIAL ATTACKS: Nil
SPECIAL DEFENSES: Nil
MAGIC RESISTANCE: Standard
INTELLIGENCE: Non-
ALIGNMENT: Neutral
SIZE: L (20'+ long)
PSIONIC ABILITY: Nil
    Attack/Defense Modes: Nil

These dinosaurs travel slowly in a bipedal manner, using their tail as a balance in order to watch for enemies as well as reach the leafy crowns of ferns, palms, etc. They can move fairly fast on all fours. These plant-eaters are fairly heavy (about 8-10 tons on the average) and panicky.

Plesiosaurus

FREQUENCY: Common
NO. APPEARING: 1-3
ARMOR CLASS: 7
MOVE: 15''
HIT DICE: 20
% IN LAIR: Nil
TREASURE TYPE: Nil
NO. OF ATTACKS: 1
DAMAGE/ATTACK: 5-20
SPECIAL ATTACKS: See below
SPECIAL DEFENSES: Nil
MAGIC RESISTANCE: Standard
INTELLIGENCE: Non-
ALIGNMENT: Neutral
SIZE: L (50'+ long)
PSIONIC ABILITY: Nil
    Attack/Defense Modes: Nil

The plesiosaurus strongly resembles a snake wearing a turtle's body (sans shell). They tend to be very aggressive and attack anything. The creature's neck is about one-third of its total length, and it is strong and fast. In a marine battle it can strike with its powerful fore flippers for 2-12 points of damage with each.

Pteranodon

FREQUENCY: Common
NO. APPEARING: 3-18
ARMOR CLASS: 7
MOVE: 3''/15''
HIT DICE: 3 + 3
% IN LAIR: Nil
TREASURE TYPE: Nil
NO. OF ATTACKS: 1
DAMAGE/ATTACK: 2-8
SPECIAL ATTACKS: Nil
SPECIAL DEFENSES: Nil
MAGIC RESISTANCE: Standard
INTELLIGENCE: Non-
ALIGNMENT: Neutral
SIZE: L (30' wing spread)
PSIONIC ABILITY: Nil
    Attack/Defense Modes: Nil

Stegosaurus

FREQUENCY: Common
NO. APPEARING: 2-8
ARMOR CLASS: 2/5
MOVE: 6''
HIT DICE: 18
% IN LAIR: Nil
TREASURE TYPE: Nil
NO. OF ATTACKS: 1
DAMAGE/ATTACK: 5-20
SPECIAL ATTACKS: Nil
SPECIAL DEFENSES: Nil
MAGIC RESISTANCE: Standard
INTELLIGENCE: Non-
ALIGNMENT: Neutral
SIZE: L (25' long, 8'+ high)
PSIONIC ABILITY: Nil
    Attack/Defense Modes: Nil

Another of the ornithischians, the stegosaurus, or "plated lizard," is a large, very stupid herbivorous dinosaur with aggressive defenses. It thrives nearly anywhere and is often found in Jurassic-like plains or jungles. Its great plates allow the creature to defend 90% of the time at armor class 2. Its spiked tail, with four or more boney spikes of one to over two feet in length, has its own brain; and the stegosaurus turns its rear continually towards an enemy, while tucking its head low. If anything near it seems threatening, it will react in this manner.

Styracosaurus

FREQUENCY: Common
NO. APPEARING: 2-8
ARMOR CLASS: 2/4
MOVE: 6''
HIT DICE: 10
% IN LAIR: Nil
TREASURE TYPE: Nil
NO. OF ATTACKS: 1
DAMAGE/ATTACK: 2-16
SPECIAL ATTACKS: Nil
SPECIAL DEFENSES: See below
MAGIC RESISTANCE: Standard
INTELLIGENCE: Non-
ALIGNMENT: Neutral
SIZE: L (18' long)
PSIONIC ABILITY: Nil
    Attack/Defense Modes: Nil

An aggressive plant-eater, styracosaurus tends to charge at anything which appears threatening. The boney plate gives the head area an armor class of 2, and there is a 50% chance that anything attempting to bite its rear portions will be stabbed by one or more of the sharp frills of the head plate, each frill inflicting 1-6 hit points of damage, 1-3 frills possibly striking. If it charges it will trample smaller creatures and do 2-16 hit points of damage.

Teratosaurus

FREQUENCY: Uncommon
NO. APPEARING: 1-3
ARMOR CLASS: 5
MOVE: 18''
HIT DICE: 10
% IN LAIR: Nil
TREASURE TYPE: Nil
NO. OF ATTACKS: 3
DAMAGE/ATTACK: 1-3/1-3/3-18
SPECIAL ATTACKS: Nil

SPECIAL DEFENSES: *Nil*
MAGIC RESISTANCE: *Standard*
INTELLIGENCE: *Non-*
ALIGNMENT: *Neutral*
SIZE: *L (20' long, 9' tall)*
PSIONIC ABILITY: *Nil*
    Attack/Defense Modes: *Nil*

A fierce carnivore found mainly on triassic plains, the teratosaurus runs nimbly after any creature which appears to be eatable. They will hunt only on dry land — plains or forest.

Triceratops

FREQUENCY: *Common*
NO. APPEARING: *2-8*
ARMOR CLASS: *2/6*
MOVE: *9''*
HIT DICE: *16*
% IN LAIR: *Nil*
TREASURE TYPE: *Nil*
NO. OF ATTACKS: *3*
DAMAGE/ATTACK: *1-8/1-12/1-12*
SPECIAL ATTACKS: *Nil*
SPECIAL DEFENSES: *Nil*
MAGIC RESISTANCE: *Standard*
INTELLIGENCE: *Non-*
ALIGNMENT: *Neutral*
SIZE: *L (24'+ long)*
PSIONIC ABILITY: *Nil*
    Attack/Defense Modes: *Nil*

The largest of the ceratopsians, and by far the most aggressive, this beaked herbivore is a plains dweller. It has a huge front plate of bone from which project two great horns (3'+ long), while a somewhat shorter horn juts from its nose. Its body is not armored, thus armor class 6. Any creature which infringes on the territory of these reptiles is likely to be charged and speared. Smaller creatures will simply be trampled for 2-24 hit points of damage.

Tyrannosaurus Rex

FREQUENCY: *Uncommon*
NO. APPEARING: *1-2*
ARMOR CLASS: *5*
MOVE: *15''*
HIT DICE: *18*
% IN LAIR: *Nil*
TREASURE TYPE: *Nil*
NO. OF ATTACKS: *3*
DAMAGE/ATTACK: *1-6/1-6/5-40*
SPECIAL ATTACKS: *Nil*
SPECIAL DEFENSES: *Nil*
MAGIC RESISTANCE: *Standard*
INTELLIGENCE: *Non-*
ALIGNMENT: *Neutral*
SIZE: *L (50' long, 20' high)*
PSIONIC ABILITY: *Nil*
    Attack/Defense Modes: *Nil*

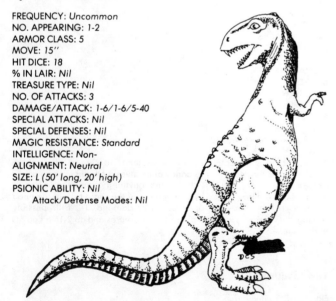

There can be no question that this reptile is the most fearsome and terrible of all carnivorous dinosaurs. Despite its huge size the monster is swift afoot. Its huge head is nearly six feet long, and its teeth are from three to six inches in length. It is a plains dweller, and so stupidly fierce that it will attack a small triceratops, kill it, and swallow its head in one gulp — thus killing itself in a matter of hours as the horns of the victim pierce the stomach of the victor. Of course, this monster will pursue and eat nearly anything, engulfing man-sized creatures whole on a roll of 18 or better.

DISPLACER BEAST

FREQUENCY: *Very rare*
NO. APPEARING: *2-5*
ARMOR CLASS: *4*
MOVE: *15''*
HIT DICE: *6*
% IN LAIR: *25%*
TREASURE TYPE: *D*
NO. OF ATTACKS: *2*
DAMAGE/ATTACK: *2-8/2-8*
SPECIAL ATTACKS: *Nil*
SPECIAL DEFENSES: *-2 on*
   opponent's attack dice
MAGIC RESISTANCE: *Save as 12th*
   level fighter +2 on die
INTELLIGENCE: *Semi-*
ALIGNMENT: *Neutral*
SIZE: *L*
PSIONIC ABILITY: *Nil*
    Attack/Defense Modes: *Nil*

A pack of these monsters always contains only full-grown beasts. The molecular vibrations of the displacer beast are such that it always appears to be 3' (left, right, ahead, or behind) its actual position. Thus, these monsters always cause opponents to subtract 2 from attack dice rolls and add 2 to their dice rolls for saving throws. These fierce creatures hate all life, but they particularly hate blink dogs. In combat the displacer beast lashes out with its two tentacles, inflicting horrible wounds with the rough, horney edges of these appendages.

Description: This vaguely puma-like creature is bluish black, its tentacles are dead black, the horney edges of the tentacles are brownish yellow, and its eyes glow a hellish green.

DJINNI

FREQUENCY: *Very rare*
NO. APPEARING: *1*
ARMOR CLASS: *4*
MOVE: *9''/24''*
HIT DICE: *7 + 3*
% IN LAIR: *Nil*
TREASURE TYPE: *Nil*
NO. OF ATTACKS: *1*
DAMAGE/ATTACK: *2-16*
SPECIAL ATTACKS: *See below*
SPECIAL DEFENSES: *Nil*
MAGIC RESISTANCE: *Standard*
INTELLIGENCE: *Average-high*
ALIGNMENT: *Chaotic good*
SIZE: *L (10½' tall)*
PSIONIC ABILITY: *Nil*
    Attack/Defense Modes: *Nil*

The djinn are creatures from the aerial plane. Their magical properties enable them to do any of the following once per day: *create nutritious food* for 2-12 persons, *create water or wine* for 2-12 persons, *create soft goods or wooden items* (up to about 16 cubic feet of the former, 9 cubic feet of the latter) with permanence, *create metal items* of short life span (the harder the metal the shorter the time it lasts, i.e. gold has about a 24 hour existence, djinni steel lasts only 1 hour) of up to about 1,000 gold pieces weight, *create an illusion* with both visual and audial components which will last without concentration until magically dispelled or touched, *become invisible, assume gaseous form, wind walk,* or *form a whirlwind.* A djinni whirlwind is cone-shaped, 1'' across the base, 3'' across the top, and up to 7'' high (according to the desire of the djinni). It requires one full turn to form the whirlwind and one full turn for it to dissolve. The whirlwind lasts 1 melee round and causes from 2-12 hit points damage to any non-aerial creature it encounters and sweeps away and kills all creatures of under two hit dice which it encounters. Djinn subjected to attacks from creatures based on the element of air take -1 on damage caused thusly, and "to hit" dice are also at a -1 penalty.

Djinn are able to carry up to 6,000 gold pieces weight, afoot or flying without tiring. They can carry double that weight for a short time — three turns afoot, but if flying with that weight the djinni can remain aloft for only one turn (for each 1,000 gold piece weight less than maximum add one turn to walking or flying time). Thereafter it must rest for six turns.

The capture and enslavement of djinn is better left to the device of the referee. It is worth noting, however, that a good master will typically *encourage* a djinni to additional effort and higher performance, while a demanding and cruel master encourages the opposite. A noble djinni (1% chance) is able to grant three wishes to his master, but he will do no other services, and upon granting the third wish he is freed of servitude. Noble djinni are as strong as the efreet, have 10 hit dice, strike for 3-24 points of damage, and their whirlwind causes 3-18 hit points of damage.

Djinn can speak their own tongue and that of any person or beast with intelligence they meet through a limited form of telepathy which enables them to speak appropriately.

Djinn can travel the elemental planes and the astral as well as the material planes. The social structure of Djinn society is based on rule by a Caliph served by various nobles and officials (vizers, beys, emirs, sheiks, sherrifs, and maliks).

DOG

	War	Wild
FREQUENCY:	Uncommon	Common
NO. APPEARING:	—	4-16
ARMOR CLASS:	6	7
MOVE:	12''	15''
HIT DICE:	2 + 2	1 + 1
% IN LAIR:	Nil	Nil
TREASURE TYPE:	Nil	Nil
NO. OF ATTACKS:	1	1
DAMAGE/ATTACK:	2-8	1-4
SPECIAL ATTACKS:	Nil	Nil
SPECIAL DEFENSES:	Nil	Nil
MAGIC RESISTANCE:	Standard	Standard
INTELLIGENCE:	Semi-	Semi-
ALIGNMENT:	Neutral	Neutral
SIZE:	M	S
PSIONIC ABILITY:	Nil	Nil
Attack/Defense Modes:	Nil	Nil

Dog, War: These are simply large dogs which are trained to fight. They are loyal to their masters and ferocious in attack. They are typically protected by light studded leather armor and a spiked collar. The number appearing depends on their masters.

Dog, Wild: Packs of wild dogs inhabit most regions, and their ranges will sometimes overlap those of wolves. If well-fed they will simply avoid contact. They can be tamed only if separated from their pack.

DOLPHIN

FREQUENCY: *Uncommon*
NO. APPEARING: *2-20*
ARMOR CLASS: *5*
MOVE: *30''*
HIT DICE: *2 + 2*
% IN LAIR: *Nil*
TREASURE TYPE: *Nil*
NO. OF ATTACKS: *1*
DAMAGE/ATTACK: *2-8*
SPECIAL ATTACKS: *Nil*
SPECIAL DEFENSES: *Save as 4th*
  level fighter
MAGIC RESISTANCE: *Standard*
INTELLIGENCE: *Very*
ALIGNMENT: *Lawful good*
SIZE: *M*
PSIONIC ABILITY: *Nil*
  Attack/Defense Modes: *Nil*

Most dolphins simply roam the oceans in nomadic schools. A small number (10%), however, have formed underwater communities, and if one is located it is 75% probable that there will be from 1-4 additional communities of dolphins within a 5 mile radius. Communal dolphins will have from 2-5 swordfish (AC 6, move 24'', 1 + 1 dice, 2-12 hit points

damage/attack) or 1-3 narwhales (AC 6, move 21'', 4 + 4 hit dice, 2-24 hit points damage/attack), depending on the climatic region, as guards.

Dolphins will attack any creature which threatens them, although they will help humans in distress. They particularly hate sharks of all sorts and will attack unless outnumbered by 2 or more to 1.

DOPPLEGANGER

FREQUENCY: *Very rare*
NO. APPEARING: *3-12*
ARMOR CLASS: *5*
MOVE: *9''*
HIT DICE: *4*
% IN LAIR: *20%*
TREASURE TYPE: *E*
NO. OF ATTACKS: *1*
DAMAGE/ATTACK: *1-12*
SPECIAL ATTACKS: *Surprise on a*
  1-4
SPECIAL DEFENSES: *See below*
MAGIC RESISTANCE: *See below*
INTELLIGENCE: *Very*
ALIGNMENT: *Neutral*
SIZE: *M*
PSIONIC ABILITY: *Nil*
  Attack/Defense Modes: *Nil*

These bipedal creatures are of mutable form so that they are able to shape themselves into the likeness of any humanoid creature of from 4' to 8' tall which they observe. Having become the double for a person they attempt to do away with that victim and assume its place. If unable to do this, the doppleganger will simply attack, counting on the confusion engendered to make it indistinguishable from the creature it is mimicking (surprise means this works). Dopplegangers are able to *ESP* and imitate with 90% accuracy. They are subject to neither *sleep* nor *charm* spells. Despite having only 4 hit dice they make all saving throws as if they were 10th level fighting men.

Note: A doppleganger actually forms itself into the likeness of the clothing and equipment of the imitated creature as well as the physical features thereof.

DRAGON

Dragons come in many colors, sizes, shapes, and alignments. Two sorts of dragons (the Chromatic Dragon and the Platinum Dragon) are singular individuals, and there are no others of their type. Each dragon sort will be treated individually herafter. General information and common characteristics will be given here.

The ten species of dragons have three general size categories (small, average, and huge) according to the size typical of each. This categorization is determined by die roll. An 8-sided die is rolled: 1-2 = small, 3-7 = average, 8 = huge. This size determination indicates the number of hit dice a dragon has.

Dragons pass through eight ages in their lives. These growth stages are:

1. Very young — 1-5 years	—	1 hit point per die
2. Young — 6-15 years	—	2 hit point per die
3. Sub-adult — 16-25 years	—	3 hit point per die
4. Young adult — 26-50 years	—	4 hit point per die
5. Adult — 51-100 years	—	5 hit point per die
6. Old — 101-200 years	—	6 hit point per die
7. Very old — 201-400 years	—	7 hit point per die
8. Ancient — 401+ years	—	8 hit point per die

To determine the age (and thus the number of hit points per die a dragon has) simply roll an 8-sided die, the number rolled indicating the age as shown above.

All dragons see equally well in daylight or darkness (infravision, 60'). They have excellent sight, smell, and hearing. Because of these keen senses, all dragons are able to *detect hidden* or *invisible* creatures within 1'' per age level. Dragons also develop the power to panic enemies as they mature. At *adult* age and older they radiate a powerful aura which causes a *fear* reaction, when a dragon flies overhead or charges, as follows:

1. All creatures under 1 hit die, as well as non-carnivorous creatures of any sort which are not trained for warfare or basically not fearless or aggressive will flee in panic. Such rout will be made at fastest speed possible, and it will continue for 4-24 turns.
2. Creatures with fewer than 3 hit dice must save versus magic or be paralyzed with *fear* (50%) or panic as above (50%).
3. Creatures with 3 or more hit dice will fight at a penalty of -1 on their hit dice unless they also save versus magic.
4. Creatures with 6 or more hit dice automatically disregard the aura affect.
5. The aura of *adult, old,* and *very old* dragons is not as powerful as that of ancient dragons, so saving throws applicable to their auras are at +5, +3, and +1 respectively. Thus, a 2nd level fighter, normally having to score 16 (75%) or better to save against magic (the dragon's aura in this case), would gain a bonus of 5 on his saving throw versus an *adult* dragon's aura; so any score of 11 or more would save him from panic.

A considerable percentage of dragons have the ability to speak one or more human languages in addition to the language of their species. Similarly, a fair number of dragons which can speak are able to employ magical spells. The chances for either of these abilities occurring in any given individual dragon are shown under the specific treatment by species. The chance that any given dragon will be asleep will likewise be so given.

Sleeping Dragon: A sleeping dragon is only found in its lair, and it will always awaken upon hearing loud noise such as talking, shouting, forcing a door, etc. if it is within 30' to 120' (depending on baffling factors; walls, doors, etc.) and the volume of sound. It will awaken if attacked. It will also awaken on a roll of 6 on a 6-sided die. If a sleeping dragon is attacked, its opponents get a bonus of +3 to strike it, but as soon as the dragon is awake, the bonus is lost.

Attacking a Dragon: Dragons may be attacked two ways: to *kill* or to *subdue.* The attack form must be announced prior to combat or it will automatically take the killing form. Once selected, attack form cannot be changed with respect to any given dragon.

Certain weapons will be more or less effective than others against the various types of dragons. This is indicated on the following chart, the number indicating the addition or subtraction for the probability of hitting as well as *the amount of damage done.*

Dragon's Breath	Air*	Earth**	Fire***	Water****	Electricity
Cold	—	—1	+1	—1	+1
Acid	—	+1	—	+1	—
Gas	+1	—	—	—	—
Electricity	—	—	+1	—1	—1
Fire	—1	+1	—1	+1	—
Multiple types	—	—	—	—	—

* Includes attack by aerial servant, air elemental, djinni, invisible stalker, or "whirlwind"
** Includes attack by earth elemental, xorn, or umber hulk
*** Includes attack by efreet, fire elemental, or salamander
**** Includes attack by triton or water elemental

Dragons can attack by claw/bite or breath weapon. The latter can be used but three times per day, maximum. If a choice is possible roll percentile dice. Any score above 50% indicates the dragon will breathe. The breath weapon causes damage equal to the dragon's hit points (half that amount if a saving throw is made) on each and every creature hit by the breath weapon. Cone shaped breath weapons are ½" diameter at point of origin.

Subduing a Dragon: An attack on a dragon to *subdue,* and thus capture it may be opted for if such intent is announced in advance of combat. Silver, gold, chromatic, and platinum dragons cannot be subdued. Note that it is impossible for creatures with less than average intelligence to attack to subdue. Subdual is accomplished as follows:

Upon announcement of intent to *strike to subdue,* all hit points of damage scored by attacks upon the dragon are considered non-fatal battering/bruising damage. The total number of hit points scored each melee round is stated as a ratio; hit points scored are ratioed over the number of hit points the dragon has, and this ratio is converted to a percentage chance; this percentage chance is the chance that the dragon

will be subdued by the hit points of subduing damage it has received at the end of any given melee round. This percentage could be 0%, 1%, 35%, 99% or whatever.

Percentile dice are then rolled, and if the number they show is equal to or less than the percentage ratio the dragon is subdued. It is always subdued when the ratio of subduing damage to hit points equals or exceeds 1:1 (100% or greater).

A maximum of one human-sized attacker per 3 linear feet of exposed dragon (excluding tail) is possible. Thus, a dragon with a 15' long body, fully exposed, would offer opportunity for a maximum of 11 humans to attack it (5 per flank plus one at its head).

Example of Subduing a Dragon: Two 8th level fighters, a 7th level dwarven fighter, an elven 4th level fighter/6th level magic-user, and a halfling thief of 9th level stumble upon a huge red dragon peacefully asleep upon a veritable mountain of treasure. After a hurried, whispered debate the party opts to strike so that will a) give them a dragon to use or sell, b) save treasure from destruction by avoiding the fireworks of a general melee, and c) the subdued dragon will have to point out and help carry out the choicest treasure items. The smaller, quiet party members circle the dragon. None stand at the beast's head. With a shout the party strikes with a general bonus of +3 to hit. They all succeed, and the halfling thief gains quadruple damage bonus of striking from behind! They score a total of 44 hit points of subduing damage. The first melee round is over. As the dragon is *ancient,* it has 8 hit points per die, as it is *huge* it has 11 dice, for a total of 88 hit points. The referee rolls percentile dice, any score of 1% to 50% indicates subdual; a 61% is rolled. Combat goes to round two. As the dragon has just awakened, the party again strikes first. Four of them hit, and another 23 hit points subduing damage is scored. The dragon chooses to breathe (dice score 99%), so he turns his head and fires right where the elf, dwarf and halfling are attacking. Saving throws indicate that each takes 44, 88, and 44 hit points damage respectively. All three char and die. The round is over, and the referee ratios 67 over 88 — 76% is the chance for subdual, but a 92 is rolled. The dragon fights on. Initiative dice are rolled, the dragon wins, decides to bite, and scores a hit doing 23 hit points of damage to the second 8th level fighter. The two fighters strike, one hits, and the dragon takes another 10 hit points of subdual. The third round is over, and the chance for the dragon being subdued is 77:88 (7/8) or 87.5% (treat as 88%). The referee rolls an 89. The fighters win initiative, strike, and score 12 hit points, so the dragon is subdued automatically before it can attack. The garnering of loot now begins.

Value of a Subdued Dragon: Larger towns and cities will usually have a market for dragons. If a dragon is sold, it usually goes out of the game, although the referee may wish to assign it to some one of his special non-playing characters whom he runs for encounter in the town/city. The selling price of a subdued dragon ranges from 100 to 800 gold pieces per hit point. This price is subject to adjustment by the referee. Offers are typically determined by rolling an 8-sided die. Subdued dragons can be ridden.

Length of Subdual: A dragon remains subdued for an indefinite period, but if the creature is not strongly held, well treated, given ample treasure, and allowed ample freedom, it will seek to kill its captor and/or escape. The older and more powerful the dragon, the less the likelihood of it remaining subdued. Likewise, an intelligent, spell-using dragon is not likely to remain subdued. In fact, the latter sort of dragon is likely to attempt to take over its captor and rule his holdings. Evil dragons will never serve a good master for long, and good dragons are 50% more likely to kill/escape from a neutral captor as opposed to one whose alignment is the same as their own. Players may always opt to sell or give a dragon to any other player or keep the monster in their own service. Note that dragons cannot be re-subdued unless they actually regain their freedom.

Encountering Multiple Dragons: If two or more dragons are encountered outside their lair it will be a mated pair if two are encountered and sub-adults if three or more are encountered. If two or more dragons are encountered in their lair it will be a mated pair — with their young if applicable. Mated pairs are always 5th through 8th age categories. Any young in lair are eggs (10%) or *very young* (90%). If young dragons are attacked both adults will automatically breathe and then melee to bite, gaining a ferocity bonus of +2 to hit and +1/+3 in clawing/biting damage. If either of the mated pair is attacked the other dragon will rush to its defense, gaining the ferocity bonuses stated above, unless it is attacked simultaneously.

Treasure: *Very* young dragons will usually have no treasure, but there is a 10% chance that they will have one-quarter the possible listed treasure. *Young* dragons have 25% chance for one-quarter the possible listed treasure. *Sub-adults* have a 50% chance for one-half the possible listed treasure. *Young adults,* and *old* dragons have normal treasure. *Very old* and *ancient* dragons are 50% and 75% likely to have 150% and 200% respectively of the listed treasure.

Weaknesses of Dragons: The innate cowardice of dragonkind is shown by the fact most can be subdued. Dragons' egoistic nature makes them subject to flattery, and it also makes the more stupid of them prone to attack other powerful creatures whom they view as disputing their dominating position. Greed and avarice are major motivating factors in all but the loftiest of dragons (40% of silver, 80% of gold, and the platinum dragon), so they are subject to manipulation by very clever persons or the prospect of actual treasure and the promise of more forthcoming.

Dragon Saving Throws: When a dragon attains 5 or more hit points per die, its saving throw is calculated by dividing its total hit points by 4, thus giving a higher number of hit dice than it actually has. This reflects the magic resistance and general toughness of this creature. Conversely, even a *very young* dragon gains the benefit of the actual number of its hit dice, even though the hit points/die are but 1 each, for determining scores required. This reflects the same nature of dragonkind, i.e. magic resistance and toughness.

Black Dragon (Draco Causticus Sputem)

FREQUENCY: *Uncommon*
NO. APPEARING: *1-4*
ARMOR CLASS: *3*
MOVE: *12"/24"*
HIT DICE: *6-8*
% IN LAIR: *30%*
TREASURE TYPE: *H*
NO. OF ATTACKS: *3*
DAMAGE/ATTACK: *1-4/1-4/3-18*
SPECIAL ATTACKS: *Breath weapon + possible magic use*
SPECIAL DEFENSES: *Nil*
MAGIC RESISTANCE: *Standard*
INTELLIGENCE: *Average*
ALIGNMENT: *Chaotic evil*
SIZE: *L (30' long)*
PSIONIC ABILITY: *Nil*
  Attack/Defense Modes: *Nil*
CHANCE OF:
  Speaking: *30%*
  Magic Use: *10%*
  Sleeping: *50%*

The black dragon is typically found in miasmal swamps or marshes, although they also inhabit subterranean lairs as well, for black dragons always seek to lair in deep, dark caves. They tend towards the mid point between law and chaos in their evil.

The black dragon attacks with a claw/claw/bite or breathes — in this case spitting acid in a ½" wide stream which extends 6" in a straight line beginning at the height of the dragon's head and traveling in the direction and at the angle which the monster's head was facing at the time of discharging the acid. Black dragons which can speak and are capable of using magic can employ one first level spell for each stage of their maturity, i.e. 1-8 spells. Roll randomly to determine which spells they know. The spells known are a special form of the ordinary spells which require only a spoken component, but each can be employed but once per day. Repeat spells are possible if random rolls so indicate.

Blue Dragon (Draco Electricus)

FREQUENCY: *Rare*
NO. APPEARING: *1-4*
ARMOR CLASS: *2*
MOVE: *9"/24"*
HIT DICE: *8-10*

% IN LAIR: *50%*
TREASURE TYPE: *H, S*
NO. OF ATTACKS: *3*
DAMAGE/ATTACK: *1-6/1-6/3-24*
SPECIAL ATTACKS: *Breath weapon + possible magic use*
SPECIAL DEFENSES: *Nil*
MAGIC RESISTANCE: *Standard*
INTELLIGENCE: *Very*
ALIGNMENT: *Lawful evil*
SIZE: *L (42' long)*
PSIONIC ABILITY: *Nil*
  Attack/Defense Modes: *Nil*
CHANCE OF:
  Speaking: *60%*
  Magic Use: *30%*
  Sleeping: *30%*

Blue dragons typically prefer deserts and arid lands; like others of their kind their lair is always some vast cave or underground cavern.

The attack of a blue dragon is a claw/claw/bite or use of its breath weapon. A blue dragon is capable of discharging a bolt of electricity (lightning) in a straight line ½" wide by 10" long. This discharge is always of the stated proportion.

Speaking blue dragons which are able to use spells do so as follows: For each stage of maturity from 1st through 3rd they gain a 1st level spell. From the 4th through 6th stages they gain a second level. At the 7th and 8th brackets they gain a 3rd level spell. Thus, an *ancient* blue dragon would have 3 1st level, 3 2nd level, and 2 3rd level spells. Determine all such spells randomly; if the same spell is rolled twice the dragon is able to use the spell twice per day.

Brass Dragon (Draco Impudentus Gallus)

FREQUENCY: *Uncommon*
NO. APPEARING: *1-4*
ARMOR CLASS: *2*
MOVE: *12"/24"*
HIT DICE: *6-8*
% IN LAIR: *25%*
TREASURE TYPE: *H*
NO. OF ATTACKS: *3*
DAMAGE/ATTACK: *1-4/1-4/4-16*
SPECIAL ATTACKS: *Breath weapon + possible magic use*
SPECIAL DEFENSES: *Nil*
MAGIC RESISTANCE: *Standard*
INTELLIGENCE: *High*
ALIGNMENT: *Chaotic good (neutral tendencies)*
SIZE: *L (30' long)*
PSIONIC ABILITY: *Nil*
  Attack/Defense Modes: *Nil*
CHANCE OF:
  Speaking: *30%*
  Magic Use: *30%*
  Sleeping: *50%*

Sandy desert regions are the typical habitat of brass dragons, whose cavernous lairs are often found therein. Brass dragons are quite forward and officious, and they love to converse. They are rather selfish and tend towards neutrality because of this.

The brass dragon attacks with a claw/claw/bite routine or by breathing either of two weapons — a cone of *sleep* gas which extends 7" from the creature's mouth to a terminating diameter of 2", or a billowing cloud of *fear* gas 4" wide by 5" across by 2" deep (ground upwards). Creatures in these gaseous clouds must save versus dragon breath regardless of their level or fall asleep/flee in fear. If the dragon is small sized, saves are at + 2, and if the dragon is of huge size saving throws are at -2, from the number rolled.

If a brass dragon can speak and employ spells, it will gain a first level spell at each odd numbered stage of maturity it attains, and a second level spell at each even numbered age. As is usual with dragons, determine spells known by random selection.

Bronze Dragon (*Draco Gerus Bronzo*)

FREQUENCY: *Rare*
NO. APPEARING: *1-4*
ARMOR CLASS: *0*
MOVE: *9''/24''*
HIT DICE: *8-10*
% IN LAIR: *45%*
TREASURE TYPE: *H, S, T*
NO. OF ATTACKS: *3*
DAMAGE/ATTACK: *1-6/1-6/4-24*
SPECIAL ATTACKS: *Breath*
   weapon + possible magic
   use
SPECIAL DEFENSES: *Nil*
MAGIC RESISTANCE: *Standard*
INTELLIGENCE: *Exceptional*
ALIGNMENT: *Lawful good*
SIZE: *L (42' long)*
PSIONIC ABILITY: *Nil*
   Attack/Defense Modes: *Nil*
CHANCE OF:
   Speaking: *60%*
   Magic Use: *60%*
   Sleeping: *25%*

Bronze dragons prefer to dwell in subterranean lairs near substantial bodies of water such as lakes or seas. Despite their love of wealth, bronze dragons are basically of beneficent nature. They often assume the form of some animal in order to observe the affairs of humans.

The attack of a bronze dragon is either a claw/claw/bite or either of two breath weapons — a bolt of lightning 10'' long and ½'' wide, or a *repulsion* gas cloud 2'' long by 3'' wide by 3'' high which affects those within it just as a *repulsion* spell (move away from the dragon for 6 melee rounds unless a saving throw versus dragon breath is made).

Magic-using bronze dragons gain a first level spell at their 1st and 2nd growth stages, an additional second level spell at their 3rd and 4th growth stages, third level spells at the 5th and 6th growth stages, and *very old* and *ancient* dragons gain additional spells of the 4th level; thus an *ancient* bronze dragon would know two each of 1st through 4th level spells. These spells should be selected randomly.

Chromatic Dragon (*Tiamat*)

FREQUENCY: *Very rare*
NO. APPEARING: *1*
ARMOR CLASS: *0*
MOVE: *6''/18''*
HIT DICE: *16 (128 hit points)*
% IN LAIR: *90%*
TREASURE TYPE: *100% H, S, T, U*
NO. OF ATTACKS: *6*
DAMAGE/ATTACK: *2-16/3-18/*
   2-20/3-24/3-30/1-6
SPECIAL ATTACKS: *Breath*
   weapons, poison and magic
   use
SPECIAL DEFENSES: *Nil*
MAGIC RESISTANCE: *Standard*
INTELLIGENCE: *Genius*
ALIGNMENT: *Lawful evil*
SIZE: *L (60' long)*
PSIONIC ABILITY: *Nil*
   Attack/Defense Modes: *Nil*
CHANCE OF:
   Speaking: *100%*
   Magic Use: *100%*
   Sleeping: *10%*

Tiamat rules the first plane of the Nine Hells where she spawns all of evil dragonkind. She hates all good as fiercely as she loves cruelty and hoards wealth. She is seldom (10%) outside her lair, but occasionally she comes to earth to place a new dragon or to seek more treasure. She can travel astrally or ethereally.

Although her sheer size prevents claw attacks, Tiamat can bite with all five of her heads and sting with her tail at the same time, breathe with one or more of these heads or cast spells with one or more heads at the same

time. Tiamat's heads are white, black, green, blue, and red. Her breath weapons correspond to the color of each head, exactly duplicating the size and shape of the appropriate dragon's breath weapon and doing damage equal to a *huge, ancient* dragon of the species applicable, i.e. 56 hit points frost (cold) damage, 64 hit points acid damage, 72 hit points gas (chlorine) damage, 80 hit points electrical (lightning) damage, and 88 hit points fire damage. She can use each breath weapon but once per day. Note that each of her heads is also capable of employing two spells. Tiamat's white head is able to cast two 1st level spells, her black head two 2nd level spells, her green head two 3rd level spells, her blue head two 4th level spells, and her red head two 5th level spells.

Each of Tiamat's heads can withstand 16 hit points damage before going out of commission until regeneration replaces it the following day. If her body takes more than 48 hit points damage she is dispelled to her own plane of Hell (or slain if fought in Hell) just as any other devil.

When encountered in her lair, Tiamat will always have five consort/guards with her — one *huge, adult* male dragon of the white, black, green, blue and red types respectively. They are all able to speak and use spells, if applicable.

Description: Tiamat's heads have already been noted. These colors run the length of each neck and into the forepart of the body as stripes, gradually blending to three stripes of gray, blue-green, and purple over her back and hind quarters, and merging into a muddy dark brown tail. Her underbelly and legs are greenish white fading into her upper body colors.

Copper Dragon (*Draco Comes Stabuli*)

FREQUENCY: *Uncommon-rare*
NO. APPEARING: *1-4*
ARMOR CLASS: *1*
MOVE: *9''/24''*
HIT DICE: *7-9*
% IN LAIR: *35%*
TREASURE TYPE: *H, S*
NO. OF ATTACKS: *3*
DAMAGE/ATTACK: *1-4/1-4/5-20*
SPECIAL ATTACKS: *Breath weapon*
   + possible magic use
SPECIAL DEFENSES: *Nil*
MAGIC RESISTANCE: *Standard*
INTELLIGENCE: *High*
ALIGNMENT: *Chaotic good*
SIZE: *L (36' long)*
PSIONIC ABILITY: *Nil*
   Attack Modes: *Nil*
CHANCE OF:
   Speaking: *45%*
   Magic Use: *40%*
   Sleeping: *40%*

Copper dragons prefer to inhabit arid rocky regions, liking warmer climes in which to locate their cavern or cave lairs. They tend to be rather selfish, and thus many copper dragons are somewhat neutral in their outlook if gain is concerned.

The normal attack of this kind of dragon is either a claw/claw/bite or the use of one or the other of its breath weapons — a discharge of acid exactly similar to that of a black dragon (7'' X ½'') or a cloud of gas 3'' long by 2'' wide by 2'' deep which will *slow* any creatures therein unless they make their saving throw vs. dragon breath. The slowing effect causes creatures to move/attack at one-half normal, and it lasts for 6 melee rounds.

Those copper dragons able to use magic gain a 1st level spell for each of their first three age brackets, a 2nd level spell in addition at each bracket of the next three ages, and at the last two an additional 3rd level at each. Thus, a magic-using *ancient* copper dragon would know three 1st level spells, three 2nd level spells, and two 3rd level spells.

Gold Dragon (*Draco Orientalus Sino Dux*)

FREQUENCY: *Very rare*
NO. APPEARING: *1-3*
ARMOR CLASS: *-2*

MOVE: 12"/30"
HIT DICE: 10-12
% IN LAIR: 65%
TREASURE TYPE: H, R, S, T
NO. OF ATTACKS: 3
DAMAGE/ATTACK: 1-8/1-8/6-36
SPECIAL ATTACKS: Breath weapon
 and magic use
SPECIAL DEFENSES: Nil
MAGIC RESISTANCE: Standard
INTELLIGENCE: Genius
ALIGNMENT: Lawful good
SIZE: L (54' long)
PSIONIC ABILITY: Nil
 Attack/Defense Modes: Nil
CHANCE OF:
 Speaking: 90%
 Magic Use: 100%
 Sleeping: 10%

Gold dragons are able to dwell in any clime, but their lairs are always of solid stone — whether a cave or a castle. Although they love precious metals and gems and use jewels and pearls as nourishment, all gold dragons are lawful, just and good. They are able to assume the form of animals or the guise of humanity, for they can *polymorph* themselves without harm. It is in some other form that they are typically encountered.

The attack of a gold dragon can be a claw/claw/bite routine or one of two breath weapons—fire in a 9" × 3" cone, or chlorine gas in a 5" × 4" × 3" cloud. Also, a gold dragon is able to cast spells of 1st through 6th level. At the *very young* age the creature has but a single 1st level spell, as a *young* dragon it has two such spells. Thereafter it gains two spells of progressively higher level at each new age bracket through *old*. At *very old* and *ancient* age they gain the use of a 6th level spell. Thus, at *ancient* age a gold dragon knows two of 1st through 6th level spells in addition to being able to *polymorph self* three times per day. As gold dragons are so intelligent their spells are always of the better sort, and at least half of them actually have regular spell books.

Green Dragon (*Draco Chlorinous Nauseous Respiratorus*)

FREQUENCY: Rare
NO. APPEARING: 1-4
ARMOR CLASS: 2
MOVE: 9"/24"
HIT DICE: 7-9
% IN LAIR: 40%
TREASURE TYPE: H
NO. OF ATTACKS: 3
DAMAGE/ATTACK: 1-6/1-6/2-20
SPECIAL ATTACKS: Breath weapon
 + possible magic use
SPECIAL DEFENSES: Nil
MAGIC RESISTANCE: Standard
INTELLIGENCE: Average to very
ALIGNMENT: Lawful evil
SIZE: L (36' long)
PSIONIC ABILITY: Nil
 Attack/Defense Modes: Nil
CHANCE OF:
 Speaking: 45%
 Magic Use: 20%
 Sleeping: 40%

The race of green dragons prefer to locate their underground lairs in or near woods or forests of the bleaker wilder sort if possible. They are very nasty tempered and thoroughly evil.

A green dragon can attack by a claw/claw/bite routine or by breathing a cloud of poisonous chlorine gas. The gas cloud is 5" long, 4" wide, and 3" high.

Those talking green dragons able to use magic gain a 1st level spell for each of their first four ages, and a 2nd level spell for each of the successive ages, until a maximum of four 1st and four 2nd level spells are known. Select these spells by random determination.

Platinum Dragon (Bahamut)

FREQUENCY: Very rare
NO. APPEARING: 1
ARMOR CLASS: -3
MOVE: 9"/30"
HIT DICE: 21 (168 hit points)
% IN LAIR: 75%
TREASURE TYPE: 100% H, I, R, S,
 T, V
NO. OF ATTACKS: 3
DAMAGE/ATTACK: 2-12/2-12/6-48
SPECIAL ATTACKS: Breath
 weapons + magic use
SPECIAL DEFENSES: Nil
MAGIC RESISTANCE: Standard
INTELLIGENCE: Supra genius
ALIGNMENT: Lawful good
SIZE: L (72' long)
PSIONIC ABILITY: Nil
 Attack/Defense Modes: Nil
CHANCE OF:
 Speaking: 100%
 Magic Use: 100%
 Sleeping: 5%

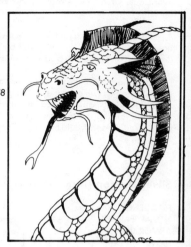

The King of Good dragons, Bahamut the platinum dragon, dwells in a great fortified palace behind the east wind. (No one knows for certain if this place is on the elemental plane of air or some plane betwixt it and the Seven Heavens or Tri-Paradises, save Bahamut and his court.) About one-quarter of the time he roams the earth in the guise of human or nearly any other form he chooses, for Bahamut is able to shape change freely. He can travel astrally or ethereally.

In attacking, the platinum dragon can opt to fight with a pair of clawing attacks and a bite, or he can breathe any one of three forms of breath weapon — cold in a cone 8" long with a base diameter of 3", a cloud of vapor which causes persons therein to save versus dragon breath or lose their substance and assume *gaseous form* for 12 full turns, or a *sonic vibration* which will *disintegrate* up to 150 hit points. He is capable of using each breath weapon twice per day. All saving throws against his breath are at a -3 due to the powerful nature of their originator.

Bahamut is able to employ any spells of 1st through 7th level; two each of magical and 1 each of clerical spells per day, or a maximum of 21 spells. He possesses books listing all known magic spells of these levels.

There are seven *huge ancient* gold dragons of highest abilities and loyalty who serve as guards, companions, and advisors to Bahamut. He seldom (10%) is without them. (A sage tells of encountering Bahamut in the guise of an old hermit, with seven canaries singing sweetly as they flitted nearby. The sage relates that he would never have known that he was anything other than what he appeared to be except that a group of ogres and trolls happened by much to their sorrow . . .)

Red Dragon (*Draco Conflagratio Horriblis*)

FREQUENCY: Rare
NO. APPEARING: 1-4
ARMOR CLASS: -1
MOVE: 9"/24"
HIT DICE: 9-11
% IN LAIR: 60%
TREASURE TYPE: H, S, T
NO. OF ATTACKS: 3
DAMAGE/ATTACK: 1-8/1-8/3-30
SPECIAL ATTACKS: Breath weapon
 + possible magic use
SPECIAL DEFENSES: Nil
MAGIC RESISTANCE: Standard
INTELLIGENCE: Exceptional
ALIGNMENT: Chaotic evil
SIZE: L (48' long)
PSIONIC ABILITY: Nil
 Attack/Defense Modes: Nil
CHANCE OF:
 Speaking: 75%
 Magic Use: 40%
 Sleeping: 20%

The red dragon is usually found dwelling in great hills or mountainous regions. As with most others of this species, they make their lairs in subterranean caves and similar places. They are very greedy and avaricious. Of all evil dragons, this sort is the worst, save for Tiamat herself.

A red dragon is able to attack by means of a claw/claw/bite routine or by breathing a cone of fire, 9″ long by 3″ base diameter. Speaking red dragons are 40% likely to be able to employ spells.

For each age bracket the dragon has attained it is able to use an additional spell. At the first two ages the red dragon gains a 1st level spell, at the next two a 2nd level spell is gained, at the fifth and sixth ages a 3rd level spell is gained, and at the last two ages a 4th level spell is gained. Thus, an *ancient* red dragon would be able to employ two spells each of spell levels 1 through 4.

Silver Dragon *(Draco Nobilis Argentum)*

FREQUENCY: *Very rare*
NO. APPEARING: *1-4*
ARMOR CLASS: *-1*
MOVE: *9″/24″*
HIT DICE: *9-11*
% IN LAIR: *55%*
TREASURE TYPE: *H, T*
NO. OF ATTACKS: *3*
DAMAGE/ATTACK: *1-6/1-6/5-30*
SPECIAL ATTACKS: *Breath weapons + possible spell use*
SPECIAL DEFENSES: *Nil*
MAGIC RESISTANCE: *Standard*
INTELLIGENCE: *Exceptional*
ALIGNMENT: *Lawful good*
SIZE: *L (48′ long)*
PSIONIC ABILITY: *Nil*
    Attack/Defense Modes: *Nil*
CHANCE OF:
    Speaking: *75%*
    Magic Use: *75%*
    Sleeping: *15%*

Silver dragons select mountain peaks, clouds, and similar locales in which to establish their abode. It is claimed that this dragon can be found in the home of the King of Good Dragons as well as behind other winds as well. Much as a gold dragon, these creatures are able to *polymorph* themselves in order to appear as an animal or human (typically a kindly old man or fair damsel if the latter).

When in combat a silver dragon is able to attack with claw and fang or use either of its two breath weapons — a cone of frost (cold) 8″ long with a 3″ base, or a cloud of paralyzing gas 5″ long by 4″ wide by 2″ high which will take immediate effect upon all within it unless they save versus dragon breath.

Silver dragons who are able to use magic are able to employ a maximum of ten spells. At each of the first two ages they gain two 1st and 2nd level spells respectively. At each age thereafter they gain an additional spell — 3rd level at *subadult* and *young adult*, 4th level at *adult* and *old*, and 5th level if *very old* and *ancient*. Thus, a *very young* silver dragon of this ability would know two 1st level spells, a *young* one would know two 1st and 2nd level spells, etc. Furthermore, 25% of magic-using silver dragons have books of spells, so they may select spells for use rather than knowing only a limited number per level.

White Dragon *(Draco Rigidus Frigidus)*

FREQUENCY: *Uncommon*
NO. APPEARING: *1-4*
ARMOR CLASS: *3*
MOVE: *12″/30″*
HIT DICE: *5-7*
% IN LAIR: *20%*
TREASURE TYPE: *E, O, S*
NO. OF ATTACKS: *3*
DAMAGE/ATTACK: *1-4/1-4/2-16*
SPECIAL ATTACKS: *Breath weapon*
SPECIAL DEFENSES: *Nil*
MAGIC RESISTANCE: *Standard*
INTELLIGENCE: *Average (low)*
ALIGNMENT: *Chaotic evil*
SIZE: *L (24′ long)*
PSIONIC ABILITY: *Nil*
    Attack/Defense Modes: *Nil*
CHANCE OF:
    Speaking: *20%*
    Magic Use: *5%*
    Sleeping: *60%*

White dragons favor chilly or cold regions in which to dwell. They lair in icy caves or deep subterranean places. Although not as intelligent as most other dragons, they are as evil and greedy as any.

The white dragon is able to attack with a claw/claw/bite or with its breath weapon — a cone of cold (frost) 7″ long with a base diameter of 2½″.

Rare magic-using white dragons are able to employ a maximum of four 1st level spells, gaining one at each even-numbered (2nd, 4th, 6th, 8th) age bracket, i.e. one spell at *young* age, a second at *young adult* stage, a third at *old* age, and the fourth at *ancient* status. To determine spells usable, select randomly from the 1st level spell list. Duplication is possible, merely indicating that the dragon can use the same spell twice, thrice, or even four times.

DRAGONNE

FREQUENCY: *Very rare*
NO. APPEARING: *1*
ARMOR CLASS: *6/2*
MOVE: *15″/9″*
HIT DICE: *9*
% IN LAIR: *40%*
TREASURE TYPE: *B, S, T*
NO. OF ATTACKS: *3*
DAMAGE/ATTACK: *1-8/1-8/3-18*
SPECIAL ATTACKS: *Roar*
SPECIAL DEFENSES: *Nil*
MAGIC RESISTANCE: *Standard*
INTELLIGENCE: *Low*
ALIGNMENT: *Neutral*
SIZE: *L (5′ at shoulder)*
PSIONIC ABILITY: *Nil*
    Attack/Defense Modes: *Nil*

A weird cross between a brass dragon and a giant lion, the dragonne is both very rare and most solitary. The beast fights with its huge claws and great fangs; but its most dreaded weapon is its horrible roar. This sound causes *weakness* to all within 12″ of the monster unless they save against paralyzation. Furthermore, any creature within 3″ or less of the dragonne will be deafened. Both effects of the dragonne's roar last for from 2-12 melee rounds. Those weak from fear from the sound lose 50% of their strength; deafened creatures cannot hear any sound and will strike at -1 on their attack dice due to disorientation. Dragonnes are able to fly only short distances (1-3 turns) with their small wings. They speak the language of brass dragons and sphinxes.

DRAGON TURTLE

FREQUENCY: *Very rare*
NO. APPEARING: *1*
ARMOR CLASS: *0*
MOVE: *3''//9''*
HIT DICE: *12-14*
% IN LAIR: *5%*
TREASURE TYPE: *B, R, S, T, V*
NO. OF ATTACKS: *3*
DAMAGE/ATTACK: *2ᴸ12/2-12/4-32*
SPECIAL ATTACKS: *See below*
SPECIAL DEFENSES: *Nil*
MAGIC RESISTANCE: *Standard*
INTELLIGENCE: *Very*
ALIGNMENT: *Neutral*
SIZE: *L (up to 30' dia.)*
PSIONIC ABILITY: *Nil*
    Attack/Defense Modes: *Nil*

Perhaps the most feared of water creatures is the dragon turtle. They are found in very large rivers and lakes as well as in the sea. Its thick shell makes it nearly impossible to harm, while its powerful claws and jaws easily rip opponents to shreds. Worse still, they can belch forth a cloud of scalding steam which covers an area 6'' long, 4'' wide, and 4'' high. This steam causes damage equal to the number of hit points the dragon turtle has, reduced by one-half if the victim makes its saving throw. Dragon turtles vary in size, age and hit points per die in the same manner as dragons (q.v.). If a dragon turtle comes up under even a large ship they are likely to capsize the vessel (chances are 95% for a small ship to 50% for a large one). They speak their own tongue.

Description: The shell of the dragon turtle is deep green with silver highlights, its legs and tail are lighter green with golden highlights, its neck is green/gold, with golden highlights, and its head and crest are green/gold.

DRYAD

FREQUENCY: *Very rare*
NO. APPEARING: *1-6*
ARMOR CLASS: *9*
MOVE: *12''*
HIT DICE: *2*
% IN LAIR: *10%*
TREASURE TYPE: *M (x 100), Q (x 10)*
NO. OF ATTACKS: *1*
DAMAGE/ATTACK: *Dagger*
SPECIAL ATTACKS: *Charm*
SPECIAL DEFENSES: *See below*
MAGIC RESISTANCE: *50%*
INTELLIGENCE: *High*
ALIGNMENT: *Neutral*
SIZE: *M*
PSIONIC ABILITY: *Nil*
    Attack/Defense Modes: *Nil*

These beautiful and alluring tree sprites are found only in the most secluded places. They are found only near oak trees and never more than 36'' from their individual tree of which they are actually a part. A dryad is shy and non-violent. Unless surprised, a dryad can disappear by stepping into a tree, slipping out on a side unseen by the intruder(s), and *dimension door* to her own tree. Dryad trees are distinguished only by their large size; they do not radiate any magic. If seriously threatened, or if near a male with a 16 or greater charisma, the dryad will use her powerful *charm person* spell which may be cast up to three times per day, once per melee round, with a minus 3 on the victim's saving throw. If a person is taken away by a dryad, there is a 50% chance they will never return, and if they do return it will be from 1-4 years later. Dryads can speak their own tongue, elven, pixieish, sprite, and also speak with plants. If carefully approached they might be persuaded to aid a person or party. Dryads have exact knowledge of the wood or forest in which they dwell.

DWARF

FREQUENCY: *Common*
NO. APPEARING: *40-400*
ARMOR CLASS: *4*
MOVE: *6''*
HIT DICE: *1*
% IN LAIR: *50%*
TREASURE TYPE: *Individuals M (x 5); G, Q (x 20), R*
NO. OF ATTACKS: *1*
DAMAGE/ATTACK: *By weapon or 1-8*
SPECIAL ATTACKS: *See below*
SPECIAL DEFENSES: *Save at 4 levels higher (See below)*
MAGIC RESISTANCE: *As above*
INTELLIGENCE: *Very*
ALIGNMENT: *Lawful good*
SIZE: *S (4' + tall)*
PSIONIC ABILITY: *Nil**
    Attack/Defense Modes: *Nil**

*possible to exist in unusual characters

Rocky hills are the favorite abode of these sturdy creatures. Dwarves typically band together in clans which are not mutually exclusive or hostile but are competitive. These creatures are able to operate in two or more classes simultaneously, so fighter/clerics, for example, are possible. Note also that the level of proficiency may vary between the two or more classes one of these creatures is capable of performing in.

For every 40 dwarves in a group there will be a fighter of 2nd through 6th level (to determine level roll a 6-sided die, 1 equalling 2 and the other numbers indicating the level). If 160 or more dwarves are in a group there will be in addition one 6th, and one 4th level fighter as chief, and lieutenant, of the group. If 200 or more are encountered there will be a fighter/cleric of 3rd to 6th level fighting ability and 4th to 7th level clerical ability in addition to the others. If 320 or more dwarves are encountered there will be the following additional dwarves with the group: an 8th level fighter, a 7th level fighter, a 6th level fighter/7th level cleric, and two 4th level fighter/clerics. If encountered in their lair (home) there will be in addition from 2-12 fighters of from 2nd to 5th level, from 2-8 fighter/clerics of from 2nd to 4th level (each category), and females and young equal to 50% and 25% respectively of the number of adult males. A dwarven lair is always an underground complex in solid rock.

Dwarves are typically armored with chainmail and shield. They have the following typical weaponing:

Sword & light crossbow	15%
Sword & pole arm	10%
Sword & spear	20%
Axe & heavy crossbow	10%
Axe & hammer	25%
Axe & mace	10%
Hammer & pick	10%

Higher level fighters and fighter/clerics have a 10% chance per level of having magic armor and/or weapons. For fighter/clerics also check at 10% per clerical level for 1-4 additional items (potion, clerical scroll, ring, wand/staff/rod, misc. magic) usable by clerics. All dwarves above normal level will have plate armor and shield.

Dwarves are 60% likely to have tamed animals to serve as guards in their lair: 5-20 wolves (25%) or 2-8 brown bears (75%).

Due to their great hatred of goblins, orcs, and hobgoblins, all dwarves gain a bonus of +1 on their dice rolls to hit these opponents. When dwarves are in melee with ogres, trolls and giants, these monsters must deduct 4 from their dice rolls to hit their dwarven opponents due to the size and skill of the latter in combatting these huge creatures.

All dwarves are resistant to both magic and poison; they therefore make saving throws at 4 levels above their actual level. Dwarves can see in the dark (infravision) noting monsters at a distance of 60'. Because of their mining skills, dwarves are good (50% to 75% likely) at detecting passages which slope upwards or downwards, sliding or shifting walls or rooms, new construction, approximate depth, or unusual stonework.

Dwarves speak their own tongue and those of gnomes, goblins, kobolds, and orcs. It is 75% likely that dwarves will also speak the common language.

Description: Dwarves are typically deep tan to light brown of skin, with ruddy cheeks and bright eyes (almost never blue). Their hair is brown, black or gray. They favor earth tones with small bits of bright color in their clothing. Although only 4 or so feet tall, they weigh no less than 150 pounds due to their stocky muscular build. They live for no less than 350 years on the average.

Mountain Dwarves: These creatures are similar to their cousins, the hill dwarves, detailed above. The only differences are size (4½′+ tall), hit dice (1 + 1), and coloration (typically lighter with brown hair). They employ fewer crossbows (20% maximum) and more spears (30%). Mountain dwarves with 16 strength can work up to 7th level, with 17 strength to 8th level, and with 18 strength to 9th level. Mountain dwarves have a life span of 400 or more years.

 EAGLE, GIANT — EAR SEEKER — EEL — EFREET — ELEMENTAL — ELEPHANT — ELF — ETTIN — EYE, FLOATING — EYE OF THE DEEP

EAGLE, *Giant*

FREQUENCY: *Rare*
NO. APPEARING: *1-20*
ARMOR CLASS: *7*
MOVE: *3″/48″*
HIT DICE: *4*
% IN LAIR: *20%*
TREASURE TYPE: *Q, C*
　　(magic only)
NO. OF ATTACKS: *3*
DAMAGE/ATTACK: *1-6/1-6/2-12*
SPECIAL ATTACKS: *See below*
SPECIAL DEFENSES: *See below*
MAGIC RESISTANCE: *Standard*
INTELLIGENCE: *Average*
ALIGNMENT: *Neutral*
SIZE: *M (20′ wing spread)*
PSIONIC ABILITY: *Nil*
　　Attack/Defense Modes: *Nil*

Giant eagles are found only in places where there are great bluffs, cliffs, mesas, or mountain crags to nest on. Their eyesight is such that they are never surprised unless encountered in their lair or at night. If they attack by diving 50 or more feet they add +4 to hit probability, do double claw damage (2-12/2-12), but get no beak attack. They can carry up to 2000 gold pieces at half speed.

If encountered outside their lair, giant eagles will typically ignore any good creatures but attack evil creatures which seem to be threatening. They are fairly friendly towards certain dwarves and elves. They have their own language and can also communicate through a limited form of telepathy. If encountered in their lair they will always be hostile. If there are young (50%) or eggs there they will attack any creature within 50′. There will be 1-4 young per nest, 1 nest per 2 giant eagles. They can be tamed. Eggs sell on the open market for 500 to 800 gold pieces each.

EAR SEEKERS

FREQUENCY: *Very rare*
NO. APPEARING: *1-4*
ARMOR CLASS: *9*
MOVE: *1″*
HIT DICE: *1 hit point*
% IN LAIR: *90%*
TREASURE TYPE: *Nil*
NO. OF ATTACKS: *1, See below*
DAMAGE/ATTACK: *See below*
SPECIAL ATTACKS: *Nil*
SPECIAL DEFENSES: *Nil*
MAGIC RESISTANCE: *Standard*
INTELLIGENCE: *Non-*
ALIGNMENT: *Neutral*
SIZE: *S(about ½″ long)*
PSIONIC ABILITY: *Nil*
　　Attack/Defense Modes: *Nil*

Ear seekers are small insectoids which are found in wood. They live by eating dead cellulose, but they need warm places in which to lay their eggs, and they favor places like ears. If this creature enters a warm place, it will always lay 9-16 tiny eggs and then crawl out to die. When the eggs hatch (4-24 hours) the larvae eat the surrounding flesh, generally burrowing inwards to where the most food and body heat is, killing their host 90% of the time. A *cure disease* spell will destroy the eggs.

EEL

	Electric	Giant	Weed
FREQUENCY:	Rare	Uncommon	Very rare
NO. APPEARING:	1-3	1-4	10-60
ARMOR CLASS:	9	6	8
MOVE:	12″	9″	15″
HIT DICE:	2	5	1-1
% IN LAIR:	Nil	Nil	100%
TREASURE TYPE:	Nil	Nil	O, P, R
NO. OF ATTACKS:	1	1	1
DAMAGE/ATTACK:	1-3	3-18	1
SPECIAL ATTACKS:	Jolt	Nil	Poison
SPECIAL DEFENSES:	Nil	Nil	Nil
MAGIC RESISTANCE:	Standard	Standard	Standard
INTELLIGENCE:	Non-	Non-	Non-
ALIGNMENT:	Neutral	Neutral	Neutral
SIZE:	M (9′ long)	M (20′ long)	S (6′ long)
PSIONIC ABILITY:	Nil	Nil	Nil
Attack/Defense Modes:	Nil	Nil	Nil

All eels are water-dwellers. They are typically aggressive only when approached too closely.

Electric eels are found in warm fresh water. They will give off a jolt of electricity in a radius of 15′. They are immune to electrical effects. Any creature within 5′ of the eel takes 3-24 hit points damage; within 5′ to 10′ the jolt delivers 2-16 hit points damage, and between 10′ and 15′ the jolt delivers 1-8 hit points. The eel can do this but once per hour (six turns). Marine species are reported to be twice the size and do twice the damage.

Giant eels are typically of the moray type. They have a nasty temper and teeth to match. Few (10%) are found in fresh water.

Weed eels are masters of camouflage, appearing as a patch of normal seaweed to any but a highly trained observer. They live in colonies, sharing food and home alike. Their bite is poisonous, and unless a saving throw is made the creature bitten will die. Weed eel colonies consist of a network of small (six to eight inch diameter) holes which all lead to several 6′ diameter tunnels, and the latter lead to a communal cave about 30′ long, 20′ wide, and 20′ high. The eels use small stones, coins, gems, metal, etc. to floor this cave with. Colonies are found in both fresh and salt water, typically in water depths of 25′ to 40′. If an attempt is made to enter any hole, the eel to whom it belongs will always strike with incredible speed. If eels note the entrance of foreign creatures, they will leave their holes to protect the cave where young are raised.

EFREETI

FREQUENCY: *Very rare*
NO. APPEARING: *1*
ARMOR CLASS: *2*
MOVE: *9"/24"*
HIT DICE: *10*
% IN LAIR: *Nil*
TREASURE TYPE: *Nil*
NO. OF ATTACKS: *1*
DAMAGE/ATTACK: *3-24*
SPECIAL ATTACKS: *See below*
SPECIAL DEFENSES: *Nil*
MAGIC RESISTANCE: *Standard*
INTELLIGENCE: *Very*
ALIGNMENT: *Neutral (tend towards lawful evil)*
SIZE: *L (12' tall)*
PSIONIC ABILITY: *Nil*
    Attack/Defense Modes: *Nil*

The efreet are creatures from the Elemental Plane of Fire, just as djinn come from Plane of Air. They are enemies of the djinn and will always attack when they encounter them. An efreeti can be forced to serve for a maximum of 1,001 days or by causing it to fulfill three wishes. They are not willing servants, and they will seek to pervert the intent of their masters by adhering to the letter of commands.

An efreeti is able to do the following once per day: *grant up to three wishes (and go free), become invisible, assume gaseous form, detect magic, enlarge* (as a 10th level magic-user), *polymorph self, create an illusion* with both visual and audial components which will last without concentration until magically dispelled or touched, or create a *wall of fire.* An efreeti can also *produce flame* or cause *pyrotechnics* as often as desired. Attacks based on fire do no harm to efreet if the fire is of the "normal" sort; magical fire attacks are at -1 on both "to hit" and damage dice.

Efreet can carry up to 7,500 gold pieces weight, afoot or flying, without tiring. They can carry double weight for only a limited time — three turns afoot or but one turn aloft. For each 1,500 gold pieces of weight under 15,000 add one turn to either walking or flying time permitted. After carrying excess weight the efreeti must rest for six full turns.

The fabled City of Brass, citadel of the Efreet, is on the plane from whence they come. Capture of an efreeti is possible there, but tens or even hundreds of efreet would possibly have to be faced also. Efreet are infamous for their dislike of servitude, their desire for revenge, their cruel nature, and their ability to mislead. A powerful Sultan rules the Efreet. He is served by many different sorts of nobles and officials (pashas, deys, amirs, valis, and maliks).

The efreet are able to communicate with any intelligent creature they encounter by means of a limited form of telepathy which enables them to understand and speak appropriately.

Efreet are able to travel the material, elemental, and astral planes.

ELEMENTAL

There are four different kinds of elementals normally encountered — air, earth, fire, and water elementals. These are strong but relatively stupid beings conjured magically from their normal habitat — the elemental planes of air, earth, etc. The strength of any type varies, and the characteristics of each elemental type are different. All differences will be dealt with separately under the appropriate headings.

More or less powerful and/or intelligent elementals exist on the elemental planes than can be summoned. Various forms of free-willed elemental plane dwellers will be found described elsewhere in this book. The outstanding true elementals dwelling on these planes will be mentioned only briefly hereunder.

Conjured elementals fall into three hit dice strength categories, and this applies to all types:

Conjured by spell	16 hit dice
Conjured by summoning device	12 hit dice
Conjured through a staff	8 hit dice

Any creature conjuring an elemental may do so but once per day per means per elemental type. For example a magic-user with two appropriate staffs could summon at least two elementals, one through each staff, once per day, each. Both elementals could not be the same kind. If the magic-user were able to employ several spells to conjure elementals, each spell would have to summon a different kind of elemental. However, if the magic-user also had a summoning device and a staff he could possibly evoke three elementals of the same type.

As elementals are stupid and resent being summoned, the conjuring party must concentrate upon controlling the creature. Failure to do so will result in the elemental turning upon the summoner 75% of the time and attacking. The turning elemental will come directly towards the conjuring party, attacking anything in its path along the way. Control can never be regained, and an uncontrolled elemental will always return to its own plane in three turns after control is lost. If an elemental does not turn (25% chance), it simply goes immediately to its own plane. Control concentration requires that the summoning party remain stationary and be neither physically nor mentally attacked, including attack by missile or distraction. In any event, only one elemental at a time can be controlled.

Elementals are impervious to attacks by normal weapons and even magical weapons under +2 bonus. Creatures without magical ability of some sort cannot harm elementals unless the creatures have four or more hit dice. Magical ability includes *paralysis, poison, acid, breath weapons,* and even the characteristic of not being subject to attack by normal weapons. Kobolds, goblins, orcs, etc. are all powerless to affect elementals because they have neither magical property nor four or more hit dice. Ogres, however, could attack an elemental with effect as they have the necessary strength (four hit dice in this case). Note, however, that if a kobold with a +2 magic sword attacked an elemental the weapon would be effective.

A conjured elemental can be taken over and controlled by a magic-user casting a dispel magic spell (ratio dispeller's level over conjuring party's level to determine chance of success), and deliberately aiming it at dispelling the control rather than the elemental. However, if the spell fails, the effect is to strengthen the elemental to a full 8 points per hit die, double the controller's ability to concentrate, and make the elemental resent the one attempting the take-over, so that if it becomes uncontrolled it will go after that magic-user.

Air Elemental

FREQUENCY: *Very rare*
NO. APPEARING: *1*
ARMOR CLASS: *2*
MOVE: *36"*
HIT DICE: *8, 12 or 16*
% IN LAIR: *Nil*
TREASURE TYPE: *Nil*
NO. OF ATTACKS: *1*
DAMAGE/ATTACK: *2-20*
SPECIAL ATTACKS: *See below*
SPECIAL DEFENSES: *+2 or better weapon to hit*
MAGIC RESISTANCE: *Standard*
INTELLIGENCE: *Low*
ALIGNMENT: *Neutral*
SIZE: *L*
PSIONIC ABILITY: *Nil*
    Attack/Defense Modes: *Nil*

Air elementals' only mode of locomotion is by "flying." They can, of course, move at slower than the speed listed. If in combat in the air they gain a +1 on hit probability and a +2 on each die of damage they cause. Upon command an air elemental can form a whirlwind — a truncated reverse cone, with a 2" bottom diameter, a 6" top diameter, and a height in inches equal to the elementals' number of hit dice, i.e. 8", 12" or 16". If the full height of the whirlwind can't be attained due to some overhead obstruction, the whirlwind is only half strength. A full strength air elemental whirlwind lasts for 1 melee round, sweeps away and kills all creatures under three hit dice, and causes 2-16 hit points of damage to all non-aerial creatures which it fails to kill outright. Formation of this whirlwind or dissipation of it requires one full turn.

On the elemental plane of air can be found certain intelligent air elementals which have special abilities beyond the above. Some are stronger than the most powerful of conjured elementals. Their queen is both powerful and has certain magical abilities.

Earth Elemental

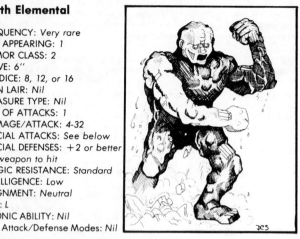

FREQUENCY: *Very rare*
NO. APPEARING: *1*
ARMOR CLASS: *2*
MOVE: *6''*
HIT DICE: *8, 12, or 16*
% IN LAIR: *Nil*
TREASURE TYPE: *Nil*
NO. OF ATTACKS: *1*
DAMAGE/ATTACK: *4-32*
SPECIAL ATTACKS: *See below*
SPECIAL DEFENSES: *+2 or better weapon to hit*
MAGIC RESISTANCE: *Standard*
INTELLIGENCE: *Low*
ALIGNMENT: *Neutral*
SIZE: *L*
PSIONIC ABILITY: *Nil*
　　Attack/Defense Modes: *Nil*

These powerful creatures travel rather slowly, and in order to cross water they must travel *through* the ground and go under the bed of the body of water (possibly a long trip). They score full damage against any creature which rests on the earth, -2 on each die of damage against other opponents (flying, levitating, etc.). Against constructions built on stone or earth they act as a super battering ram, causing 2-8 points of structural damage (a typical cottage having about 7 structural points). They can be summoned from earth or stone.

On the elemental plane of earth there exists a boss rumored to be of astounding size.

Fire Elemental

FREQUENCY: *Very rare*
NO. APPEARING: *1*
ARMOR CLASS: *2*
MOVE: *12''*
HIT DICE: *8, 12, or 16*
% IN LAIR: *Nil*
TREASURE TYPE: *Nil*
NO. OF ATTACKS: *1*
DAMAGE/ATTACK: *3-24*
SPECIAL ATTACKS: *See below*
SPECIAL DEFENSES: *+2 or better weapon to hit*
MAGIC RESISTANCE: *Standard*
INTELLIGENCE: *Low*
ALIGNMENT: *Neutral*
SIZE: *L*
PSIONIC ABILITY: *Nil*
　　Attack/Defense Modes: *Nil*

Fire elementals are terrible to behold and fierce opponents. They set fire to any inflammable material they touch. Against fire-using opponents they score -1 on their damage dice. Fire elementals are checked by water, being unable to pass over non-inflammable liquids.

On the elemental plane of fire exist many sorts of different fire elementals and similar beings. The ruler of all fire elementals is reported to be known as the tyrant.

Water Elemental

FREQUENCY: *Very rare*
NO. APPEARING: *1*
ARMOR CLASS: *2*
MOVE: *6''//18''*
HIT DICE: *8, 12, or 16*
% IN LAIR: *Nil*
TREASURE TYPE: *Nil*
NO. OF ATTACKS: *1*
DAMAGE/ATTACK: *5-30*
SPECIAL ATTACKS: *See below*
SPECIAL DEFENSES: *+2 or better weapon to hit*
MAGIC RESISTANCE: *Standard*
INTELLIGENCE: *Low*
ALIGNMENT: *Neutral*
SIZE: *L*
PSIONIC ABILITY: *Nil*
　　Attack/Defense Modes: *Nil*

Water elementals are, for all practical purposes, limited to water operations, for they can stray only 6'' from their element. It normally requires a considerable volume of water (or watery liquid) to create a water elemental — a pool of water of at least 1,000 cubic feet in volume, but several large barrels of ale or wine would suffice. Outside their element water elementals are less effective, and they lose 1 point from each die of damage they inflict. In a body of water they attack at full effect, move more swiftly, can upset small craft (1 ton of craft per hit die of elemental), or slow or stop craft (1 ton of vessel can be stopped per hit point of elemental; if greater tonnage, simply ratio the tons to hit points to find the rate the vessel is slowed).

There are many other elemental forms on the plane of water. Free-willed, intelligent beings are common as well as much more powerful elementals of the sort dealt with here. It is possible that they are ruled by a god-like king.

ELEPHANT

	(Asiatic) Elephant	Loxodont (African Elephant)
FREQUENCY:	Common	Common
NO. APPEARING:	1-20	1-12
ARMOR CLASS:	6	6
MOVE:	12''	15''
HIT DICE:	10	11
% IN LAIR:	Nil	Nil
TREASURE TYPE:	Nil	Nil
NO. OF ATTACKS:	5	5
DAMAGE/ATTACK:	2-12/2-12/2-12/ 2-12/2-12	2-16/2-16/2-12/ 2-12/2-12
SPECIAL ATTACKS:	Nil	Nil
SPECIAL DEFENSES:	Nil	Nil
MAGIC RESISTANCE:	Standard	Standard
INTELLIGENCE:	Semi-	Semi-
ALIGNMENT:	Neutral	Neutral
SIZE:	L (9' + tall)	L (11' tall)
PSIONIC ABILITY:	Nil	Nil
Attack/Defense Modes:	Nil	Nil

The elephant is found only in warm climates. They attack by means of a stab with two tusks, a grab and squeeze with their trunk, and then two tramplings with their front feet. One opponent can be subject to no more than two of these attacks at the same time, but several opponents can be fought simultaneously — 6 or more man-sized opponents for example. Ogre-sized opponents will not be affected by trunk attacks. Elephants are relatively intelligent, and will not trunk-attack creatures which will harm their trunk, i.e. spikey, hot, etc. They fear fire. An elephant can easily break open a great gate by pushing unless the gate is spiked to prevent this. They can be trained to carry equipment and/or men.

Elephant tusks have a value of 100 to 600 gold piece value each. Each gold piece of value equals one-quarter pound of weight.

If more than one-half the possible number is encountered, there will be young animals in the herd — from 1 to 4, 20% to 70% mature. If a single animal is encountered it will be a rogue bull, with no fewer than 6 hit points per die, and a very nasty and aggressive temper. Rogues will attack 90% of the time.

(See also the headings **MAMMOTH** *and* **MASTODON** *for information on elephants.)*

ELF

FREQUENCY: *Uncommon*
NO. APPEARING: *20-200*
ARMOR CLASS: *5*
MOVE: *12''*
HIT DICE: *1 + 1*
% IN LAIR: *10%*
TREASURE TYPE: *Individuals N;*
   G, S, T in lair
NO. OF ATTACKS: *1*
DAMAGE/ATTACK: *By weapon or*
   1-10
SPECIAL ATTACKS. *+1 with*
   normal bow or sword
SPECIAL DEFENSES: *See below*
MAGIC RESISTANCE: *90% to*
   charm and sleep only
INTELLIGENCE: *High and up*
ALIGNMENT: *Chaotic good*
SIZE: *M (5'+ tall)*
PSIONIC ABILITY: *Nil*
   Attack/Defense Modes: *Nil*

Elves are of various sorts, including a marine race, all of which are detailed here. These creatures are able to operate in two or more classes simultaneously, so fighter/clerics, for example, are possible. Note also that the level of proficiency may vary between the two or more classes one of these creatures is capable of performing in. They have only a loose social structure based on independent bands which owe allegiance to an overlord (duke, princess, king or queen).

For every 20 elves in a band there will be one with above average fighting ability (2nd, or 3rd level). For every 40 elves encountered there will be one with this fighting ability plus 1st or 2nd level magic-user ability. If 100 or more elves are encountered there will be the following additional figures: a 4th level fighter/8th level magic-user, two 4th level fighter/5th level magic-user elves, and a 4th level fighter/4th level magic-user/4th level cleric. If over 160 elves are encountered their leaders will be a 6th level fighter/9th level magic-user, and a 6th level fighter/6th level magic-user/6th level cleric; and these leaders will have two special retainers each — 4th level fighter/5th level magic-user, 3rd level fighter/3rd level magic-user/3rd level cleric. These are also in addition to the group indicated. If encountered in their lair there will also be these extra figures: a 4th level fighter/7th level magic-user, a 4th level fighter for every 40 elves in the group, a 2nd level fighter/2nd level magic-user/2nd level cleric for every 40 elves in the group, a 5th level fighter, a 6th level fighter, and females and young equal to 100% and 5% respectively.

Elves of all sorts seek to make their home secure by locating it in secluded copse, wood or forest. They typically (65%) have from 2-12 giant eagles as guards for their lair.

The composition of a band of elves by weaponing is given below: (They are usually in scale, ring, or chain mail, and most carry shields.)

sword and bow	10%
sword and spear	20%
sword	20%
two-handed sword	5%
spear	30%
bow	15%

Higher level fighters, fighter/magic-users, and fighter/magic-user/clerics have a 10% chance per level per class of magical items of a usable sort. Thus, a 4th level fighter/5th level magic-user/5th level cleric would have a 40% chance for magic armor (including shield, possibly, or possibly shield only) and/or weapon (sword or miscellaneous weapon); a 40% chance for any other item not covered by the first class, i.e. armor and weapons; and a 50% chance for any sort of magical item usable by a cleric. Furthermore, if above 4th level of magical ability the elf will have from 2-5 magic items for magic-user use if the required score is rolled on the percentile dice.

Although elves do not favor horses, certain bands of elves will have female fighters who will be mounted on unicorns, although this is rare (5%) and only from 10-30 of such warrior elfmaids are typically encountered.

When in natural surroundings such as a wood or meadow, elves can move silently (surprise on a 1-4) and blend into the vegetation so as to be invisible (requiring the ability to see invisible objects to locate them) as long as they are not attacking. Note the bonus elves gain with bow or sword. Elves are also very quick and agile, so they can move, fire their bows, and move back all in the same round.

Elves are 90% resistant to charm and sleep spells of all sorts. They have infravision to 60'. They note secret or hidden doors and the like from one-third to half of the time, depending on the care or magic with which they are hidden.

Elves are able to speak the tongue of goblins, orcs, hobgoblins, and gnolls, in addition to common, alignment, elvish, halflingish, and gnomish.

Description: Elves are slim of build and pale complected. Their hair is dark, and their eyes are green. Their garb is typically pastel and of blue or green or violet (but often covered by a greenish gray cloak). The life span of these creatures is a dozen centuries long.

Aquatic Elf: Also called sea elves, they are akin to mermen as land elves are to men. Found almost exclusively among heavy weed beds in quiet sheltered salty waters, they are great friends of the dolphins. They fashion caverns in lagoon bottoms and reefs where they live and work. They trade with land elves — metal goods (they are unable to forge underwater) for rare items found in the sea. For every 20 sea elves, there is a 50% chance that they are accompanied by 1-3 friendly dolphins.

Aquatic elves use spears and tridents as weapons, usually in combination with nets. They do not use magic. They speak only elvish.

They are humanoid in appearance, with gill slits on the throat and greenish-silver skin and green or blue-green hair. Seaweed affords little or no hindrance to their movement. They are invisible in weeds or on reefs. They are mortal enemies of sharks and sahuagin, and will attack either if the elves outnumber them. They are friends to dolphins and land elves, and neutral to all others, except for fishermen, whom they dislike due to the number of sea elves snared in nets and killed mistakenly as sahuagin by these ignorant humans.

Drow: The "Black Elves," or drow, are only legend. They purportedly dwell deep beneath the surface in a strange subterranean realm. The drow are said to be as dark as faeries are bright and as evil as the latter are good. Tales picture them as weak fighters but strong magic-users.

Gray Elf *(Faerie):* These noble elves are the rarest and most powerful of their kind. They are more intelligent than other sorts (+1 on dice roll for intelligence), and those few with supra-genius abilities can become wizards. They are very reclusive, live in isolated meadowlands, and never associate with any other humanoids, other than elves, for long — or with frequency. They usually are armored with chain mail and shield, and all carry swords. Grey elves often (50%) have hippogriffs as steeds (70%) or actually use griffons (3-12) as guards/mounts (30%). They speak the same languages as do high elves. Grey elves have either silver hair and amber eyes or pale golden hair and violet eyes. The latter sort are generally called faeries. They favor white, yellow, silver, or gold garments. Their cloaks are often deep blue or purple. They live beyond the age of 1,500 years.

Half-Elf: All half-elves are of human stock. They are handsome folk, with the good features of each of their races. They mingle freely with either race, being only slightly taller than the average elf (5½') and weighing about 150 pounds. They are able to detect secret entrances and the like as elves do (one-third to one-half the time). Half-elves have normal infravision. They do not gain the sword and bow advantages of their elven stock, but half-elves are able to progress simultaneously in two or three categories, i.e. fighter/magic-user or fighter/magic-user/cleric (if wisdom is 13 or greater). Half-elves normally may attain maximum levels of 6/6/4; if strength is 17 or 18, the level of fighting ability can go to 7th or 8th. Similarly, if intelligence is 17 or 18, half-elves can attain 7th or 8th level magic-user. Thus a half-elf can be a superhero/warlock/vicar (8/8/4). Half-elves are able to speak the same languages as elves — goblin, orcish, gnoll, halflingish, gnomish, and elvish (plus alignment and common). Half-elves live 250 years.

Wood Elf: Sometimes called sylvan elves, these creatures are very reclusive and generally (75%) avoid all contact. Wood elves are more neutral than are other elves. They are unusually strong for elves (add +1 to all die rolls, treating 19 as 18), but they are not quite as intelligent (treat 18 intelligence as 17). They usually wear studded leather or ring mail (armor class 6) and fully 50% of any band is equipped with bows. Only 20% carry swords. 40% of wood elves use spears. The lair of a band of wood elves is usually (70%) guarded by 2-8 giant owls (80%) or by 1-6 giant lynx (20%). They live in primaeval forests and distant woodlands. Wood elves speak only elvish and the languages of certain woods animals and treants. Their complexions are fair, their hair is yellow to coppery red and their eyes are light brown, light green, or hazel. They wear russets, reds, brown and tans. Their cloaks are usually green or greenish brown. Wood elves have a life span of centuries.

ETTIN

FREQUENCY: *Very rare*
NO. APPEARING: *1-4*
ARMOR CLASS: *3*
MOVE: *12"*
HIT DICE: *10*
% IN LAIR: *20%*
TREASURE TYPE: *Individual O, C,*
    Y in lair
NO. OF ATTACKS: *2*
DAMAGE/ATTACK: *2-16/3-18*
SPECIAL ATTACKS: *Nil*
SPECIAL DEFENSES: *Surprised only*
    on a 1
MAGIC RESISTANCE: *Standard*
INTELLIGENCE: *Low*
ALIGNMENT: *Chaotic evil*
SIZE: *L (13'+ tall)*
PSIONIC ABILITY: *Nil*
    Attack/Defense Modes: *Nil*

Ettins are giant-like creatures which dwell only in remote areas. Their lairs

are always underground, for they prefer darkness and are nocturnal.

An ettin attacks with both arms, its left head directing the left arm and the right head the right. Blows from the former arm cause 2-16 points of damage; the right inflicting 3-18. One of the ettin's heads is always likely to be alert, so they are difficult to surprise.

Description: It is evident from their appearance that ettins are closely related to orcs. Their animal skin dress is typically moth eaten and filthy. Ettins use spiked clubs and similar weapons.

EYE, *Floating*

FREQUENCY: *Rare*
NO. APPEARING: *1-12*
ARMOR CLASS: *9*
MOVE: *30"*
HIT DICE: *1-4 hit points*
% IN LAIR: *Nil*
TREASURE TYPE: *Nil*
NO. OF ATTACKS: *Nil*
DAMAGE/ATTACK: *Nil*
SPECIAL ATTACKS: *Hypnotism*
SPECIAL DEFENSES: *Nil*
MAGIC RESISTANCE: *Standard*
INTELLIGENCE: *Non-*
ALIGNMENT: *Neutral*
SIZE: *S (1' long)*
PSIONIC ABILITY: *Nil*
    Attack/Defense Modes: *Nil*

Floating eyes are salt water fish of very unusual nature. They have transparent bodies and a single large eye of about three inch diameter. The latter is all that is readily visible of this fish, and when it is gazed at the creature so doing must save versus paralyzation or become *hypnotized* and remain stationary. Predatory fish (always near floating eyes) then eat the helpless prey, while the floating eyes feed upon the scraps. Naturally, these creatures also eat any small marine creatures they come upon and hypnotize.

EYE OF THE DEEP

FREQUENCY: *Very rare*
NO. APPEARING: *1*
ARMOR CLASS: *5*
MOVE: *6"*
HIT DICE: *10-12*
% IN LAIR: *20%*
TREASURE TYPE: *R*
NO. OF ATTACKS: *3*
DAMAGE/ATTACK: *2-8/2-8/1-6*
SPECIAL ATTACKS: *See below*
SPECIAL DEFENSES: *Nil*
MAGIC RESISTANCE: *Standard*
INTELLIGENCE: *Very*
ALIGNMENT: *Lawful evil*
SIZE: *L (3'-5' dia.)*
PSIONIC ABILITY: *Nil*
    Attack/Defense Modes: *Nil*

It is possible that this monster is a relative of the beholder, for there are remarkable similarities between the two species. The eye of the deep dwells only at great depths of the ocean, floating slowly about, stalking prey. It has two huge crab-like pincers to seize its victims and a mouth full of small sharp teeth. Its primary weapons, however, are its eyes. The creature has a large central eye which emits a blinding flash of light to dazzle and *stun* those in its ray (cone ½" at eye extending 3" to a 2" diameter base) for 2-8 melee rounds unless a saving throw versus death ray/poison is made. The eye of the deep also has two smaller eyes on long stalks with which it is able to *create an illusion*; or, acting independently, the small eyes are able to cast *hold person* and *hold monster* spells respectively.

Because it inhabits the deeps, this monster has an armor class of 5 everywhere, including eyes and eye stalks. It can withstand 10 to 12 dice of damage before being killed. If its eyestalks are severed they will, as with those of a beholder, grow back in about a week of time.

Nature: The eye of the deep is hateful and aggressive, generally conforming to its land-dwelling cousin, the beholder, as regards temperament.

 FLIGHTLESS BIRD — FROG, GIANT — FUNGI, VIOLET

FLIGHTLESS BIRD

FREQUENCY: *Common*
NO. APPEARING: *2-20*
ARMOR CLASS: *7*
MOVE: *18"*
HIT DICE: *1-3*
% IN LAIR: *Nil*
TREASURE TYPE: *Nil*
NO. OF ATTACKS: *1 or 1, See below*
DAMAGE/ATTACK: *1-4 or 2-8*
SPECIAL ATTACKS: *Nil*
SPECIAL DEFENSES: *Nil*
MAGIC RESISTANCE: *Standard*
INTELLIGENCE: *Animal*
ALIGNMENT: *Neutral*
SIZE: *M*
PSIONIC ABILITY: *Nil*
    Attack/Defense Modes: *Nil*

These large avian creatures are typified by the ostrich, emu, and rhea. They live in warm climates in open grasslands. The ostrich-sized have 3 hit dice, emu-like birds have 2, and rhea-sized types 1 hit die. All flightless birds are non-aggressive and run from danger. If cornered they can peck (1-4 hit points) or kick (2-8 hit points).

FROG, *Giant*

	Frog, Giant	Killer	Poisonous
FREQUENCY:	*Uncommon*	*Very rare*	*Rare*
NO. APPEARING:	5-40	3-18	2-12
ARMOR CLASS:	7	8	8
MOVE:	3"//9"	6"//12"	3"//9"
HIT DICE:	1-3	1+4	1
% IN LAIR:	Nil	Nil	Nil
TREASURE TYPE:	Nil	Nil	Nil
NO. OF ATTACKS:	1	3	1
DAMAGE/ATTACK:	1-3/1-6/2-8	1-2/1-2/2-5	1
SPECIAL ATTACKS:	See below	See below	See below
SPECIAL DEFENSES:	Nil	Nil	Nil
MAGIC RESISTANCE:	Standard	Standard	Standard
INTELLIGENCE:	Non-	Non-	Non-
ALIGNMENT:	Neutral	Neutral	Neutral
SIZE:	S to M 6'	S	S
PSIONIC ABILITY:	Nil	Nil	Nil
Attack/Defense Modes:	Nil	Nil	Nil

Giant frogs are found in marshes, swamps, large ponds, river banks, and lake shores. The smallest are only about 2' long (body), medium-sized frogs (2 hit dice) are about 4' long, and the largest are some 6' long. Because of their coloration they surprise on a 1-4. These creatures can leap up to 18" to attack. A giant frog has a tongue which is equal to three times its body length. This sticky member strikes at +4 to hit but does no damage. The tongue is used to draw prey to the frog's mouth. Any creature hit by the tongue gets the opportunity to hit it, and if it does, the frog will withdraw it and not use it against the creature again. If the tongue is not struck, the creature contacted by this member is drawn to the frog next turn and automatically takes maximum damage.

Exception: Creatures weighing more than the frog have a second opportunity to strike the tongue and will not be dragged to the frog's mouth until the third melee round. Furthermore, creatures weighing more than twice the weight of the frog will not be dragged at all, and the frog will release its hold on the third melee round.

Frogs weigh from 50 to 250 pounds, (figure 50 pounds additional weight for every foot of body length over 2'). For each 50 pounds of weight over 50, subtract 2" from leaping distance maximum (18"). A giant frog can jump to a maximum of 30' high, regardless of weight. The direction of a jump can be up to 45° to either side of their direct facing.

Giant frogs eat large insects, birds, rats, or just about any other creature small enough to swallow. A giant frog can swallow a small human, elf, halfling, etc. This is indicated by a score of 20. If a giant frog swallows an opponent whole, there is a chance for it to cut its way out if it has a sharp edged weapon and can score an 18 or better (this also kills the frog). The victim has three chances to so escape. Hits upon a giant frog with whole prey inside have a one-third probability of hitting the creature inside, thus inflicting whatever damage scored on the giant frog on that creature also. They aggressively hunt, but fear such predators as giant fish, giant turtles, giant snakes, etc. If severely wounded they will retreat. They fear fire.

Killer Frog: These smallish giant frogs employ talons and teeth in attack. They are man-eating, specially bred mutants. Only their cannibalistic habits keep them from becoming common and thus a real threat.

Poisonous Frog: This is a rare variety of the normal frog. It secretes a poison from its skin, so that its touch as well as its bite can prove fatal. However, as the poison is weak, all creatures gain a +4 on their saving throws.

FUNGI, *Violet*

FREQUENCY: *Rare*
NO. APPEARING: *1-4*
ARMOR CLASS: 7
MOVE: *1''*
HIT DICE: 3
% IN LAIR: *Nil*
TREASURE TYPE: *Nil*
NO. OF ATTACKS: *1-4*
DAMAGE/ATTACK: *See below*
SPECIAL ATTACKS: *See below*
SPECIAL DEFENSES: *Nil*
MAGIC RESISTANCE: *Standard*
INTELLIGENCE: *Non-*

ALIGNMENT: *Neutral*
SIZE: *S to M*
PSIONIC ABILITY: *Nil*
    Attack/Defense Modes: *Nil*

Violet fungus growths resemble shriekers, and are usually (75%) encountered with them. The latter are immune to the touch of violet fungi, and the two types of creatures complement each other's existence. Violet fungi favors rotted animal matter to grow upon. Each fungus has 1 to 4 branches which it will flail out with if any animal comes within their 1' to 4' range. The excretion from these branches *rots* flesh in but one melee round unless a saving throw versus poison is made or a *cure disease* is used. The branch length of this growth depends upon size. Violet fungi range from 4' to 7' tall, the smallest having 1' branches, the 5' sort having 2' branches, etc. Any sized growth can have 1 to 4 branches.

GAR, GIANT — GARGOYLE — GAS SPORE — GELATINOUS CUBE — GHAST — GHOST — GHOUL — GIANT — GNOLL — GNOME — GOAT, GIANT — GOBLIN — GOLEM — GORGON — GRAY OOZE — GREEN SLIME — GRIFFON — GROANING SPIRIT

GAR, *Giant*

FREQUENCY: *Rare*
NO. APPEARING: *1-6*
ARMOR CLASS: 3
MOVE: *30''*
HIT DICE: 8
% IN LAIR: *Nil*
TREASURE TYPE: *Nil*
NO. OF ATTACKS: *1*
DAMAGE/ATTACK: *5-20*
SPECIAL ATTACKS: *See below*
SPECIAL DEFENSES: *Nil*
MAGIC RESISTANCE: *Standard*
INTELLIGENCE: *Non-*
ALIGNMENT: *Neutral*
SIZE: *L (21'-30' long)*
PSIONIC ABILITY: *Nil*
    Attack/Defense Modes: *Nil*

Unlike their smaller relatives, giant gar tend to be aggressive hunters. They inhabit only large, deep lakes and rivers. They are capable of swallowing prey whole, and any hit of 20 indicates they have done so. Note that a small giant gar can swallow an elf or dwarf whole. If a creature is swallowed whole there is a 5% chance/melee round that it will die. A creature so swallowed must have a sharp-edged weapon in hand to have any chance of cutting its way out. The swallowed creature must be able to inflict damage equal to 25% of the fish's total hit points to get free. Attacks which pierce the gar can hit the creature swallowed whole (assume 20% chance), and this will cause appropriate damage to both the gar and the creature swallowed.

GARGOYLE

FREQUENCY: *Uncommon*
NO. APPEARING: *2-16*
ARMOR CLASS: 5
MOVE: *9''/15''*
HIT DICE: 4 + 4
% IN LAIR: *20%*
TREASURE TYPE: *Individuals M*
    (×10), C in lair
NO. OF ATTACKS: 4
DAMAGE/ATTACK: *1-3/1-3/1-6/1-4*
SPECIAL ATTACKS: *Nil*
SPECIAL DEFENSES: *+1 or better weapon to hit*
MAGIC RESISTANCE: *Standard*
INTELLIGENCE: *Low*
ALIGNMENT: *Chaotic evil*
SIZE: *M*
PSIONIC ABILITY: *Nil*
    Attack/Defense Modes: *Nil*

These monsters are ferocious predators of a magical nature. They are typically found amidst ruins or dwelling in underground caverns. They will attack anything they detect, regardless of whether it is good or evil, 90% of the time. They love best to torture prey to death when it is helpless. Because they are fairly intelligent and evil they will sometimes serve an evil master of some sort.

Kopoacinth: This creature is a marine variety of gargoyle which uses its wings to swim. They conform in all respects to a normal gargoyle. They dwell in relatively shallow waters, lairing in undersea caves.

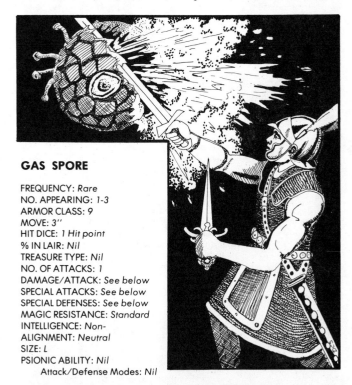

GAS SPORE

FREQUENCY: *Rare*
NO. APPEARING: *1-3*
ARMOR CLASS: 9
MOVE: *3''*
HIT DICE: *1 Hit point*
% IN LAIR: *Nil*
TREASURE TYPE: *Nil*
NO. OF ATTACKS: *1*
DAMAGE/ATTACK: *See below*
SPECIAL ATTACKS: *See below*
SPECIAL DEFENSES: *See below*
MAGIC RESISTANCE: *Standard*
INTELLIGENCE: *Non-*
ALIGNMENT: *Neutral*
SIZE: *L*
PSIONIC ABILITY: *Nil*
    Attack/Defense Modes: *Nil*

At any distance greater than 10' a gas spore is 90% likely to be mistaken for a beholder. Even at close ranges there is a 25% possibility that the creature will be viewed as the eye tyrant, for a gas spore has a false central eye and rhizome growths atop it which strongly resemble the eye stalks of a beholder. If the spore is struck for even one point of damage it will explode, its gaseous contents react violently to air, and every creature within a 20' radius takes 6-36 hit points of damage (3-18 if saving throw versus wands is made). If a gas spore makes contact with exposed flesh the spore shoots tiny rhizomes into the living matter and grows throughout the victim's system in but one melee round. The gas spore dies immediately. The victim must get a *cure disease* within 24 hours or die, sprouting 2-8 gas spores.

GELATINOUS CUBE

FREQUENCY: *Uncommon*
NO. APPEARING: *1*
ARMOR CLASS: *8*
MOVE: *6''*
HIT DICE: *4*
% IN LAIR: *Nil*
TREASURE TYPE: *See below*
NO. OF ATTACKS: *1*
DAMAGE/ATTACK: *2-8*
SPECIAL ATTACKS: *Paralyzation,
   surprise on 1-3*
SPECIAL DEFENSES: *See below*
MAGIC RESISTANCE: *See below*
INTELLIGENCE: *Non-*
ALIGNMENT: *Neutral*
SIZE: *L (10' cube)*
PSIONIC ABILITY: *Nil*
   Attack/Defense Modes: *Nil*

The gelatinous cube is one of the scavengers not uncommon in dungeons. Its cubic form is ideal for cleaning all living organisms, as well as carrion, from the floor and walls of underground passageways. Certain very large cubes are taller so as to be able to garner mosses and the like from ceilings as well.

Gelatinous cubes are nearly transparent and are difficult to see (thus surprise on 1-3). As these monsters travel about they sweep up metallic and other items which are ''indigestible'' to them. This includes treasure types J, K, L, M, N, Q as well as a potion, dagger, or similar items. Such material will remain in the body of a gelatinous cube for several weeks before being cast out (thus deposited somewhere on the floor).

If a gelatinous cube touches (hits) an opponent, a saving throw versus paralyzation must be made, or the creature touched is anesthetized for 5-20 melee rounds. The 'cube then surrounds the victim, secretes digestive fluids, and digests a meal. Damage caused to opponents is due to the digestive secretions.

Gelatinous cubes can be hit by all forms of weapons, and attacks by fire have normal effects. Cold will have no effect on these monsters unless they fail their saving throw, in which case they are slowed 50% and do only 1-4 hit points of damage. Electricity, fear, holds, paralyzation, polymorph, and sleep based attacks have no effect on gelatinous cubes.

GHAST

FREQUENCY: *Rare*
NO. APPEARING: *1-6*
ARMOR CLASS: *4*
MOVE: *15''*
HIT DICE: *4*
% IN LAIR: *10%*
TREASURE TYPE: *B, Q, R, S, T*
NO. OF ATTACKS: *3*
DAMAGE/ATTACK: *1-4/1-4/1-8*
SPECIAL ATTACKS: *See below*
SPECIAL DEFENSES: *See below*
MAGIC RESISTANCE: *Standard*
INTELLIGENCE: *Very*
ALIGNMENT: *Chaotic evil*
SIZE: *M*
PSIONIC ABILITY: *Nil*
   Attack/Defense Modes: *Nil*

These creatures are so like ghouls as to be completely indistinguishable from them, and they are usually found only with a pack of ghouls. When the pack attacks it will quickly become evident that ghasts are present, however, for they exude a carrion stench in a 10' radius which causes retching and nausea unless a saving throw versus poison is made. Those failing to make this save will attack at a penalty of -2 on ''to hit'' dice rolls. Worse, the ghast attacks as a ghoul with regard to paralyzation, and this attack will affect elves as well.

Ghasts are of the ''undead'' class so *sleep* and *charm* spells do not affect them. They are struck by any sort of weapon; cold iron causes double damage, and clerics can turn them. The circle of *protection from evil* does

not keep them at bay unless it is used in conjunction with cold iron (such as a circle of powdered iron, an iron ring, etc.).

These creatures are often used as slaves by powerful demons.

GHOST

FREQUENCY: *Very rare*
NO. APPEARING: *1*
ARMOR CLASS: *0 (or 8) See
   below*
MOVE: *9''*
HIT DICE: *10*
% IN LAIR: *25%*
TREASURE TYPE: *E, S*
NO. OF ATTACKS: *1*
DAMAGE/ATTACK: *Age 10-40
   years*
SPECIAL ATTACKS: *See below*
SPECIAL DEFENSES: *See below*
MAGIC RESISTANCE: *See below*
INTELLIGENCE: *High*
ALIGNMENT: *Lawful evil*
SIZE: *M*
PSIONIC ABILITY: *Nil*
   Attack/Defense Modes: *Nil*

Ghosts are the spirits of evil humans who were so awful in their badness that they have been rewarded (or perhaps cursed) by being given undead status. Thus they roam about at night or in places of darkness. These spirits hate goodness and life, hungering to draw the living essences from humans. As ghosts are non-corporeal (ethereal), they are usually encountered by creatures in a like state, although they can be seen by non-ethereal creatures. The supernatural power of a ghost is such, however, that the mere sight of one causes any humanoid being to age 10 years and flee in panic for 2-12 turns unless a saving throw versus magic is made. Clerics above 6th level are immune to this effect, and all other humanoids above 8th level add +2 to their saving throws.

Ghosts attack by two means: Any creature within 6'' of one is subject to attack by *magic jar* spell from the ghost. Unless the ghost becomes semi-material to attack by other means, it can otherwise only be combatted by another in the ethereal plane (in which case the ghost has an armor class of 8) or by telepathic means. If the ghost fails to *magic jar* its chosen victim, it will then semi-materialize in order to attack by touch (in which case the ghost is armor class 0). Semi-materialized ghosts can only be struck by silver (doing 50% of normal damage) or magical weapons. If they strike an opponent it ages him 10-40 years. Note that ghosts can be attacked with spells only from creatures who are in an ethereal state. Any human — including dwarves, elves, gnomes, and halflings — killed by a ghost is forever dead.

GHOUL

FREQUENCY: *Uncommon*
NO. APPEARING: *2-24*
ARMOR CLASS: *6*
MOVE: *9''*
HIT DICE: *2*
% IN LAIR: *20%*
TREASURE TYPE: *B, T*
NO. OF ATTACKS: *3*
DAMAGE/ATTACK: *1-3/1-3/1-6*
SPECIAL ATTACKS: *Paralyzation*
SPECIAL DEFENSES: *See below*
MAGIC RESISTANCE: *Standard*
INTELLIGENCE: *Low*
ALIGNMENT: *Chaotic evil*
SIZE: *M*
PSIONIC ABILITY: *Nil*
   Attack/Defense Modes: *Nil*

Ghouls are ''undead,'' once human creatures which feed on human and other corpses. Although their change from human to ghoul has deranged and destroyed their minds, ghouls have a terrible cunning which enables them to hunt their prey most effectively. Ghouls attack by clawing with their filthy nails and with fangs. Their touch causes humans — including dwarves, gnomes, half-elves, and halflings, but excluding elves — to become rigid *(paralysis)* unless a saving throw versus paralyzation is successful. Any human killed by a ghoulish attack will become a ghoul unless blessed (or blessed and then resurrected). Ghoul packs always attack without fear.

These creatures are subject to all attack forms except *sleep* and *charm* spells. They can be turned by clerics. The magic circle of protection from evil actually keeps these monsters completely at bay.

Lacedon: The lacedon is a marine form of the ghoul. It conforms in all other respects to ghouls.

GIANT

Giants are huge humanoids. There are six major races of giants, each race having some similarities and many differences from the others. Common characteristics will be given here, while the unique features of each race will be detailed under the heading appropriate to each.

All giants are very strong, with strengths ranging from 19 to 25 as compared with humans. Because of this strength, they are able to pick up rocks and hurl them as if the missile were shot from a catapult, but without the minimum range restrictions of the device.

Most giants are cave dwellers. Whenever they leave their lair giants of all sorts will always have a huge sack with them. Giant's bags contain various odds and ends of things precious only to the giant: a large rock or two, and from 1,000 to 6,000 coins of some type — usually gold.

Although giants are often stupid, they are usually cunning, too. They can sometimes be tricked and will be likely to bargain if approached from a position of strength. It is not unusual for giants to agree to share in an undertaking with a group of creatures of similar alignment to that of the giant, for these huge monsters are eager for treasure.

Young giants will have hit points and do damage according to the percentage of a normal adult male indicated by the dice roll.

Each race of giants speaks its own particular dialect which is unintelligible to other races. They also speak their appropriate alignment tongue.

Cloud Giant

FREQUENCY: *Rare*
NO. APPEARING: *1-6*
ARMOR CLASS: *2*
MOVE: *15"*
HIT DICE: *12 + 2-7*
% IN LAIR: *40%*
TREASURE TYPE: *E, Q (×5)*
NO. OF ATTACKS: *1*
DAMAGE/ATTACK: *6-36*
SPECIAL ATTACKS: *Hurling rocks for 2-24 hit points*
SPECIAL DEFENSES: *Surprised only on 1*
MAGIC RESISTANCE: *Standard*
INTELLIGENCE: *Average to very*
ALIGNMENT: *Neutral (good 50%, evil 50%)*
SIZE: *L (18' tall)*
PSIONIC ABILITY: *Nil*
    Attack/Defense Modes: *Nil*

Unlike the commoner sorts of giants, cloud giants usually reside in crude castles built atop mountains or on magical cloud islands. When found in their lair it is 60% likely that cloud giants will have 1-4 spotted lions as pets/guards. If more than 1 cloud giant is encountered in their lair it is 75% likely that the second will be a giantess (treat as firegiant for hit dice and damage/attack) and the others young giants (roll percentile dice to determine state of maturity). If 6 giants are thus encountered, one of the young will be a full-grown male, one a full-grown female, and the other two sub-adults of either sex (1-3 male, 4-6 female).

Adult cloud giants can hurl rocks from 1" to 24" distance, inflicting from 2-24 hit points of damage when they hit. They have a 60% chance of catching like missiles. All cloud giants have a keen sense of smell, thus they are surprised only on a roll of 1 on a 6-sided die. 10% of cloud giants are very intelligent. These will be the ones found dwelling on cloud islands. All such cloud giants are able to *levitate* themselves and additional weight of up to 20,000 gold pieces twice per day.

There is a 50% chance that evil cloud giants will have 1-3 captives as slaves in their lair.

Description: Cloud giants have pale blue white to light blue skin, silver white or brass colored hair, and wear various items of clothing and jewelry. They are armed with great clubs.

Fire Giant

FREQUENCY: *Uncommon*
NO. APPEARING: *1-8*
ARMOR CLASS: *3*
MOVE: *12"*
HIT DICE: *11 + 2-5*
% IN LAIR: *35%*
TREASURE TYPE: *E*
NO. OF ATTACKS: *1*
DAMAGE/ATTACK: *5-30*
SPECIAL ATTACKS: *Hurling rocks for 2-20 hit points*
SPECIAL DEFENSES: *Impervious to fire*
MAGIC RESISTANCE: *Standard*
INTELLIGENCE: *Average to low*
ALIGNMENT: *Lawful evil*
SIZE: *L (12' tall)*
PSIONIC ABILITY: *Nil*
    Attack/Defense Modes: *Nil*

Fire giants are as often found in castles as in caverns. If found in their lair it is 25% likely that they will have 1-4 hell hounds of the largest size as watch dogs. If more than 4 fire giants are encountered in their lair the additional ones will be females (corresponding to frost giants for hit dice and damage/attack), except that if 7 or 8 are encountered the last one or two will be young (roll percentile dice for size).

Adult fire giants are able to hurl rocks from 1" to 20" distances, inflicting 2-20 hit points of damage. They can catch like missiles 50% of the time. Fire giants are impervious to fire, even red dragon breath.

Description: Fire giants are very broad (about 6' at the shoulders), looking almost like dwarves. Their skins are coal black, hair is flaming red or bright orange, and eyes are deep red. Their teeth are usually yellow orange. They wear armor or dragon hides. They favor huge swords.

Frost Giant

FREQUENCY: *Rare*
NO. APPEARING: *1-8*
ARMOR CLASS: *4*
MOVE: *12"*
HIT DICE: *10 + 1-4*
% IN LAIR: *30%*
TREASURE TYPE: *E*
NO. OF ATTACKS: *1*
DAMAGE/ATTACK: *4-24*
SPECIAL ATTACKS: *Hurling rocks for 2-20 hit points*
SPECIAL DEFENSES: *Impervious to cold*
MAGIC RESISTANCE: *Standard*
INTELLIGENCE: *Average to low*
ALIGNMENT: *Chaotic evil*
SIZE: *L (15' tall)*
PSIONIC ABILITY: *Nil*
    Attack/Defense Modes: *Nil*

Frost giants more commonly inhabit castles, although they often lair in large frigid caverns. There is a 50% probability that they will have from 1-6 winter wolves in their lair as watchdogs. If more than 4 frost giants are encountered in their lair numbers 5 and 6 will be females (treat as stone giants with respect to hit dice and damage/attack), and 7 and 8 will be young giants (roll percentile dice to determine size).

Adult frost giants are able to hurl rocks from 1″ to 20″ distances, inflicting 2-20 hit points of damage. They can catch like missiles 40% of the time. Frost giants are impervious to cold, even white dragon breath.

Description: Frost giants have dead white or ivory skin color, blue-white or yellow hair, and pale blue or yellow eyes. Their build is basically similar to a muscular human, with appropriate size differences. Frost giants wear armor and bear arms similar to those of humans of the northern barbarian sort.

Hill Giant

FREQUENCY: *Common*
NO. APPEARING: *1-10*
ARMOR CLASS: *4*
MOVE: *12″*
HIT DICE: *8 + 1-2*
% IN LAIR: *25%*
TREASURE TYPE: *D*
NO. OF ATTACKS: *1*
DAMAGE/ATTACK: *2-16*
SPECIAL ATTACKS: *Hurling rocks for 2-16 hit points*
SPECIAL DEFENSES: *See below*
MAGIC RESISTANCE: *Standard*
INTELLIGENCE: *Low*
ALIGNMENT: *Chaotic evil*
SIZE: *L (10½′ tall)*
PSIONIC ABILITY: *Nil*
    Attack/Defense Modes: Nil

Hill giants always dwell in caves or similar underground habitations. These lairs are typically of foresaken areas. Hill giants sometimes have other creatures in their lairs to act as guards; this is 50% likely, and the guarding creatures will be 2-8 dire wolves (50%), 1-3 giant lizards (30%) or a group of 2-8 ogres (20%). If more than 4 hill giants are encountered in their lair numbers 5, 7, and 9 will be giantesses (6 hit dice, and treat as ogres for damage/attack) and 6, 8, and 10 will be young hill giants (roll percentile dice for size).

Adult hill giants are able to hurl rocks from 1″ to 20″ distances, inflicting 2-16 hit points of damage. They are able to catch similar missiles 30% of the time. 50% of hill giants also speak ogre.

Description: Hill giants have tan to reddish brown skins, brown to black hair, and red-rimmed eyes. They typically dress in rough hides or skins. They use any form of weapon available but favor clubs.

Stone Giant

FREQUENCY: *Uncommon*
NO. APPEARING: *1-8*
ARMOR CLASS: *0*
MOVE: *12″*
HIT DICE: *9 + 1-3*
% IN LAIR: *30%*
TREASURE TYPE: *D*
NO. OF ATTACKS: *1*
DAMAGE/ATTACK: *3-18*
SPECIAL ATTACKS: *Hurling rocks for 3-30 hit points*
SPECIAL DEFENSES: *See below*
MAGIC RESISTANCE: *Standard*
INTELLIGENCE: *Average*
ALIGNMENT: *Neutral*
SIZE: *L (12′ tall)*
PSIONIC ABILITY: *Nil*
    Attack/Defense Modes: Nil

Stone giants inhabit mountainous regions in most cases, dwelling in caves

or caverns. They are fond of cave bears and are 75% likely to have 1-4 guarding their lair. If more than 4 stone giants are encountered in their lair numbers 5 and 6 will be females (treat as hill giants with regard to hit dice and damage/attack), and numbers 7 and 8 will be young (roll percentile dice to determine size).

Stone giants are playful at times — especially at night. The adults find great sport hurling rocks from 1″ to 30″ distances, causing 3-30 hit points of damage when striking a creature, and stone giants are 90% likely to catch similar types of missiles hurled at them.

Description: With their gray to gray-brown skins, dark gray to blue-gray hair, and metallic-looking eyes (silver to steel), stone giants are both striking in appearance and able to blend easily into stoney settings. The latter effect is enhanced by their choice of rock-colored garments. Stone giants are typically armed with stone weapons.

Storm Giant

FREQUENCY: *Rare*
NO. APPEARING: *1-4*
ARMOR CLASS: *1*
MOVE: *15″*
HIT DICE: *15 + 2-7*
% IN LAIR: *55%*
TREASURE TYPE: *E, Q (× 10), S*
NO. OF ATTACKS: *1*
DAMAGE/ATTACK: *7-42*
SPECIAL ATTACKS: *See below*
SPECIAL DEFENCES: *See below*
MAGIC RESISTANCE: *Standard*
INTELLIGENCE: *Exceptional*
ALIGNMENT: *Chaotic good*
SIZE: *L (21′ tall)*
PSIONIC ABILITY: *Nil*
    Attack/Defense Modes: Nil

The most powerful and respected true giant is the storm giant. These great, generally reclusive creatures inhabit only out-of-the-way places. Their abodes are typically cloud islands (60%), mountain peaks (30%) or underwater (10%), and there the storm giants build their spacious castles. It is 30% probable that the lairs of storm giants will have animals as guards and/or pets. Storm giants dwelling on cloud islands or mountain peaks will have 1 or 2 rocs (70%) which they will also employ as a riding animal or 1-4 griffons (30%). Those storm giants who dwell underwater will have 2-8 sea lions.

Unlike other sorts of giants, storm giants do not hurl rocks, for they have magical properties and spells which they employ instead. A storm giant is able to hurl a lightning bolt of 8 (8-sided) dice effect once per day. All storm giants are able to *levitate* twice per day, lifting weights up to 30,000 gold pieces equivalent in addition to their own body weight. They are able to breathe normally underwater as desired. Note that storm giants dwelling underwater are able to cast lightning bolts and move at normal speed. When they desire to do so, storm giants are able to perform any of the following spells, one at a time, once each per day: *predict weather, call lightning* (3 bolts of 10-15 6-sided dice each), *control winds, weather summoning.* When aroused for combat, it is probable that a storm giant will summon a storm and call lightning, for this weather is most favored by an angry storm giant in battle.

Storm giants are not harmed by electrical energy, even including such discharges as blue dragon breath.

Description: The skin coloration of storm giants ranges from pale light green to violet, the former being typical of those specimens which are marine. Green colored storm giants have dark green hair and emerald green eyes, while other storm giants tend towards deep violet or blue-black hair coloration with silvery gray or purple eyes.

GNOLL

FREQUENCY: *Uncommon*
NO. APPEARING: *20-200*
ARMOR CLASS: *5*
MOVE: *9''*
HIT DICE: *2*
% IN LAIR: *20%*
TREASURE TYPE: *Individuals L, M;*
   D, Q (× 5), S in lair
NO. OF ATTACKS: *1*
DAMAGE/ATTACK: *2-8 or by*
   weapon
SPECIAL ATTACKS: *Nil*
SPECIAL DEFENSES: *Nil*
MAGIC RESISTANCE: *Standard*
INTELLIGENCE: *Low-average*
ALIGNMENT: *Chaotic evil*
SIZE: *L (7'+ tall)*
PSIONIC ABILITY: *Nil*
   Attack/Defense Modes: *Nil*

Gnolls travel and live in rapacious bands of loose organization, with the largest dominating the rest. These bands recognize no other gnoll as supreme, but they do not necessarily dislike other bands, and on occasion two or more such groups will join together briefly in order to fight, raid, loot, or similarly have greater chance of success against some common foe or potential victim. They are adaptable and inhabit nearly any area save those which are arctic and/or arid. They have a so-called king, very powerful personally and with a double normal-sized following, but his authority extends only as far as his reach.

For every 20 gnolls encountered there will be a leader-type with 16 hit points (attacks as a 3 hit dice creature). If 100 or more of these creatures are encountered there will be the following additional gnolls with the band: a chieftain (armor class 3, 22 hit points, attack as a 4 hit dice creature and does 4-10 hit points damage/attack) and 2-12 guards (armor class 4, 20 hit points, attack as 3 hit dice monsters, and do 3-9 hit points damage). If the gnolls are encountered in their lair there will always be a chieftain there, and there will be from 5-20 guards with him. The lair will also contain females and young equal to 50% and 200% respectively of the number of males present.

Gnolls are subterranean 85% of the time, but occasionally (15%) they will take up residence in an abandoned (or cleared) village or building of some sort. In the former case they are 30% likely to have 1-3 trolls living with them and acting as guards. In the case where gnolls are found above ground, they are quite likely (65%) to have 4-16 hyenas (80%) or 2-12 hyaenodons (20%) as pets and guards. They always have a number of captives for food or slave labor (1 per 10 gnolls is minimum).

Gnolls employ a great variety of weapons, all carry swords, and a typical force will have the following percentages:

great bow	15%
pole arm	35%
two-handed sword	15%
battle axe	20%
morning star	15%

Gnolls will generally be on friendly terms with orcs, hobgoblins, bugbears, ogres, and even trolls — providing the weaker types are not very much weaker in numbers and the gnolls are relatively equal in strength to the stronger monsters.

Gnolls are strong, but they dislike work and are not good miners. They have infravision. They speak their racial tongue, chaotic evil, troll, and often (60%) orcish and/or hobgoblin.

Description: There is a great resemblance between gnolls and hyenas. Gnolls have greenish gray skins, darker near the muzzle, with reddish gray to dull yellow mane. Eyes are dull black and nails are amber colored. Their armor is of horn, metal plates, and leather; like their fur capes and vests, it is shabby, and the latter are moth-eaten and dingy, being brown, black or grayish pelts. Gnolls have short life spans — 35 years being average.

GNOME

FREQUENCY: *Rare*
NO. APPEARING: *40-400*

ARMOR CLASS: *5*
MOVE: *6''*
HIT DICE: *1*
% IN LAIR: *50%*
TREASURE TYPE: *Individuals M*
   (x 3); C, Q (x 20) in lair
NO. OF ATTACKS: *1*
DAMAGE/ATTACK: *By weapon or*
   1-6
SPECIAL ATTACKS: *See below*
SPECIAL DEFENSES: *Save at 4*
   levels higher
MAGIC RESISTANCE: *As above*
INTELLIGENCE: *Very*
ALIGNMENT: *Neutral to lawful*
   good
SIZE: *S (3'+ tall)*
PSIONIC ABILITY: *Nil*
   Attack/Defense Modes: *Nil*

Similar to their larger cousins, dwarves, the social organization of gnomes is based on clans, and these groups are likewise neither exclusive nor hostile to each other, although there does exist a rivalry wherein each tries to outdo the other groups. For every 40 gnomes encountered there will be a fighter of a 2nd, 3rd, or 4th level (die roll 1-2, 3-4, or 5-6). If 160 or more gnomes are in a group there will be in addition one 5th level and one 3rd level fighter as chief and lieutenant of the band. If 200 or more are encountered they will have a gnomish cleric of 4th, 5th, or 6th level in addition to the others. If 320 or more gnomes are encountered there will be the following additional gnomes in the group: a 6th level fighter, two 5th level fighters, a 7th level cleric, and four 3rd level clerics. If encountered in their lair (home) there will be the following additional gnomes: from 2-8 fighters of 2nd or 3rd level, 1-4 clerics of 2nd level, and females and young equal to 50% and 25% respectively of the number of adult males. A gnomish lair is sometimes based upon earthen burrows, although 75% of the time it will be made in rocky hill formations.

Gnomes are typically armored with leather armor which is ringed or well studded with metal and shield (armor class 5). They have the following typical weaponing:

short sword and short bow	10%
short sword and spear	20%
club and sling	15%
club and spear	40%
club and short sword	15%

All gnomes above normal level will have chainmail and shield. Those above 5th level will have plate armor and shield. Higher level fighters will have a 10% chance per level of having magic armor and/or weapons. Gnomish clerics will likewise have a 10% chance per level for 1-3 additional items (potion, clerical scroll, ring, wand/staff/rod, misc. magic) usable by clerics.

Gnomes are 80% likely to have tamed animals to serve as guards in their lair: 5-30 badgers (70%) or 3-12 giant badgers (20%) or 2-8 wolverines (10%).

Due to their great hatred of kobolds and goblins, all gnomes gain a bonus of +1 on their dice rolls to hit these opponents. When gnomes are in melee with gnolls, bugbears, ogres, trolls, or giants their opponents must deduct 4 from their dice rolls to hit the gnomes because of their small size and their combat skill against these much bigger creatures.

All gnomes are highly resistant to magic and poison, so they make saving throws at 4 levels above their actual level. Gnomes can see in the dark (infravision), noting monsters at 60'. Because of their mining skills gnomes are excellent (50% to 80% likely) in detection of passages which slope upwards or downwards, unsafe walls, floors, and ceilings, and approximate depth and direction. It is rumored that there exist gnomes with magical abilities up to 4th level, but this has not been proved.

Besides their alignment and racial tongues, gnomes speak kobold, goblin, halflingish, dwarvish, and can speak with burrowing mammals as well.

Description: Most gnomes are wood brown, a few range to gray brown, of skin. Their hair is medium to pure white, and their eyes are gray-blue to bright blue. They wear leather and earth tones of cloth and like jewelry. The average gnome will live for 600 years.

GOAT, *Giant*

FREQUENCY: *Rare*
NO. APPEARING: *1-12*
ARMOR CLASS: *7*
MOVE: *18''*
HIT DICE: *3 + 1*
% IN LAIR: *Nil*
TREASURE TYPE: *Nil*
NO. OF ATTACKS: *1*
DAMAGE/ATTACK: *2-16*
SPECIAL ATTACKS: *Charge*
SPECIAL DEFENSES: *Nil*
MAGIC RESISTANCE: *Standard*
INTELLIGENCE: *Semi-*
ALIGNMENT: *Neutral*
SIZE: *L (5'+ at shoulder)*
PSIONIC ABILITY: *Nil*
    Attack/Defense Modes: *Nil*

These reclusive herbivores dwell in hilly country. They will aggressively defend themselves from any threat. If giant goats charge, they add + 4 to damage inflicted when they hit (6-20 hit points). Their weapons are two long, sharp horns. They attack by butting with them. In rare cases these creatures have been tamed to serve as steeds.

If more than 7 of these creatures are encountered the remainder will be young (roll percentile dice to determine size, halving the number rolled and adding it to 50%).

GOBLIN

FREQUENCY: *Uncommon*
NO. APPEARING: *40-400*
ARMOR CLASS: *6*
MOVE: *6''*
HIT DICE: *1-7 Hit points*
% IN LAIR: *40%*
TREASURE TYPE: *Individuals K,*
    Lair C
NO. OF ATTACKS: *1*
DAMAGE/ATTACK: *1-6 or by*
    weapon
SPECIAL ATTACKS: *Nil*
SPECIAL DEFENSES: *Nil*
MAGIC RESISTANCE: *Standard*
INTELLIGENCE: *Average (low)*
ALIGNMENT: *Lawful evil*
SIZE: *S (4' tall)*
PSIONIC ABILITY: *Nil*
    Attack/Defense Modes: *Nil*

Goblins have a tribal society, the strongest ruling the rest, allowing fealty to the goblin king. It is possible that goblins are distantly related to kobolds. Like the latter, goblins enjoy dwelling in dismal surroundings, although they tend to inhabit caves and similar underground places in preference to any habitation above ground. They too hate full daylight and attack at a -1 when in sunlight. Goblins have normal infravision (60' range).

For every 40 goblins encountered there will be a leader and 4 assistants who are equal to orcs, each having 7 hit points and attacking as monsters with a full hit die. If 200 or more goblins are encountered there will be the following additional figures: a sub-chief and 2-8 guards, each fighting as hobgoblins and having 8 hit points, armor class 5, and doing 1-8 hit points damage. There is a 25% chance that any force of goblins encountered will have 10% of its strength mounted on huge wolves (qv) and if this is the case there will also be from 10-40 of these creatures without riders. In their lair there will be the following additional figures: a goblin chief and 2-8 bodyguards (9-14 hit points, armor class 4, fight as gnolls doing 2-8 hit points of damage), females and young equal to 60% and 100% respectively of the number of male goblins encountered. As is usual with creatures of this sort, the females and young do not fight. A goblin lair will be protected by from 5-30 huge wolves not less than 60% of the time. There is a 20% chance that 2-12 bugbears will be in a goblin lair.

Goblins are typically armed with:

short sword and military pick	10%
short sword and sling	10%
short sword and spear	10%
sling	10%
morning star	20%
military pick	10%
spear	30%

Leaders and guards will typically have the best weapons, bearing two each.

Goblins are fair miners, and they are able to note new or unusual construction 25% of the time. They hate gnomes and dwarves and will attack them in preference to any other creature. All goblins are slave takers and fond of torture.

The languages spoken by goblins are: their own, lawful evil, kobold, orcish, and hobgoblin.

Description: Goblins range from yellow through dull orange to brick red in skin color. Their eyes are reddish to lemon yellow. They dress in dark leather gear, and their garments tend towards dull, soiled-looking colors (brown drab, dirty gray, stained maroon). Goblins reach the age of 50 years or so.

GOLEM

Golems are magically created monsters. There are four different sorts, and each will be detailed separately. All but the flesh golem are created from earthen components. The former is created from the remains of humans. The creation of a golem involves ultra-powerful spells and elemental forces.

Magical creatures with hit dice equal to or greater than those of the golem are able to attack with effect. For purposes of determination of hit dice, figure 4.5 hit points per hit die, and points being rounded up. Thus a flesh golem has 9 dice, a clay golem 11, a stone golem 14, and an iron golem 18.

Clay Golem

FREQUENCY: *Very rare*
NO. APPEARING: *1*
ARMOR CLASS: *7*
MOVE: *7''*
HIT DICE: *50 Hit points*
% IN LAIR: *Nil*
TREASURE TYPE: *Nil*
NO. OF ATTACKS: *1*
DAMAGE/ATTACK: *3-30*
SPECIAL ATTACKS: *See below*
SPECIAL DEFENSES: *See below*
MAGIC RESISTANCE: *See below*
INTELLIGENCE: *Non-*
ALIGNMENT: *Neutral*
SIZE: *L (8' tall)*
PSIONIC ABILITY: *Nil*
    Attack/Defense Modes: *Nil*

A clay golem can be created by a lawful good cleric of 17th or higher level (unless a magical tome is used, in which case a lower level cleric can create one). It requires a *resurrection* spell, an *animate objects* spell, a *commune* spell, a *prayer* spell, and a *bless* spell. The cleric must first fashion a man-shaped clay statue, and once this is sculpted the cleric must go through an uninterrupted ritual using the spells delineated. Materials to do the spell require an outlay of 20,000 gold pieces. Vestments for the ritual cost another 30,000 gold pieces, minimum.

Once created the clay golem is under the command of the cleric who created it. Each melee round the clay golem is in combat there is a 1% cumulative chance that it will be imbued with a chaotic evil spirit. If this happens, the clay golem immediately passes from the control of the cleric and attacks any living thing, moving to the closest one to attack, and proceeding on to the next after killing it. This behavior will continue until the golem is destroyed, for control can never be regained.

Damage inflicted upon living matter by a clay golem is only repairable by means of a *healing* spell from a cleric of 17th or greater level.

Attacks by a clay golem are based on 11 hit dice. Once per day the golem can be *hasted* for three melee rounds after engaging in at least one round of combat. During this period it strikes twice per round. (If out of control, the golem will immediately *haste* itself if it has not previously done so.)

Clay golems can be struck only by blunt magical weapons such as hammers or maces. Other weapons do not affect it. Spells do not affect it, except as follows: *move earth* will drive the golem back 12" and inflicts 3-36 hit points of damage, *disintegrate* will slow the golem 50% and inflicts 1-12 hit points of damage, and an *earthquake* cast directly at a clay golem will stop it from moving that turn and inflict 5-50 hit points of damage.

Iron Golem

FREQUENCY: *Very rare*
NO. APPEARING: *1*
ARMOR CLASS: *3*
MOVE: *6"*
HIT DICE: *80 Hit points*
% IN LAIR: *Nil*
TREASURE TYPE: *Nil*
NO. OF ATTACKS: *1*
DAMAGE/ATTACK: *4-40*
SPECIAL ATTACKS: *See below*
SPECIAL DEFENSES: *See below*
MAGIC RESISTANCE: *See below*
INTELLIGENCE: *Non-*
ALIGNMENT: *Neutral*
SIZE: *L (12' tall)*
PSIONIC ABILITY: *Nil*
    Attack/Defense Modes: *Nil*

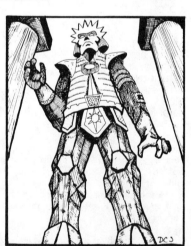

Construction of an iron golem, bipedal and manlike, requires a magical tome or a magic-user of 18th or higher level employing the following spells: *wish, polymorph any object, geas,* and *cloud kill*. The cost in materials is 1,000 gold pieces per hit point, and it requires 3 months construction time.

The golem created always remains under the control of the magic-user who created it. It can obey any simple commands. It will stand, non-functioning, as a guard until some event takes place, i.e. until a door is opened, a book read, etc.

In addition to striking, an iron golem will breathe out a cloud of poisonous gas, 1" × 1" × 1", directly before it, once every 7 melee rounds.

The strength of an iron golem is three times greater than that of a flesh golem. An iron golem can do 1 point of structural damage per melee round.

An iron golem can be struck only by magical weapons of +3 or greater enchantment. Normal and magical weapons under +3 do no damage. The only magical attacks which affect the iron golem are electrical, such as a *lightning bolt*, which slows the monster 50% for 3 melee rounds. Magical fire attacks repair damage on a 1 hit point for 1 hit point basis. Iron golems are subject to attack from the rust monsters.

Flesh Golem

FREQUENCY: *Very rare*
NO. APPEARING: *1*
ARMOR CLASS: *9*
MOVE: *8"*
HIT DICE: *40 Hit points*
% IN LAIR: *Nil*
TREASURE TYPE: *Nil*
NO. OF ATTACKS: *2*
DAMAGE/ATTACK: *2-16/2-16*
SPECIAL ATTACKS: *See below*
SPECIAL DEFENSES: *See below*
MAGIC RESISTANCE: *See below*
INTELLIGENCE: *Semi-*
ALIGNMENT: *Neutral*
SIZE: *L (7½" tall)*
PSIONIC ABILITY: *Nil*
    Attack/Defense Modes: *Nil*

A flesh golem can be created by means of a magical tome or by a high-level magic-user employing a *wish* spell, a *polymorph any object*, a *geas*, a *protection from normal missiles* and a *strength* spell. The latter case demands a level of magic-use of at least the 14th. The cost in materials is 1,000 gold pieces per hit point of the golem. It requires 1 month to fashion the creature.

The creator of the flesh golem controls the monster, being able to have it follow simple commands (go ahead, stop, kill, etc.). The master of the golem can have it suspend its functioning until a set event takes place (such as someone entering its room).

However, for each turn of melee a flesh golem engages in there is a 1% per melee round cumulative chance it will go berserk, attacking at random anything in sight. The monster's master has a 10% per melee round chance of regaining control of the golem.

The flesh golem is very powerful and able to smash through doors and wooden structures of normal construction. For example, a flesh golem would break through an oaken door with iron reinforcing bands and hinges, in 5-8 melee rounds. It does 1 point of structural damage to wooden constructions only every 3 melee rounds.

Normal weapons do not harm flesh golems, but magical weapons have normal effect. Spells of most sorts have no effect on such monsters, but fire or cold based spells (such as *wall of fire, fire ball, ice storm,* etc.) slow the golem by 50% for 2-12 melee rounds. Electrical attacks restore damage to the golem in direct relation to the number of dice of damage normally done, i.e. a 6 die lightning bolt restores 6 hit points of damage which the golem might have sustained.

Stone Golem

FREQUENCY: *Very rare*
NO. APPEARING: *1*
ARMOR CLASS: *5*
MOVE: *6"*
HIT DICE: *60 Hit points*
% IN LAIR: *Nil*
TREASURE TYPE: *Nil*
NO. OF ATTACKS: *1*
DAMAGE/ATTACK: *3-24*
SPECIAL ATTACKS: *See below*
SPECIAL DEFENSES: *See below*
MAGIC RESISTANCE: *See below*
INTELLIGENCE: *Non-*
ALIGNMENT: *Neutral*
SIZE: *L (9½' tall)*
PSIONIC ABILITY: *Nil*
    Attack/Defense Modes: *Nil*

Stone golems of man-like shape are constructed by means of a magical tome or a magic-user of 16th or higher level employing the following spells: *wish, polymorph any object, geas,* and *slow*. The cost in materials is 1,000 gold pieces per hit point, and it requires 2 months construction time.

Once created the stone golem can be controlled by its creator, and it will understand and obey simple commands, i.e. attack, stop, wait, go, etc. The golem can be made to stand and wait to attack until someone does something to trigger the golem.

In addition to its normal attack, the stone golem is able to cast a *slow* spell on any opponent within 1" of its front facing every other melee round.

The strength of a stone golem is twice that of a flesh golem. It does 1 point of structural damage every other melee round.

Normal weapons do not harm stone golems. In fact, it requires weapons of +2 or greater enchantment to damage them. The only spells which affect a stone golem are: *rock to mud* slows the golem 50% for 2-12 melee rounds, *mud to rock* restores all damage suffered by the golem, and *stone to flesh* makes the golem vulnerable to normal attacks on the following melee round.

GORGON

FREQUENCY: *Rare*
NO. APPEARING: *1-4*
ARMOR CLASS: *2*
MOVE: *12''*
HIT DICE: *8*
% IN LAIR: *40%*
TREASURE TYPE: *E*
NO. OF ATTACKS: *1*
DAMAGE/ATTACK: *2-12*
SPECIAL ATTACKS: *Breath turns to stone*
SPECIAL DEFENSES: *Nil*
MAGIC RESISTANCE: *Standard*
INTELLIGENCE: *Animal*
ALIGNMENT: *Neutral*
SIZE: *L*
PSIONIC ABILITY: *Nil*
    Attack/Defense Modes: *Nil*

Gorgons are bull-like creatures covered with thick metal scales. They prefer the fastness of a wilderness or dreary caverns for habitation. A gorgon is able to breathe out a cloud of noxious vapors which will turn any creature to stone unless they make the appropriate saving throw. The breath shoots forth in truncated cone-shape, ½'' diameter at the beasts' mouth, 6'' in length, to an end diameter of 2''. A gorgon is able to use such breath up to 4 times per day. Gorgons will always use this attack form in preference to other sorts of attack.

The awareness of gorgons extends into the astral and ethereal planes. So do the effects of their breath weapon.

GRAY OOZE

FREQUENCY: *Rare*
NO. APPEARING: *1-3*
ARMOR CLASS: *8*
MOVE: *1''*
HIT DICE: *3 + 3*
% IN LAIR: *Nil*
TREASURE TYPE: *Nil*
NO. OF ATTACKS: *1*
DAMAGE/ATTACK: *2-16*
SPECIAL ATTACKS: *See below*
SPECIAL DEFENSES: *See below*
MAGIC RESISTANCE: *See below*
INTELLIGENCE: *Animal*
ALIGNMENT: *Neutral*
SIZE: *M to L*
PSIONIC ABILITY: *21-121*
    Attack/Defense Modes: *E/Nil*

Gray ooze is a slimy horror which inhabits subterranean places. It closely resembles wet stone or sedimentary cave formations.

This creature corrodes metal at the same rate a black pudding (qv) does, i.e. chainmail is eaten through in a single melee round. Its acids do no harm to stone or wood. Spells do not harm this creature, and it is impervious to heat or cold. Lightning, however, causes full damage to gray ooze, as do blows from weapons. Note, however, that in the latter case the weapons striking the creature may corrode and break. They strike like snakes when attacking.

Large specimens (over 18 hit points) are larger than a full grown man, some (those over 21 hit points) are fully 3' wide and 12' long, although only about 6 or 8 inches thick.

In exceptionally large individuals intelligence of a sort is well developed. Furthermore, these exceptional individuals have a latent psionic ability, and if psionic powers are used within 6'' of them they will prepare a psychic crush of from 21 to 121 psionic strength attack points and direct it at any individual within range who uses psionic abilities. After loosing its psionic attack the gray ooze can be psionically attacked.

GREEN SLIME

FREQUENCY: *Rare*
NO. APPEARING: *1-6*
ARMOR CLASS: *9*
MOVE: *0''*
HIT DICE: *2*
% IN LAIR: *Nil*
TREASURE TYPE: *Nil*
NO. OF ATTACKS: *0*
DAMAGE/ATTACK: *Nil*
SPECIAL ATTACKS: *See below*
SPECIAL DEFENSES: *See below*
MAGIC RESISTANCE: *See below*
INTELLIGENCE: *Non-*
ALIGNMENT: *Neutral*
SIZE: *S*
PSIONIC ABILITY: *Nil*
    Attack/Defense Modes: *Nil*

Green slimes are strange plant growths found in subterranean places. Although they cannot move, they slowly grow, feeding on animal, vegetable and metallic substances. They are sensitive to vibrations and will often drop upon passing creatures from above.

Green slime will attach itself to living flesh, and in 1-4 melee rounds thereafter turn the creature into green slime (no resurrection possible). It eats away wood slowly, consuming but one inch thickness in an hour. Green slime eats metals quickly, going through plate armor in 3 melee rounds.

It can be scraped off quickly (if the scraper is then discarded), excised, frozen, or burned. A *cure disease* spell kills green slime. Other forms of attack — including weapons or spell — do it no harm.

Occasionally huge slimes or colonies of dozens have been reported.

GRIFFON

FREQUENCY: *Uncommon*
NO. APPEARING: *2-12*
ARMOR CLASS: *3*
MOVE: *12"/30"*
HIT DICE: *7*
% IN LAIR: *25%*
TREASURE TYPE: *C, S*
NO. OF ATTACKS: *3*
DAMAGE/ATTACK: *1-4/1-4/2-16*
SPECIAL ATTACKS: *Nil*
SPECIAL DEFENSES: *Nil*
MAGIC RESISTANCE: *Standard*
INTELLIGENCE: *Semi-*
ALIGNMENT: *Neutral*
SIZE: *L*
PSIONIC ABILITY: *Nil*
    Attack/Defense Modes: *Nil*

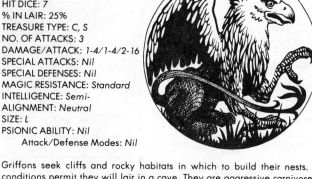

Griffons seek cliffs and rocky habitats in which to build their nests. If conditions permit they will lair in a cave. They are aggressive carnivores, and their favorite prey are horses. If they come within sighting or smelling distance (36" as a general rule) of horseflesh, the griffons will wing to the hunt. They are much sought after in their fledgling state, for they can be tamed for use as fierce, loyal, steeds if obtained before maturity. If encountered in their lair, there is a 75% chance that there will be 1 or 2 eggs or young for every 2 griffons. The young are non-combative, but the adults will attack until killed. Fledglings sell for 5,000 gold pieces, eggs for 2,000, on the open market.

GROANING SPIRIT (Banshee)

FREQUENCY: *Very rare*
NO. APPEARING: *1*
ARMOR CLASS: *0*
MOVE: *15"*
HIT DICE: *7*
% IN LAIR: *10%*
TREASURE TYPE: *D*
NO. OF ATTACKS: *1*
DAMAGE/ATTACK: *1-8*
SPECIAL ATTACKS: *See below*
SPECIAL DEFENSES: *+1 or better*
    weapon to hit
MAGIC RESISTANCE: *50%*
INTELLIGENCE: *Exceptional*
ALIGNMENT: *Chaotic evil*
SIZE: *M*
PSIONIC ABILITY: *Nil*
    Attack/Defense Modes: *Nil*

The groaning spirit, or banshee, is the spirit of an evil female elf — a very rare thing indeed. The spirit returns to harm the living. It is found only in desolate countrysides, moors, etc. The groaning spirit can attack by its chilling touch, causing 1-8 hit points of damage/attack when it strikes. Its more fearsome mode of attack, however, is its wail, or keening, which will cause the hearers within 3" to save versus magic or die on the spot. The sight of a groaning spirit causes fear unless an appropriate saving throw is made. It can wail but once per day, and only during darkness. Groaning spirits cannot be affected by *charm, sleep,* or *hold* spells. They are impervious to attack by cold or electricity. Exorcism kills them.

HALFLING — HARPY — HELL HOUND — HERD ANIMAL — HIPPOCAMPUS — HIPPOGRIFF — HIPPOPOTAMUS — HOBGOBLIN — HOMONCULOUS — HORSE — HYDRA — HYENA

HALFLING

FREQUENCY: *Rare*
NO. APPEARING: *30-300*
ARMOR CLASS: *7*
MOVE: *9"*
HIT DICE: *1-6 hit points*
% IN LAIR: *70%*
TREASURE TYPE: *Individuals K, B*
    in lair
NO. OF ATTACKS: *1*
DAMAGE/ATTACK: *By weapon*
    or 1-6
SPECIAL ATTACKS: *+3 with bow*
    or sling
SPECIAL DEFENSES: *Save at 4*
    levels higher
MAGIC RESISTANCE: *As above*
INTELLIGENCE: *Very*
ALIGNMENT: *Lawful good*
SIZE: *S (3+ ' tall)*
PSIONIC ABILITY: *Nil**
    Attack/Defense Modes: *Nil**
*possible to exist in unusual characters

Halflings are basically hard-working, orderly and peaceful citizens of communities similar to humans — although their villages usually contain many burrow homes as well as surface cottages. For every 30 halflings encountered there will be two 2nd level fighters. If more than 90 are encountered there will be an additional leader of 3rd level fighting ability. If more than 150 are encountered there will also be the following additional halflings in the group: one 4th level fighter, two 3rd level fighters and three 2nd level fighters. If encountered in their lair there will be females and children equal to 100% and 60% respectively of the adult males indicated. A typical halfling lair will be in pastoral countryside.

The usual protection worn by halflings consists of padded or leather armor. Halflings are typically weaponed as follows:

small sword and short bow	10%
small sword and spear	10%
short bow	10%
sling	20%
small sword	10%
spear	20%
hand axe	20%

All halflings of above normal level will have armor class 6, while those of 3rd or 4th level will have armor class 5 and 4 respectively. All such higher levels will have a 10% chance per level of having magic armor and/or miscellaneous weapons.

Halflings encountered in their lair will have from 1-4 dogs (treat them as wild dogs for statistical purposes) per halfling.

The magic and poison resistance of halflings causes them to save at four levels above their actual. They are exceedingly clever at both quiet movement and hiding. They will surprise on a die roll of 1-4 on a 6-sided die. In natural terrain they must be treated as invisible if they have any form of vegetation in which to conceal themselves. They have no infravision. They shun water.

Halflings speak their own language, their alignment tongue, and the common speech. In addition they speak the language of gnomes, goblins, and orcs.

Description: Of ruddy complexion, halflings tend toward brown or sandy brown hair coloration, and have brown or hazel eyes. Their dress is usually colorful, but their trousers and coats are likely to be serviceable grey, tan, or brown material. Halflings have a life expectancy of 150 or more years.

Tallfellow: A taller (4+'), slimmer halfling, with fairer skin and hair. Tallfellows are very rare. They use more armor (AC 6), ride ponies and carry more spears. It is possible for exceptionally strong (17, 18) tallfellows to work to 5th or 6th level of fighting ability. They can speak elvish and are very friendly with elves. They live for about 180 years on the average.

Stout: This kind of halfling is a bit smaller (3½ +') and stockier than the typical (hairfeet). They use more armor also (AC 6), and employ morning stars in addition to the usual halflingish arms. Very strong stouts (18) are able to work up to 5th level fighting ability. Stouts have infravision and can detect sloping passageways. They have no fear of water and can swim. These halflings are able to speak dwarvish and enjoy dwarven company. Stouts reach the age of 200 or more years.

HARPY

FREQUENCY: *Rare*
NO. APPEARING: *2-12*
ARMOR CLASS: *7*
MOVE: *6"/15"*
HIT DICE: *3*
% IN LAIR: *25%*
TREASURE TYPE: *C*
NO. OF ATTACKS: *3*
DAMAGE/ATTACK: *1-3/1-3/1-6*
SPECIAL ATTACKS: *Singing & charm*
SPECIAL DEFENSES: *Nil*
MAGIC RESISTANCE: *Standard*
INTELLIGENCE: *Low*
ALIGNMENT: *Chaotic evil*
SIZE: *M*
PSIONIC ABILITY: *Nil*
    Attack/Defense Modes: *Nil*

Harpies have the bodies of vultures but the upper torsos and heads of women. They are voracious carnivores and foul creatures. Those that dwell along seacoasts are generally known as sirens. All harpies are able to emit sweet-sounding calls. Any creature hearing these calls will proceed towards the harpies unless they save versus magic. Similarly, the touch of a harpy *charms* those creatures which fail to make their saving throw versus magic. The harpies attack, torture, and devour their charmed prey. What they do not want they foul with excrement. A harpy attacks with her vulture claws and some form of weapon — often a bone club or some weapon left from one of her former victims. They speak their own language and none other.

HELL HOUND

FREQUENCY: *Very rare*
NO. APPEARING: *2-8*
ARMOR CLASS: *4*
MOVE: *12"*
HIT DICE: *4-7*
% IN LAIR: *30%*
TREASURE TYPE: *C*
NO. OF ATTACKS: *1*
DAMAGE/ATTACK: *1-10*
SPECIAL ATTACKS: *Breathe fire*
SPECIAL DEFENSES: *See below*
MAGIC RESISTANCE: *Standard*
INTELLIGENCE: *Low*
ALIGNMENT: *Lawful evil*
SIZE: *M*
PSIONIC ABILITY: *Nil*
    Attack/Defense Modes: *Nil*

Hell hounds are not normally from the material plane, but some few now dwell on it, having been brought along by various creatures who wished their evil service.

In addition to a normal attack (simply biting with their great black teeth), hell hounds breathe out a scorching fire on an opponent up to a 1" distance, causing 1 hit point of damage for each hit die they possess, unless the opponent is able to save versus dragon breath, in which case only one-half damage is inflicted, i.e. a 7 hit dice hell hound breathes for 7 or 4 hit points of damage/attack.

Hell hounds move with great stealth, so they surprise opponents on a die roll of 1-4 (out of 6). They have keen hearing, and they are surprised on a die roll of 1 only (out of 6). Their exceptional sight allows them to *locate*

hidden or invisible creatures 50% of the time. For these reasons they are favored as watchdogs by monsters and fire giants.

Description: Hell hounds are rusty red to red brown in color. Their eyes are glowing red. Teeth and tongues are sooty black.

HERD ANIMAL

FREQUENCY: *Common*
NO. APPEARING: *20-200 (or more)*
ARMOR CLASS: *8-7*
MOVE: *15" to 24"*
HIT DICE: *1-5*
% IN LAIR: *Nil*
TREASURE TYPE: *Nil*
NO. OF ATTACKS: *Variable*
DAMAGE/ATTACK: *Variable*
SPECIAL ATTACKS: *Stampede*
SPECIAL DEFENSES: *Nil*
MAGIC RESISTANCE: *Standard*
INTELLIGENCE: *Animal*
ALIGNMENT: *Neutral*
SIZE: *S, M, or L*
PSIONIC ABILITY: *Nil*
    Attack/Defense Modes: *Nil*

Herd animals live in all climes — musk oxen and reindeer at the North Pole, giraffe and antelopes at the equator. The smallest will have but 1 hit die, the largest will have 5. Attacks are simply a matter of the animals' in question modes of defense (horns, butting, hooves, flight). Damage is a factor of defense (attack) mode and size/strength. As herd animals are not aggressive, they will stampede away from what they perceive to be the greatest threat to their safety. Humans or humanoids of about man-size or less, will be trampled to death if caught in the path of a stampede.

HIPPOCAMPUS

FREQUENCY: *Rare*
NO. APPEARING: *2-8*
ARMOR CLASS: *5*
MOVE: *24"*
HIT DICE: *4*
% IN LAIR: *Nil*
TREASURE TYPE: *Nil*
NO. OF ATTACKS: *1*
DAMAGE/ATTACK: *1-4*
SPECIAL ATTACKS: *Nil*
SPECIAL DEFENSES: *Nil*
MAGIC RESISTANCE: *Standard*
INTELLIGENCE: *Average*
ALIGNMENT: *Chaotic good*
SIZE: *L*
PSIONIC ABILITY: *Nil*
    Attack/Defense Modes: *Nil*

The hippocampus is the most prized of marine steeds, for they are strong, swift, and intelligent. They differ from the normal seahorse in that they have a long rear body similar to that of a great fish, and the hippocampus has forelegs ending in powerful fins. Their bodies are covered with fine scales in the fore parts, large scales elsewhere. They speak their own language and can learn another if properly trained. Tritons are often found in possession of these creatures.

HIPPOGRIFF

FREQUENCY: *Rare*
NO. APPEARING: *2-16*
ARMOR CLASS: *5*
MOVE: *18''/36''*
HIT DICE: *3 +3*
% IN LAIR: *10%*
TREASURE TYPE: *Q (×5)*
NO. OF ATTACKS: *3*
DAMAGE/ATTACK: *1-6/1-6/1-10*
SPECIAL ATTACKS: *Nil*
SPECIAL DEFENSES: *Nil*
MAGIC RESISTANCE: *Standard*
INTELLIGENCE: *Semi-*
ALIGNMENT: *Neutral*
SIZE: *L*
PSIONIC ABILITY: *Nil*
    Attack/Defense Modes: *Nil*

Hippogriffs dwell only in places uninhabited by men, generally nesting on rocky crags and similar places. They are fierce fighters and will defend themselves resolutely. As the hippogriff is an omnivore, it will never be found with pegasi. Griffons will attack and eat hippogriffs on occasion. The hippogriff is able to fight well with its two great fore claws and powerful beak, however, and they are not easy prey. If encountered in their lair (nesting area) they will attack immediately. There will be one nest for every 2 creatures, each nest containing 1 or 2 eggs or fledglings. Hippogriff eggs are valued at 1,000 gold pieces each on the open market, fledglings at 2,000 to 3,000 gold pieces.

HIPPOPOTAMUS

FREQUENCY: *Uncommon*
NO. APPEARING: *2-12*
ARMOR CLASS: *6*
MOVE: *9''//12''*
HIT DICE: *8*
% IN LAIR: *Nil*
TREASURE TYPE: *Nil*
NO. OF ATTACKS: *1*
DAMAGE/ATTACK: *2-12 or 3-18*
SPECIAL ATTACKS: *See below*
SPECIAL DEFENSES: *Nil*
MAGIC RESISTANCE: *Standard*
INTELLIGENCE: *Animal*
ALIGNMENT: *Neutral*
SIZE: *L*
PSIONIC ABILITY: *Nil*
    Attack/Defense Modes: *Nil*

As their name implies, hippopotomi are found in rivers and lakes of tropical regions. They are herbivores, but they aggressively defend their own territory. A hippo' bites with exceedingly strong jaws, and a bull will do 3-18 hit points of damage/attack. There will be 1-3 bulls in a herd, 1 for every 4 animals. If a boat or canoe passes over submerged hippopotomi there is a 50% chance that a bull will emerge under it and tip the craft over. Hippopotomi travel underwater by running along the bottom. They can stay submerged for 15 minutes.

HOBGOBLIN

FREQUENCY: *Uncommon*
NO. APPEARING: *20-200*
ARMOR CLASS: *5*
MOVE: *9''*
HIT DICE: *1 + 1*
% IN LAIR: *25%*
TREASURE TYPE: *Individuals J, M, D, Q (× 5) in lair*
NO. OF ATTACKS: *1*
DAMAGE/ATTACK: *1-8 or by weapon*
SPECIAL ATTACKS: *Nil*
SPECIAL DEFENSES: *Nil*
MAGIC RESISTANCE: *Standard*
INTELLIGENCE: *Average*
ALIGNMENT: *Lawful evil*
SIZE: *M (6½' tall)*
PSIONIC ABILITY: *Nil*
    Attack/Defense Modes: *Nil*

Tribal bands of hobgoblins are likely to be encountered nearly anywhere as these creatures are equally at home in sunlight or subterranean setting. They fight well in full daylight and have infravision (60') so as to be able to fight in total darkness as well. Each tribe is jealous of its status, and if two tribal bands of hobgoblins meet there will be at least catcalls and derision (85%) and open fighting might break out (15%) unless a strong leader such as a powerful monster or fighter or evil high priest, etc. is on hand to control them. Similarly, the hobgoblins will bully nearby orcs or goblins given the opportunity, and hobgoblin leaders are sometimes used in bodies of goblins or orcish troops to keep them in order and drive them into battle.

The better known (more infamous) hobgoblin tribes include: rippers, leg breakers, skull smashers, flesh renders, marrow suckers, flayers, and slow killers.

For every 20 hobgoblins in a group there is a leader (sergeant) and 2 assistants. These hobgoblins will have 9 hit points each. If 100 or more hobgoblins are encountered there will be the following additional figures with the group: a subchief (armor class 3, 16 hit points, and 1 + 2 damage (3-10 hit points)). These additional hobgoblins fight as 3 hit dice monsters. If hobgoblins are encountered in their lair there will also be, in addition, a chief and 5-20 bodyguards. Hobgoblin chiefs are armor class 2, 22 hit points, do 2-11 hit points of damage, and fight as 4 hit dice monsters. Their bodyguards are the same as those of sub-chiefs. There are females and young in the lair equal to 150% and 300% respectively of the number of males.

Hobgoblin lairs are underground 80% of the time and above ground 20% of the time. In the latter case the lair will be a village with a ditch, rampart, and palisade of stones, earth and logs. There will be two gates and 3-6 guard towers. The dwellings inside are usually a mixture of wood and stone. As they seek to build on the ruins of human or other more sophisticated creatures, a hobgoblin village may be of better construction than indicated, possibly having solid stone works, buildings or a keep. In any event, hobgoblins will have 2 heavy catapults, 2 light catapults, and 1 ballista per 50 warriors. If the lair is underground, there is a 60% chance that there will be from 2-12 carnivorous apes (qv) as guards.

Hobgoblins have the following typical weapon distribution.

sword and composite bow	20%
sword and spear	10%
sword and morning star	5%
sword and whip	5%
polearm	30%
spear	10%
morning star	20%

Leaders will always bear two weapons. The tribal standard will be with a sub-chief 20% of the time. It is always present with the chief. The tribal standard causes hobgoblin warriors within 6″ to fight harder, thus giving them +1 on their attack dice rolls and +1 on morale (reaction) dice rolls.

If elves are nearby, hobgoblins will attack them in preference to any other troops because of the great hatred they bear.

Hobgoblins are highly adept at mining, and they can detect new construction, sloping passages, and even shifting walls 40% of the time.

Most hobgoblins speak goblin, orcish, and the rudimentary tongue of carnivorous apes in addition to their racial and alignment languages. 20% of hobgoblins can speak the common tongue as well.

Description: The hairy hides of hobgoblins range from dark reddish-brown to gray black. Their faces are bright red-orange to red. Large males will have blue-red noses. Eyes are either yellowish or dark brown. Teeth are yellowed white to dirty yellow. Hobgoblins favor bright, bloody colors and black leather. They keep weapons well polished. Hobgoblins live for 60 years.

Koalinth: A marine species of hobgoblin with gills. They are similar to their land-dwelling cousins in most respects. They dwell in shallow water in caverns and sea caves. They use spears and pole arms adapted to their marine environment. Koalinth speak only their racial language (hobgoblin) and lawful evil. They prey on any available creatures. Koalinth are of lighter coloration, having green faces, and have webbed hands and feet.

HOMONCULOUS

FREQUENCY: Very rare
NO. APPEARING: 1
ARMOR CLASS: 6
MOVE: 6″/18″
HIT DICE: 2
% IN LAIR: Nil
TREASURE TYPE: Nil
NO. OF ATTACKS: 1
DAMAGE/ATTACK: 1-3
SPECIAL ATTACKS: Bite causes sleep
SPECIAL DEFENSES: See below
MAGIC RESISTANCE: See below
INTELLIGENCE: See below
ALIGNMENT: See below
SIZE: S (1½′)
PSIONIC ABILITY: Nil
    Attack/Defense Modes: Nil

This creature is created and animated through a special process by a magic-user and an alchemist (described hereafter). The homonculous travels on its hind legs or by flying. Its bite causes 1-3 points of damage, and forces the victim to save versus magic or fall into a comatose sleep which lasts for 5-30 minutes. The creature makes all of its saving throws at the same level as its creator. Although the homonculous cannot speak, it knows what the magic-user knows, and the latter is able to see and hear through the creature's eyes and ears. There is a telepathic link between the magic-user and his creature, and the homonculous can be controlled up to 48″ away from its master. It will never willingly pass from this maximum range. If the homonculous is killed the magic-user immediately suffers 2-20 points of damage.

When a homonculous is desired the magic-user must hire an alchemist, and the latter will require from 1-4 weeks to create fluids for forming the creature. This will cost 1 pint of the magic-user's blood and 500-2,000 gold

pieces. The magic-user must then cast a *mending spell*, a *mirror image*, and a *wizard eye* upon the fluid to form the homonculous.

Description: When the homonculous is finished it will be man-like in form, about 18″ tall, have a greenish, reptilian skin, leathery wings, and a bat-like mouth with teeth passing on a venom which causes sleep unless the party bitten saves vs. magic.

HORSE

	Draft	Heavy	Light	Medium	Pony	Wild
FREQUENCY:	Common	Uncommon	Uncommon	Uncommon	Uncommon	Uncommon
NO. APPEARING:	1	1	1	1	1	5-30
ARMOR CLASS:	7	7	7	7	7	7
MOVE:	12″	15″	24″	18″	12″	24″
HIT DICE:	3	3 + 3	2	2 + 2	1 + 1	2
% IN LAIR:	Nil	Nil	Nil	Nil	Nil	Nil
TREASURE TYPE:	Nil	Nil	Nil	Nil	Nil	Nil
NO. OF ATTACKS:	1	3	2	3	1	1
DAMAGE/ATTACK:	1-3	1-8/1-8/ 1-3	1-4/1-4	1-6/1-6/ 1-3	1-2	1-3
SPECIAL ATTACKS:	Nil	Nil	Nil	Nil	Nil	Nil
SPECIAL DEFENSES:	Nil	Nil	Nil	Nil	Nil	Nil
MAGIC RESISTANCE:	Std.	Std.	Std.	Std.	Std.	Std.
INTELLIGENCE:	Anl.	Anl.	Anl.	Anl.	Anl.	Anl.
ALIGNMENT:	Ntl.	Ntl.	Ntl.	Ntl.	Ntl.	Ntl.
SIZE:	L	L	L	L	L	L
PSIONIC ABILITY:	Nil	Nil	Nil	Nil	Nil	Nil
Attack/Defense Modes:	Nil	Nil	Nil	Nil	Nil	Nil

Various forms of horses are found nearly everywhere. They are panicked by raging fire, sudden movement, loud noises, or strange smells 90% of the time. Note, however, that warhorses are only 10% likely to panic, rear, and run away. Ponies and wild horses can be trained for war, about 10% of these animals being fit for such training. A pony will never fight well, but it will be less likely to panic.

Warhorses fight on the second and succeeding rounds of melee, as long as their rider remains mounted. Their attack consists of two hoof thrusts and a bite.

The various types of horses can carry the following maximum loads, indicated in gold pieces of weight. The number before the slash is normal movement, the number after is encumbered movement maximum load. Encumbrance slows speed one-half.

draft horse	4,000/8,000
heavy warhorse	5,000/7,500
light warhorse	3,000/5,000
medium warhorse	4,000/6,500
pony	2,000/3,000
wild horse	3,000/6,000

Horses (and ponies) are not sufficiently agile to take into dungeons.

HYDRA

FREQUENCY: Uncommon
NO. APPEARING: 1
ARMOR CLASS: 5
MOVE: 9″
HIT DICE: 5 to 12
% IN LAIR: 20%
TREASURE TYPE: B
NO. OF ATTACKS: 5 to 12
DAMAGE/ATTACK: 1-6, 1-8, or 1-10 according to size
SPECIAL ATTACKS: See below
SPECIAL DEFENSES: See below
MAGIC RESISTANCE: Standard
INTELLIGENCE: Semi-
ALIGNMENT: Neutral
SIZE: L
PSIONIC ABILITY: Nil
    Attack/Defense Modes: Nil

Hydrae are reptilian monsters found in marshes, swamps, and similar places, as well as in subterranean lairs. Their large, four-legged bodies are surmounted by from 5 to 12 heads (roll an 8-sided die to determine number). Each head has 1 hit die of a full 8 hit points. When all of a hydra's heads are killed, the body dies, but not until each and every head is killed. The hydra attacks according to the number of heads it has, each head being considered as a hit die. Thus, a hydra of 7 heads attacks as a monster of 7 hit dice. It is possible for the hydra to attack several opponents at once, and up to 4 heads are able to attack the same target simultaneously. Damage scored is based on the number of heads the hydra has: hydrae of 5 or 6 heads do 1-6 hit points of damage/attack, those with 7 to 10 heads score 1-8 points of damage, and hydrae with 11 or 12 heads do 1-10 hit points of damage.

Description: Hydrae are gray brown to blackish brown with lighter underbellies tinged towards yellow or tan. Their eyes are amber to orange. The teeth are yellowish white.

Lernaean Hydra: These creatures are very rare. The lernaean hydra is indistinguishable from a normal hydra until it is attacked. Every time one of the heads of these creatures is cut off or killed, it grows two new ones in 1-4 melee rounds unless fire is applied to the dead member or neck stump. Thus, a 5-headed lernaean hydra could grow to a 12-headed monster in a single combat, gaining the appropriate hit dice and attack potential in the process.

Pyrohydra: Pyrohydrae also appear quite similar to normal hydrae, although their coloration may be tinged with more red. They seldom exceed 7 heads, 10% having 8, and no 9-headed pyrohydra has ever been recorded. Each head of a pyrohydra is able to breathe fire twice per day,

the breath shooting out in a cone ½" diameter at the mouth, 1" diameter at the end, and 2" long. This fire causes 8 hit points of damage (4 if saving throw versus dragon breath is made). They can, of course, strike normally as well.

HYENA

	Hyena	Giant (Hyaenodon)
FREQUENCY:	Common	Very rare
NO. APPEARING:	2-12	2-8
ARMOR CLASS:	7	7
MOVE:	12"	12"
HIT DICE:	3	5
% IN LAIR:	Nil	Nil
TREASURE TYPE:	Nil	Nil
NO. OF ATTACKS:	1	1
DAMAGE/ATTACK:	2-8	3-12
SPECIAL ATTACKS:	Nil	Nil
SPECIAL DEFENSES:	Nil	Nil
MAGIC RESISTANCE:	Standard	Standard
INTELLIGENCE:	Animal	Animal
ALIGNMENT:	Neutral	Neutral
SIZE:	M	L
PSIONIC ABILITY:	Nil	Nil
Attack/Defense Modes:	Nil	Nil

Hyenas are pack animals dwelling on warm plains. They are hunter/scavengers with very strong jaws and aggressive if hungry.

Hyaenodons are simply huge (prehistoric) hyenas.

IMP — INTELLECT DEVOURER — INVISIBLE STALKER — IRISH DEER — IXITXACHITL

IMP

FREQUENCY: *Very rare*
NO. APPEARING: *1*
ARMOR CLASS: *2*
MOVE: *6"/18"*
HIT DICE: *2 + 2*
% IN LAIR: *0%*
TREASURE TYPE: *0*
NO. OF ATTACKS: *1*
DAMAGE/ATTACK: *1-4*
SPECIAL ATTACKS: *See below*
SPECIAL DEFENSES: *See below*
MAGIC RESISTANCE: *25%*
INTELLIGENCE: *Average*
ALIGNMENT: *Lawful evil*
SIZE: *S (2' tall)*
PSIONIC ABILITY: *Nil*
    Attack/Defense Modes: *Nil*

Imps are very rare on the material plane, but on the planes of Acheron and Hell they are not uncommon. An imp is created from a larva. It is a very minor devil created to spread evil in the form of a familiar to a lawful evil magic-user or cleric. The imp is given the power to *polymorph itself* into animal form at will. The shape it can assume is limited to two of the following: large spider, raven, giant rat, or goat.

In an unpolymorphed state the imp attacks with its tail, and any creature struck by it must save versus poison or die. For hit determination the tail is considered a dagger. In animal form the imp attacks accordingly, the raven and goat having no effective attacks.

All magical powers of an imp are usable whatever form it is in. Imps are able to *detect good* and *detect magic.* They regenerate at 1 hit point per melee round. Imps can *become invisible* at will. Once per day they are able to use a *suggestion.* Only silver or magical weapons are effective against imps. Magical attacks employing cold, fire, or electricity do not harm imps, and for purposes of spell attacks upon them imps are considered 7 hit dice creatures.

Imps have average intelligence plus devilish cunning. As familiars they are also able to call upon the intelligence of arch-devils.

When an imp assumes the role of a familiar, its "master" gains the following benefits: A telepathic link is established between the pair, and the "master" is able to receive all sensory impressions of the imp, including visual images of infrared spectrum, up to a mile distance. The presence of an imp within 1" allows its "master" to gain a 25% magic resistance and regenerate at 1 hit point per melee round. If the imp is within 1 mile its "master" gains an additional level of ability, but if the imp is over a mile distant the character loses 1 level, and if the familiar is killed the character drops 4 ability levels. Also, in addition to its normal aid and advice, the imp familiar is able to contact a lower plane once per week in order to help its "master" decide some course of action. This contact is like a *commune* spell, but 6 questions are allowed.

INTELLECT DEVOURER

FREQUENCY: *Very rare*
NO. APPEARING: *1-2*
ARMOR CLASS: *4*
MOVE: *15"*
HIT DICE: *6 + 6*
% IN LAIR: *60%*
TREASURE TYPE: *D*
NO. OF ATTACKS: *4*
DAMAGE/ATTACK: *1-4 (× 4)*
SPECIAL ATTACKS: *See below*
SPECIAL DEFENSES: *See below*
MAGIC RESISTANCE: *See below*
INTELLIGENCE: *Very*
ALIGNMENT: *Chaotic evil*
SIZE: *M*
PSIONIC ABILITY: *200*
    Attack/Defense Modes: *C, E/F, G*

The intellect devourer is one of the most feared of monsters. They are found dwelling deep beneath the ground or in dark and dismal lairs in the wilderness. Although they are able to attack with their great claws, their primary offensive means is psionic, for they subsist on the psychic energy of their prey — whether gained from the dying shriek or by more subtle means. If psionic energy (from abilities or magical means) is in use nearby (6") they will stalk the user, seeking a time to attack him alone and by surprise. The monster then leaps upon his victim, tearing with his claws and psionically attacking with ego whip or id insinuation. If psionically successful the 'devourer will then house itself within the mindless body, seeking to deceive others by assuming the character of the person it has slain. The intellect devourer will then seek opportunities to attack and devour others.

They are able to hide in shadow as well as a 10th level thief. Normal weapons and most spells have no effect upon these monsters. Magical weapons +3 or more cause 1 point of damage upon them when they hit. Bright light will drive them off, and a *protection from evil* will keep them at a distance. *Fireballs* serve only as a bright light, but *lightning bolts* will cause them pain and some small damage (1 point per die of lightning bolt strength). A *death spell* has a 25% chance of success, and a *power word kill* will slay them. Of course, they can be psionically attacked, and their psionic strength of 200 total makes this not too difficult. However, if seriously threatened they will seek to flee and save themselves.

Their awareness extends to the astral and ethereal planes, and intellect devourers often roam the astral and ethereal planes. They are able to speak any human language.

INVISIBLE STALKER

FREQUENCY: *Very rare*
NO. APPEARING: *1*
ARMOR CLASS: *3*
MOVE: *12''*
HIT DICE: *8*
% IN LAIR: *Nil*
TREASURE TYPE: *Nil*
NO. OF ATTACKS: *1*
DAMAGE/ATTACK: *4-16*
SPECIAL ATTACKS: *Surprise on 1-5*
SPECIAL DEFENSES: *Invisibility*
MAGIC RESISTANCE: *30%*
INTELLIGENCE: *High*
ALIGNMENT: *Neutral*
SIZE: *L (8' tall)*
PSIONIC ABILITY: *Nil*
    Attack/Defense Modes: *Nil*

The invisible stalker is a creature from the elemental plane of air, normally encountered on the material plane only due to the conjuration of some magic-user. This conjuration causes the creature to serve for a period on this plane. Invisible stalkers roam the astral and ethereal planes, and if they are encountered there on the elemental planes, they can be dimly seen. Otherwise or unless their opponents are able to *detect/see invisible objects*, their invisibility causes opponents to subtract 2 from "to hit" dice rolls. Unless slain on their own plane, invisible stalkers are simply sent back to the elemental plane when damage accrued exceeds their total hit points.

The conjuring party retains full command of the invisible stalker summoned until it fulfills its duties or is killed. Once set upon a mission, an invisible stalker will follow through unceasingly until it is accomplished. They are faultless trackers within one day of a quarry's passing. They must be destroyed to make them cease an ordered attack. Once a mission is finished, the creature is freed to return to its own plane. The invisible stalker is at best an unwilling servant but will not resent a brief, uncomplicated task. Service involving a period of a week tries the creature severely, and anything longer is certain to make it attempt to fulfill the letter of command by perverting the spirit of it. This is not to say that impelling the invisible stalker to serve for extended periods is impossible, but the compulsion to cause it to do so fully and properly must be great, i.e. a carefully worded command from a very powerful magic-user. A simple command such as "Follow me, and guard me from any attack," could be interpreted to mean follow at 100' distance if the invisible stalker had been on duty over a week — or perhaps even if it hadn't been that long, for dealing with such creatures is always a hazard. Similarly, a command to: "Keep me safe from all harm," can be construed by the invisible stalker to mean that it is to carry the conjuring party to its own plane and place them in suspended animation in a secret room in its own abode, thus carrying out its duties to the letter.

Each day of duty which an invisible stalker serves will see a 1% cumulative chance of the creature seeking to pervert the intent of its commands in order to be free of servitude. If no option remains open, the stalker must continue to serve.

Invisible stalkers understand the common speech, but they do not talk any language but their own.

IRISH DEER

FREQUENCY: *Rare*
NO. APPEARING: *1-8*
ARMOR CLASS: *7*
MOVE: *18''*
HIT DICE: *4*
% IN LAIR: *Nil*
TREASURE TYPE: *Nil*
NO. OF ATTACKS: *1 (2)*
DAMAGE/ATTACK: *2-12 (2-12)*
SPECIAL ATTACKS: *Nil*
SPECIAL DEFENSES: *Nil*
MAGIC RESISTANCE: *Standard*
INTELLIGENCE: *Animal*
ALIGNMENT: *Neutral*
SIZE: *L*
PSIONIC ABILITY: *Nil*
    Attack/Defense Modes: *Nil*

These moose-sized creatures of the Pleistocene epoch dwell in temperate climes. Their antlers spread to 10' width, and they can actually gore two opponents within this span if they are directly before the deer. They are not generally aggressive, but are very dangerous during rutting season (early spring).

IXITXACHITL

FREQUENCY: *Very rare*
NO. APPEARING: *10-100*
ARMOR CLASS: *6*
MOVE: *12''*
HIT DICE: *1 + 1*
% IN LAIR: *60%*
TREASURE TYPE: *See below*
NO. OF ATTACKS: *1*
DAMAGE/ATTACK: *3-12*
SPECIAL ATTACKS: *Evil clerical spells*
SPECIAL DEFENSES: *Nil*
MAGIC RESISTANCE: *Standard*
INTELLIGENCE: *Average to high*
ALLIGNMENT: *Chaotic evil*
SIZE: *M*
PSIONIC ABILITY: *Nil*
    Attack/Defense Modes: *Nil*

Ixitxachitl are a race of intelligent rays which dwell in shallow tropical seas. They are of evil disposition, and clerical in nature. For every 10 encountered there will be one which is the equivalent of a 2nd level human cleric with regard to spell use; for every 20 encountered there will be a 3rd level equivalent; and for every 50 encountered there will be a 5th level equivalent. If more than 50 are encountered there will be the following additional ixitxachitl with the group: a leader with 8th level clerical spell ability and quadruple normal hit dice, two guards with 6th level clerical spell ability and triple normal hit dice. Also, some of these monsters are vampiric. For every 20 ixitxachitl encountered there is a 50% chance that there will be a vampiric form in the group. Vampiric ixitxachitl are similar to their fellows, but they regenerate 3 hit points per melee round and drain an energy level each time they strike an opponent, and they have double hit dice.

Discovering an ixitxachitl lair is difficult, for they are typically made in coral reefs and hidden by a secret entrance. Inside the lair will be various items as shown for treasure types P, R, and S. If a leader is encountered there is the possibility that it and its guards will possess type U magic items which can be worn, or used without hands if the creatures are in their lair.

JACKAL — JACKALWERE — JAGUAR

JACKAL

FREQUENCY: *Common*
NO. APPEARING: *1-6*
ARMOR CLASS: *7*
MOVE: *12''*
HIT DICE: *1-4 Hit points*
% IN LAIR: *Nil*
TREASURE TYPE: *Nil*
NO. OF ATTACKS: *1*
DAMAGE/ATTACK: *1-2*
SPECIAL ATTACKS: *Nil*
SPECIAL DEFENSES: *Nil*
MAGIC RESISTANCE: *Standard*
INTELLIGENCE: *Semi-*
ALIGNMENT: *Neutral*
SIZE: *S*
PSIONIC ABILITY: *Nil*
    Attack/Defense Modes: *Nil*

Jackals are small, dog-like scavengers found in warm regions. They are not particularly fierce nor are they brave. They appear here because of the magical *bag of tricks* (qv).

JACKALWERE

FREQUENCY: *Rare*
NO. APPEARING: *1-4*
ARMOR CLASS: *4*
MOVE: *12''*
HIT DICE: *4*
% IN LAIR: *30%*
TREASURE TYPE: *C*
NO. OF ATTACKS: *1*
DAMAGE/ATTACK: *2-8*
SPECIAL ATTACKS: *Gaze causes sleep*
SPECIAL DEFENSES: *Iron or +1 weapons to hit*
MAGIC RESISTANCE: *Standard*
INTELLIGENCE: *Very*
ALIGNMENT: *Chaotic evil*
SIZE: *S (M)*
PSIONIC ABILITY: *Nil*
    Attack/Defense Modes: *Nil*

The jackalwere is a malign foe of humankind, a jackal able to assume the form of a man. In this guise they roam about seeking to waylay and murder humans. They then steal their riches and eat the slain victims. The jackalwere can use human weapons. Its gaze will have the effect of a *sleep* spell on any unsuspecting creature which fails its saving throw versus magic. Note: a hostile creature is not unsuspecting! Jackalwere will sometimes (20%) be found with normal jackals.

JAGUAR

FREQUENCY: *Uncommon*
NO. APPEARING: *1-2*
ARMOR CLASS: *6*
MOVE: *15''*
HIT DICE: *4 + 1*
% IN LAIR: *5%*
TREASURE TYPE: *Nil*
NO. OF ATTACKS: *3*
DAMAGE/ATTACK: *1-3/1-3/1-8*
SPECIAL ATTACKS: *Rear claws for 2-5/2-5*
SPECIAL DEFENSES: *Surprised only on a 1*
MAGIC RESISTANCE: *Standard*
INTELLIGENCE: *Semi-*
ALIGNMENT: *Neutral*
SIZE: *L*
PSIONIC ABILITY: *Nil*
    Attack/Defense Modes: *Nil*

These jungle predators are very ferocious. They will attack any creature which they believe threatens them. If found in their lair, there is a 75% chance that there will be 1-3 young (10% to 40% grown). The cubs will not fight effectively. When hungry they will hunt prey much larger than themselves, including snakes and crocodiles. They climb well, swim well, and can leap 30' to attack. If in close combat the jaguar will grasp its opponent with both forepaws (two paw hits in the same melee round) and rake with its rear claws (2 additional attacks at 2-5 hit points each that turn).

KI-RIN — KOBOLD

KI-RIN

FREQUENCY: *Very rare*
NO. APPEARING: *1*
ARMOR CLASS: *-5*
MOVE: *24''/48''*
HIT DICE: *12*
% IN LAIR: *5%*
TREASURE TYPE: *I, S, T*
NO. OF ATTACKS: *3*
DAMAGE/ATTACK: *2-8/2-8/3-18*
SPECIAL ATTACKS: *Magic use*
SPECIAL DEFENSES: *See below*
MAGIC RESISTANCE: *90%*
INTELLIGENCE: *Supra-genius*
ALIGNMENT: *Lawful good*
SIZE: *L*
PSIONIC ABILITY: *130 to 200*
   Attack/Defense Modes: *All/all*

The ki-rin are a race of aerial creatures whose hooves rarely touch the earth, for they dwell amongst the clouds and behind the winds. Females are never encountered, and ki-rin are always solitary. They sometimes aid humans if properly abjured or the need to combat evil is great. They sometimes travel the astral and ethereal planes.

The attack of a ki-rin can take the form of two powerful hoof-blows and a thrust with a magically sharp (+3) horn much resembling that of a unicorn. The ki-rin can also attack in other ways.

Ki-rin are able to employ spells of all levels at 18th level quality, 9 of the 1st, 8 of the 2nd, 7 of the 3rd, 6 of the 4th, 5 of the 5th, 4 of the 6th, 3 of the 7th, 2 of the 8th, and 1 of the 9th during any given day. They also command 4 major and 6 minor psionic disciplines, operating at ninth level of mastery in all. Ki-rin can, once per day, do each of the following: create nutritious food for 2-24 persons, create drinkable beverages for 2-24 persons, create soft goods or wooden items (up to 32 cubic feet of the former, 18 cubic feet of the latter) which are permanent, create metal items of relatively short life span (gold which lasts 2-5 days to adamanite which lasts but 1 hour) of up to 2,000 gold pieces weight, create an *illusion* with audial, visual, and olfactory components which lasts without concentration until magically dispelled or touched in disbelief, *assume gaseous form, wind walk, call lightning,* and *summon weather.*

When a ki-rin conjures things of the sky or which involve air, the creature or magic is at twice normal strength, including hit points and damage inflicted.

Ki-rin speak their own tongue, but with their special telepathic speaking ability they are able to converse with virtually any living thing.

Description: The coat of the ki-rin is luminous gold, much as a sunrise on a clear day. Its mane and tail are darker gold. Its horn and hooves are golden pink. Its eyes are violet. (The skin of this creature is worth 25,000 gold pieces if it is perfectly intact.)

KOBOLD

FREQUENCY: *Uncommon*
NO. APPEARING: *40-400*
ARMOR CLASS: *7*
MOVE: *6''*
HIT DICE: *1-4 Hit points*
% IN LAIR: *40%*
TREASURE TYPE: *Individuals J, O,*
   Q (×5) in lair
NO. OF ATTACKS: *1*
DAMAGE/ATTACK: *1-4 or by*
   weapon
SPECIAL ATTACKS: *Nil*
SPECIAL DEFENSES: *Nil*
MAGIC RESISTANCE: *Standard*
INTELLIGENCE: *Average (low)*
ALIGNMENT: *Lawful evil*
SIZE: *S (3' tall)*
PSIONIC ABILITY: *Nil*
   Attack/Defense Modes: *Nil*

The society of these creatures is tribal with war bands based on gens. The stronger tribes rule weaker ones. Kobolds are usually found in dank, dark places such as dismal overgrown forests or subterranean settings. They hate bright sunlight, not being able to see well in it, but their night vision is excellent, and they have infra-red vision which operates well up to 60'. If they are in bright sunlight they have a lesser chance to fight well (-1 from dice rolls to hit opponents).

For every 40 kobolds encountered there will be a leader and two guards who are equal to goblins, each having 4 hit points, armor class 6, and doing 1-6 points of damage. If 200 or more kobolds are encountered in their lair there will be the following additional creatures there: 5-20 guards (as bodyguards above), females equal to 50% of the total number, young equal to 10% of the total number, and 30-300 eggs. There will always be a chief and his bodyguard in the kobold lair. It is also probable (65%) that there will be from 2-5 wild boars (70%) or 1-4 giant weasels (30%) in a kobold lair; the animals will serve as guards.

A force of kobolds is typically equipped as follows:

short sword and javelin	5%
short sword and spear	10%
short sword	10%
axe	20%
spiked wooden club	30%
javelins (2-3)	15%
spear	10%

Chief and guard types always have the best available weapons. All kobold shields are of wood or wickerwork.

Kobolds hate most other life, delighting in killing and torture. They particularly hate such creatures as brownies, pixies, sprites and gnomes. They war continually with the latter, and will attack them on sight.

In addition to the tongues of lawful evil and kobolds, these monsters can usually (75%) speak goblin and orcish.

Description: The hide of kobolds runs from very dark rusty brown to a rusty black. They have no hair. Their eyes are reddish and their small horns are tan to white. They favor red or orange garb. Kobolds live for up to 135 years.

LAMIA — LAMMASU — LAMPREY — LARVA — LEECH, GIANT — LEOPARD — LEPRECHAUN — LEUCROTTA —
LICH — LION — LIZARD — LIZARD MAN — LOCATHAH — LURKER ABOVE — LYCANTHROPE — LYNX, GIANT

LAMIA

FREQUENCY: *Very rare*
NO. APPEARING: *1*
ARMOR CLASS: *3*
MOVE: *24"*
HIT DICE: *9*
% IN LAIR: *60%*
TREASURE TYPE: *D*
NO. OF ATTACKS: *1*
DAMAGE/ATTACK: *1-4*
SPECIAL ATTACKS: *See below*
SPECIAL DEFENSES: *Nil*
MAGIC RESISTANCE: *Standard*
INTELLIGENCE: *High*
ALIGNMENT: *Chaotic evil*
SIZE: *M*
PSIONIC ABILITY: *Nil*
    Attack/Defense Modes: *Nil*

Lamias prefer to dwell in deserts — in ruined cities, caves, or the like. Their upper torso, arms, and head resemble a human female, while their lower body is that of a beast. Lamias are very fast and powerful. They usually are armed with daggers.

A lamia is able to use the following spells once per day: *charm person, mirror image, suggestion,* and *illusion* (as a wand). These spells are typically used to lure persons to the lamia and then hold them there for the creature to devour. The lamia's touch permanently drains 1 point of wisdom from a victim, and when wisdom drops below 3 they willingly do whatever the lamia tells them to do. Lamias first drain their prey of blood and then feast upon the flesh. They can speak their alignment language and the common tongue.

LAMMASU

FREQUENCY: *Rare*
NO. APPEARING: *2-8*
ARMOR CLASS: *6*
MOVE: *12"/24"*
HIT DICE: *7 + 7*
% IN LAIR: *30%*
TREASURE TYPE: *R, S, T*
NO. OF ATTACKS: *2*
DAMAGE/ATTACK: *1-6/1-6*
SPECIAL ATTACKS: *See below*
SPECIAL DEFENSES: *See below*
MAGIC RESISTANCE: *30%*
INTELLIGENCE: *Genius*
ALIGNMENT: *Lawful good*
SIZE: *L*
PSIONIC ABILITY: *Nil*
    Attack/Defense Modes: *Nil*

Lammasu dwell in warm regions, but they occasionally visit every clime. It is the nature of these creatures to aid and protect lawful good persons and they are of generally kind and friendly disposition to all good creatures.

A lammasu is able to become *invisible* and/or *dimension door* at will. They radiate a *protection from evil* in a 10' radius which has double strength (-2 on evil attacks, +2 on saving throws against evil attacks). Additionally, they are able to use clerical spells up to 4th level, doing so at a 6th level proficiency. A lammasu can employ 4 spells of the 1st level, 3 of the 2nd, 2 of the 3rd, and 1 of the 4th. They have *cure wounds* spells of double effect (4-14 and 8-28). 10% of these creatures can speak a *holy word* as well. Lammasu communicate in their own tongue, the language of lawful good, and through a limited form of telepathy.

LAMPREY

	Normal	Giant
FREQUENCY:	*Uncommon*	*Rare*
NO. APPEARING:	*1-2*	*1-4*
ARMOR CLASS:	*7*	*6*
MOVE:	*12"*	*9"*
HIT DICE:	*1 + 2*	*5*
% IN LAIR:	*Nil*	*Nil*
TREASURE TYPE:	*Nil*	*Nil*
NO. OF ATTACKS:	*1*	*1*
DAMAGE/ATTACK:	*1-2*	*1-6*
SPECIAL ATTACKS:	*Drain blood*	*Drain blood*
SPECIAL DEFENSES:	*Nil*	*Nil*
MAGIC RESISTANCE:	*Standard*	*Standard*
INTELLIGENCE:	*Non-Neutral*	*Non-Neutral*
ALIGNMENT:		
SIZE:	*S*	*M*
PSIONIC ABILITY:	*Nil*	*Nil*
Attack/Defense Modes:	*Nil*	*Nil*

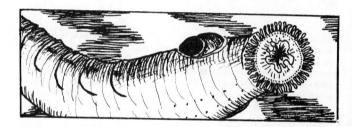

Lampreys are leech-like eels which inhabit both fresh and salt water: They do not inhabit shallow bodies of water. They feed by biting their victims, fastening themselves to the hapless creatures with sphincter-like mouths ringed with cruel teeth. Once attached the lamprey will begin to drain blood on the next and each successive melee round. The rate of blood drain is equivalent to 2 hit points of damage per hit die the lamprey has. Thus, a giant specimen will drain blood causing 10 hit points of damage per melee round.

LARVA

FREQUENCY: *Common*
NO. APPEARING: *10-40*
ARMOR CLASS: *7*
MOVE: *6"*
HIT DICE: *1*
% IN LAIR: *100%*
TREASURE TYPE: *Nil*
NO. OF ATTACKS: *1*
DAMAGE/ATTACK: *2-5*
SPECIAL ATTACKS: *Nil*
SPECIAL DEFENSES: *Nil*
MAGIC RESISTANCE: *Standard*
INTELLIGENCE: *Low*
ALIGNMENT: *Evil*
SIZE: *M*
PSIONIC ABILITY: *Nil*
    Attack/Defense Modes: *Nil*

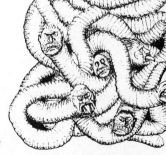

The larvae are the most selfishly evil of all souls who sink to lower planes after death. They abide in the gloom of Hades, controlled by the night hags. These creatures are desired by demons and devils alike, as they are used to form *quasits* (qv) or *imps* (qv) respectively. Liches employ their essence in order to retain their un-dead status and powers. Because of the value of larva the night hags use them to trade off and thus maintain the freedom of their planes.

Larvae appear as sickly yellow worms with distorted human faces.

LEECH, Giant

FREQUENCY: Uncommon
NO. APPEARING: 4-16
ARMOR CLASS: 9
MOVE: 3''
HIT DICE: 1-4
% IN LAIR: Nil
TREASURE TYPE: Nil
NO. OF ATTACKS: 1
DAMAGE/ATTACK: 1-4
SPECIAL ATTACKS: Drain blood
SPECIAL DEFENSES: Nil
MAGIC RESISTANCE: Standard
INTELLIGENCE: Non-
ALIGNMENT: Neutral
SIZE: S to M
PSIONIC ABILITY: Nil
    Attack/Defense Modes: Nil

Found only in the fetid waters of swamps and marshes, giant leeches are a threat to any warm-blooded creature which passes within their movement range of 3''. These horrors wait in the mud and slime for prey, and as it passes they strike. Giant leeches range from 1 to 4 hit dice in size; various sized creatures usually are found in the same group. The initial attack also attaches the sucker mouth of the giant leech, and on the next melee round, and on each round thereafter, it will drain blood the equivalent of 1 hit point damage per hit die it possesses. There is only a 1% chance that the victim will be aware of the attack unless it comes out of the water, for the leech has anesthetizing saliva, and its bite and blood drain are not usually felt until weakness (loss of 50% of hit points) makes the victim aware that something is amiss. Giant leeches will come out of water at night to attack prey within 3''. They can be killed by attack or with quantities of salt sprinkled on their bodies. There is a 50% chance that the bite of one of these creatures will cause disease which will be fatal in 2-5 weeks unless cured.

LEOPARD

FREQUENCY: Uncommon
NO. APPEARING: 1-2
ARMOR CLASS: 6
MOVE: 12''
HIT DICE: 3 + 2
% IN LAIR: 5%
TREASURE TYPE: Nil
NO. OF ATTACKS: 3
DAMAGE/ATTACK: 1-3/1-3/1-6
SPECIAL ATTACKS: Rear claws for
    1-4/1-4
SPECIAL DEFENSES: Surprised only
    on a 1
MAGIC RESISTANCE: Standard
INTELLIGENCE: Semi-
ALIGNMENT: Neutral
SIZE: M
PSIONIC ABILITY: Nil
    Attack/Defense Modes: Nil

These carnivores live in tropical woodlands and jungles. They hunt by laying in wait and leaping upon their prey, surprising on a 1-3. Leopards can spring 20' upwards or ahead 25'. If they score hits with both forepaws during a melee round, the leopard gains 2 additional attacks that round, each attack at 1-4 hit points damage.

If found in their lair, there is a 25% chance that there will be 1-3 cubs there. These young will have no effective attack.

LEPRECHAUN

FREQUENCY: Uncommon
NO. APPEARING: 1 or 1-20
ARMOR CLASS: 8
MOVE: 15''
HIT DICE: 2-5 Hit points
% IN LAIR: 10%
TREASURE TYPE: F
NO. OF ATTACKS: 0
DAMAGE/ATTACK: Nil
SPECIAL ATTACKS: See below
SPECIAL DEFENSES: See below
MAGIC RESISTANCE: 80%
INTELLIGENCE: Exceptional
ALIGNMENT: Neutral
SIZE: S (2' tall)
PSIONIC ABILITY: Nil
    Attack/Defense Modes: Nil

Leprechauns normally dwell only in fair, green lands with lush hills and dales for them to frolic through. Occasionally a party of adventurous ones will reside elsewhere for a time. These small creatures of magical talent and mischievous nature can become invisible at will, polymorph non-living objects, create illusions, and use ventriloquism spells as often as they like. Their keen ears prevent them from being surprised. Being full of mischief they will often (75%) snatch valuable objects from persons, turn invisible and dash away. The object stolen will be valuable, and there is 75% chance of such theft being successful. If pursued closely there is a 25% chance per turn of pursuit that the leprechaun will drop the stolen goods.

If caught or discovered in its lair the leprechaun will attempt to mislead its captor into believing he is giving over his treasure while he actually is duping the captor. It will require great care to actually obtain the leprechaun's treasure.

Note: Leprechauns have a great fondness for wine, and this weakness may be used to outwit them.

Rumor has it leprechauns are a species of halfling with a strong strain of pixie.

LEUCROTTA

FREQUENCY: Rare
NO. APPEARING: 1-4
ARMOR CLASS: 4
MOVE: 18''
HIT DICE: 6 + 1
% IN LAIR: 40%
TREASURE TYPE: D
NO. OF ATTACKS: 1
DAMAGE/ATTACK: 3-18
SPECIAL ATTACKS: See below
SPECIAL DEFENSES: Kick in retreat
MAGIC RESISTANCE: Standard
INTELLIGENCE: Average
ALIGNMENT: Chaotic evil
SIZE: L
PSIONIC ABILITY: Nil
    Attack/Defense Modes: Nil

This weird creature haunts deserted and desolated places, for it is so ugly most other creatures cannot bear the sight of it. The body of a leucrotta resembles that of a stag, its tail being rather lion-like, and its legs end in cloven hooves. Its head is that of a huge badger, but instead of teeth it has sharp, jagged boney ridges. This monster is very sly and can imitate the voice of a man or woman. They will do this to trick prey to approach within attack distance. When retreating the leucrotta can kick backwards with booth hooves, causing 1-6 hit points damage with each that hits. The monster speaks the language of its alignment as well as the common tongue.

LICH

FREQUENCY: *Very rare*
NO. APPEARING: *1*
ARMOR CLASS: *0*
MOVE: *6"*
HIT DICE: *11+*
% IN LAIR: *90%*
TREASURE TYPE: *A*
NO. OF ATTACKS: *1*
DAMAGE/ATTACK: *1-10*
SPECIAL ATTACKS: *See below*
SPECIAL DEFENSES: *+1 or better weapon to hit*
MAGIC RESISTANCE: *Standard*
INTELLIGENCE: *Supra-genius*
ALIGNMENT: *Neutral (evil)*
SIZE: *M*
PSIONIC ABILITY: *See below*
   Attack/Defense Modes: *See below*

A lich exists because of its own desires and the use of powerful and arcane magic. The lich passes from a state of humanity to a non-human, non-living existence through force of will. It retains this status by certain conjurations, enchantments, and a phylactery. A lich is most often encountered within its hidden chambers, this lair typically being in some wilderness area or vast underground labyrinth, and in any case both solidly constructed of stone and very dark. Through the power which changes this creature from human to lich, the armor class becomes the equivalent of +1 plate armor and +1 shield (armor class 0). Similarly, hit dice are 8-sided, and the lich can be affected only by magical attack forms or by monsters with magical properties or 6 or more hit dice.

Liches were formerly ultra powerful magic-users or magic-user/clerics of not less than 18th level of magic-use. Their touch is so cold as to cause 1-10 points of damage and *paralyze* opponents who fail to make their saving throw. The mere sight of a lich will cause any creature below 5th level (or 5 hit dice) to flee in panic from *fear*. All liches are able to use magic appropriate to the level they had attained prior to becoming non-human.

The following spells or attack forms have no effect on liches: *charm, sleep, enfeeblement, polymorph, cold, electricity, insanity* or *death spells/symbols.*

Description: A lich appears very much as does a wight or mummy, being of skeletal form, eyesockets mere black holes with glowing points of light, and garments most often rotting (but most rich).

LION

	Lion	Mountain Lion	Spotted Lion
FREQUENCY:	*Uncommon*	*Uncommon*	*Rare*
NO. APPEARING:	*2-12*	*1-2*	*2-8*
ARMOR CLASS:	*5/6*	*6*	*5/6*
MOVE:	*12"*	*15"*	*12"*
HIT DICE:	*5+2*	*3+1*	*6+2*
% IN LAIR:	*25%*	*10%*	*25%*
TREASURE TYPE:	*Nil*	*Nil*	*Nil*
NO. OF ATTACKS:	*3*	*3*	*3*
DAMAGE/ATTACK:	*1-4/1-4/1-10*	*1-3/1-3/1-6*	*1-4/1-4/1-12*
SPECIAL ATTACKS:	*Rear claws for 2-7/2-7*	*Rear claws for 1-4/1-4*	*Rear claws for 2-8/2-8*
SPECIAL DEFENSES:	*Surprised only on a 1*	*Surprised only on a 1*	*Surprised only on a 1*
MAGIC RESISTANCE:	*Standard*	*Standard*	*Standard*
INTELLIGENCE:	*Semi-*	*Semi-*	*Semi-*
ALIGNMENT:	*Neutral*	*Neutral*	*Neutral*
SIZE:	*L*	*M*	*L*
PSIONIC ABILITY:	*Nil*	*Nil*	*Nil*
Attack/Defense Modes:	*Nil*	*Nil*	*Nil*

Lions generally inhabit warmer climates — warm temperate to tropical. They will thrive in any region, from desert to jungle, swamp to savannah. Lions hunt in packs (prides), the males seldom doing any actual stalking/killing of prey. The lioness is the real huntress. All these creatures can spring up to 30'. Males, however, are ferocious fighters, and will actively defend their group territory. Male lions have armor class 5 forequarters and armor class 6 hindquarters, lionesses have the latter armor class. A typical pride consists of 1-3 males and 1-9 females. If found in their lair there will be 1-10 cubs from 30% to 60% grown which will not fight. There will be 1-4 lionesses with these cubs which will immediately attack.

Lions do not climb trees well and they dislike swimming.

If a lion scores two paw hits during melee it gains the advantage of raking with its two rear claws that turn, each rake causing 2-7 points of damage.

Mountain Lion: This creature is not actually a true lion, but a species of great cat. They inhabit forests and deserts as well as mountains. They are somewhat cautious, but they are fierce fighters if threatened or cornered. They can spring upwards 15' or ahead at least 20' to attack. Their rear claws each rake for 1-4 hit points damage.

Spotted Lion: Also known as cave lions, spotted lions are larger, spotted specimens of the common lion. They roam the plains of the pleistocene epoch, with but few being found elsewhere. Their hunting traits and group closely resemble those of their smaller, more modern kin.

LIZARD

	Fire	Giant	Minotaur	Subterranean
FREQUENCY:	*Very rare*	*Uncommon*	*Rare*	*Uncommon*
NO. APPEARING:	*1-4*	*2-12*	*1-8*	*1-6*
ARMOR CLASS:	*3*	*5*	*5*	*5*
MOVE:	*9"*	*15"*	*6"*	*12"*
HIT DICE:	*10*	*3+1*	*8*	*6*
% IN LAIR:	*50%*	*Nil*	*80%*	*20%*
TREASURE TYPE:	*B, Q (×10) S, T*	*Nil*	*J-N, Q, C (magic)*	*O, P, Q (×5)*
NO. OF ATTACKS:	*3*	*1*	*3*	*1*
DAMAGE/ATTACK:	*1-8/1-8/ 2-16*	*1-8*	*2-12/2-12/ 3-18*	*2-12*
SPECIAL ATTACKS:		*See below for each type of lizard*		
SPECIAL DEFENSES:	*See below*	*Nil*	*Nil*	*Nil*
MAGIC RESISTANCE:	*Standard*	*Standard*	*Standard*	*Standard*
INTELLIGENCE:	*Animal*	*Non-*	*Non-*	*Non-*
ALIGNMENT:	*Neutral*	*Neutral*	*Neutral*	*Neutral*
SIZE:	*L (30' long)*	*L (15' long)*	*L (40' long)*	*L (20' long)*
PSIONIC ABILITY:	*Nil*	*Nil*	*Nil*	*Nil*
Attack/Defense Modes:	*Nil*	*Nil*	*Nil*	*Nil*

Fire Lizard: These reptiles may be an ancestral dragon type or an offshoot of a common ancestor. In any case these creatures resemble red dragons, are sometimes called "false dragons," and the latter seem to avoid confrontation with fire lizards. They are slow-moving creatures and often (50%) sleep for long periods. They are found in subterranean lairs, coming forth every fortnight or so to hunt. As shiny things attract them, fire lizards collect metals and gems in their den. There is a 10% chance that the lair will contain 1-4 eggs (market value 5,000 gold pieces each), but the fire lizard does not otherwise care for its young which depart after hatching.

While the fire lizard usually attacks with a combination of two raking claws and a bite, it can also breathe forth a puff of flame from its mouth, a truncated cone ½" diameter at the mouth by 1" diameter, by 1½" long, which causes 2-12 hit points damage (1-6 if saving throw is made). Fire-based attacks do not harm a fire lizard.

Fire lizards are typically a neutral gray in color, with mottlings of red brown on the back and reddish undersides. Younger ones are lighter, old (50 to 100 years) specimens are darker.

Giant Lizards: The giant lizard is remarkable only for its size. They dwell in marshes and swamps by preference. Because of their large maws, they are able to engulf prey. Any "to hit" score of 20 indicates the creature has snapped both jaws onto its opponent, thus causing double damage (2-16 hit points).

Minotaur Lizard: These huge reptiles are very aggressive carnivores, usually inhabiting only warm regions. While moving slowly, they hide and quickly snatch at prey, surprising it on a 1-4. They have long sharp talons and teeth which inflict terrible wounds. Subdued prey is dragged into the lizards' den to be devoured at leisure. Because of the mouth-size of these creatures, a roll of 20 indicates a minotaur lizard attack has picked up any creature of man-size and weight or less (7' or less, 300 pounds or less) and has it fast in its mouth where it will be helpless to attack next round, but where the lizard is certain to be able to bite the creature again.

Subterranean: A variety of giant lizard which is found only underground, the subterranean lizard is most aggressive and dreaded, for it is able to run along ceilings or walls as easily as floors because of its suction cupped toes. Worse still, its horrible teeth inflict great wounds, and it can cause double damage on hits where it clamps both jaws firmly on its victim (indicated by a die roll of 20). As with most other lizards, it typically drags its prey to its lair before devouring it.

LIZARD MAN

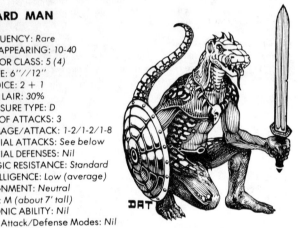

FREQUENCY: *Rare*
NO. APPEARING: *10-40*
ARMOR CLASS: *5 (4)*
MOVE: *6''//12''*
HIT DICE: *2 + 1*
% IN LAIR: *30%*
TREASURE TYPE: *D*
NO. OF ATTACKS: *3*
DAMAGE/ATTACK: *1-2/1-2/1-8*
SPECIAL ATTACKS: *See below*
SPECIAL DEFENSES: *Nil*
MAGIC RESISTANCE: *Standard*
INTELLIGENCE: *Low (average)*
ALIGNMENT: *Neutral*
SIZE: *M (about 7' tall)*
PSIONIC ABILITY: *Nil*
　　Attack/Defense Modes: *Nil*

Lizard men are semi-aquatic, breathing air but often (35%) dwelling totally underwater and having caves which are not water filled in which they lair. They are typically found in swamps, marshes, and similar places. They band together in rough tribal form. They are omnivorous, but lizard men are likely to prefer human flesh to other foods. In this regard they have been known to ambush humans, gather up the corpses and survivors as captives, and take the lot back to their lair for a rude and horrid feast. About 1 tribe in 10 has evolved to a higher state. These lizard men will dwell in crude huts, use shields (thus armor class 4) and hurl barbed darts (3'' range, 1-4 points damage) or javelins (1-6 hit points damage) before closing with enemies. In combat these advanced lizard men employ clubs (treat as morning stars). They speak their own language.

LOCATHAH

FREQUENCY: *Rare*
NO. APPEARING: *20-200*
ARMOR CLASS: *6*
MOVE: *12''*
HIT DICE: *2*
% IN LAIR: *10%*
TREASURE TYPE: *A*
NO. OF ATTACKS: *1*
DAMAGE/ATTACK: *By weapon*
SPECIAL ATTACKS: *Nil*
SPECIAL DEFENSES: *Nil*
MAGIC RESISTANCE: *Standard*
INTELLIGENCE: *Very*
ALIGNMENT: *Neutral*
SIZE: *M*
PSIONIC ABILITY: *Nil*
　　Attack/Defense Modes: *Nil*

The locathah are a humanoid race of aquatic nomads. They roam shallow sea waters, hunting and gathering food from bountiful warm waters.

For every 40 locathah encountered there will be a leader with 18 hit points (treat as a 4th level fighter) and 4 assistants with 14 hit points (treat as 3rd level fighters). If more than 120 are encountered there will be in addition

a chief with 22 points (treat as a 5th level fighter) and 12 guards (12-14 hit points, 3rd level fighters).

Locathah are always mounted upon giant eels, their steeds. These creatures also fight. (See Eel for statistics.) A typical force of locathah will be armed as follows:

lance	20%
crossbow	30%
trident	30%
net & dagger	20%

The lair of these aquatic nomads is typically some castle-like undersea rock which the locathah have hollowed out into rooms, passages, etc. It will be guarded by stout doors and have the additional protection of moray eels (4-16) as warders and it is 50% likely that there will be a Portuguese man o' war trap as well.

Description: Locathah are scaled in hues of pale yellow. Their ears are fanned with fins to increase hearing, and their eyes are large in order to see better in their watery domain. Their back scales and fins are darker than those in front.

LURKER ABOVE

FREQUENCY: *Uncommon*
NO. APPEARING: *1 (1-4)*
ARMOR CLASS: *6*
MOVE: *1''/9''*
HIT DICE: *10*
% IN LAIR: *50%*
TREASURE TYPE: *C, Y*
NO. OF ATTACKS: *1*
DAMAGE/ATTACK: *1-6*
SPECIAL ATTACKS: *See below*
SPECIAL DEFENSES: *Nil*
MAGIC RESISTANCE: *Standard*
INTELLIGENCE: *Non-*
ALIGNMENT: *Neutral*
SIZE: *L (20' ''wing'' spread)*
PSIONIC ABILITY: *Nil*
　　Attack/Defense Modes: *Nil*

The lurker above is a carnivorous creature found only in subterranean places. If the chamber or cave is large there might be as many as 4 of them, but normally only 1 is encountered. A lurker' can creep along surfaces but slowly (1'') or by using a gas which it generates and excretes into sacs about its body. This gives the lurker above a neutral bouyancy, and it then flaps its wing-like appendages and flies about.

They surprise prey on a 1-4 (on a 6-sided die). When disturbed the lurker' drops from the ceiling, smothering all creatures beneath in the tough folds of its ''wings.'' This constriction causes 1-6 points of damage per round, and the victims will smother in 2-5 rounds in any event unless they kill the lurker' and thus break free. Unintelligent, the lurker' will fight until dead. Prey caught in its grip cannot fight unless the weapons used are both short and in hand at the time the creature falls upon them.

Description: This terrible beast somewhat resembles a large manta ray. Its greyish belly is so textured as to appear to be stone, and the lurker' typically attaches itself to a ceiling where it is almost impossible to detect (90%) unless actually prodded.

LYCANTHROPE

	Werebear	Wereboar	Wererat	Weretiger	Werewolf
FREQUENCY:	Rare	Rare	Uncommon	Very rare	Common
NO. APPEARING:	1-4	2-8	4-24	1-6	3-18
ARMOR CLASS:	2	4	6	3	5
MOVE:	9''	12''	12''	12''	15''
HIT DICE:	7+3	5+2	3+1	6+2	4+3
% IN LAIR:	10%	20%	30%	15%	25%
TREASURE TYPE:	R, T, X	B, S	C	D, Q (× 5)	B
NO. OF ATTACKS:	3	1	1	3	1
DAMAGE/ATTACK:	1-3/1-3/	2-12	1-8	1-4/1-4/	2-8
	2-8		(sword)	1-12	
SPECIAL ATTACKS:	Hug for	Nil	Surprise	Rake for	Surprise
	2-16		on 1-4	2-5/2-5	on 1-3
SPECIAL DEFENSES:	All are hit only by silver or + 1 or better magic weapons				
MAGIC RESISTANCE:	All lycanthropes have standard resistance				
INTELLIGENCE:	Exceptional	Average	Very	Average	Average
ALIGNMENT:	Chaotic	Neutral	Lawful	Neutral	Chaotic
	good		evil		evil
SIZE:	L	L	S-M	L	M
PSIONIC ABILITY:	No lycanthrope possesses psionic abilities				
Attack/Defense Modes:					

Lycanthropes are humans with the ability to assume animal form. During the hours of darkness, they most commonly shape change to their animal form. In periods of a full moon lycanthropes are 90% likely to be compelled to assume their alter-shape. They usually move about as humans for whatever purposes they may have. Each type has its own language which is spoken in addition to common.

Any humanoid creature bitten by a lycanthrope for damage equal to or greater than 50% of its total potential, but not actually killed (and eaten), is infected by the disease of *lycanthropy.* If the person is carrying belladonna there is a 25% chance that this will cure the affliction if eaten within one hour. Note that this infusion will incapacitate the person for 1-4 days and there is a 1% chance of the poison in it killing the creature. Otherwise, a *cure disease* spell from a 12th or higher level patriarch must be placed upon the creature within 3 days or it will become a lycanthrope in 7-14 days. There are some other forms of lycanthropes, but these are very rare in the extreme.

Wereboar: Found in dense woodlands and similar areas, wereboars are of ugly temper and likely to attack. In their human shape they are usually hot tempered and irascible — typical berserker nature. Wereboars seldom mingle with normal boarkind (15% chance).

Werebear: Great werebears are the most powerful of all lycanthropes. They never are found in other than full-grown state. Werebears alone are 50% likely to be in company with 1-6 brown bears. They are able to *summon* 1-6 brown bears in 2-12 turns if any such creatures are within one mile of the werebear. Their human form is typically large, hirsute, and of solitary temperament. These creatures heal their wounds at three times the normal rate and are not subject to disease. They can *cure disease* in another creature in 1-4 weeks if they so desire.

Wererat: Sometimes known as ratmen, these sly and evil creatures inhabit subterranean tunnel complexes beneath cities. Wererats are able to take three forms — human, human-sized ratman, and giant rat. They are typically sword-armed. They use their human form to dupe humans, luring them to a place where they can be captured to be held for ransom or possibly eaten. Wererats prefer to move about in a rat-like shape, smaller than a man but much larger than a normal rat. They are capable of *summoning* and controlling giant rats, each wererat doing so with 2-12 of the creatures.

Weretiger: Weretigers are quite similar to normal tigers in their habitat. They are most often female. It is only 5% likely that weretigers will mingle with the normal sort of cat. They have the power to speak with all sorts of cats, however, and cats are 75% likely to be friendly with the weretiger because of this.

60% to 90% growth. The male will fight at +2 to hit and full damage each time he hits if the female is attacked. If the cubs are attacked the female will attack at +3 to hit and do full damage possible each time she hits. The young fight at -4 to -1 to hit, according to their maturity, and inflict 2-5 points of damage/attack.

Werewolf: In their human form, werewolves are very difficult to detect, for they can be of nearly any build and of either sex. Werewolves are prone to retain bipedal form in their wolf state, but wolweres (wolves which can become men) always take normal wolf form. Both sorts are likely to be found in a pack. Werewolf packs can be family groups if they number 5 to 8. Family packs consist of a male, female and 3 to 6 young of

LYNX, *Giant*

FREQUENCY: *Rare*
NO. APPEARING: *1-4*
ARMOR CLASS: *6*
MOVE: *12''*
HIT DICE: *2 + 2*
% IN LAIR: *5%*
TREASURE TYPE: *Nil*
NO. OF ATTACKS: *3*
DAMAGE/ATTACK: *1-2/1-2/1-4*
SPECIAL ATTACKS: *Rear claws for
        1-3/1-3*
SPECIAL DEFENSES: *See below*
MAGIC RESISTANCE: *Standard*
INTELLIGENCE: *Very*
ALIGNMENT: *Neutral*
SIZE: *M*
PSIONIC ABILITY: *Nil*
        Attack/Defense Modes: *Nil*

These forest cats prefer cold regions. They are aggressive and compete well with other predators because of their intelligence. If found in their lair there is a 25% chance that there will be 1-4 kittens there, 10% to 30% grown, with no effective attack. Giant lynx climb very well, swim reasonably well, and they can leap 15'. If the lynx strikes with both forepaws, it will then get two additional attacks, raking with the rear claws, each causing 1-3 hit points of damage.

Giant lynx speak their own language. They have also learned to hide themselves in order to avoid detection (90% unlikely in normal circumstances) or surprise prey (surprise on 1-5). They are 75% accurate in detecting traps.

"Whaddya mean we gotta talk to this lynx?? The last monster we talked to ate half of the party!"

MAMMOTH — MANTICORE — MASHER — MASTODON — MEDUSA — MEN — MERMAN — MIMIC — MIND FLAYER — MINOTAUR — MOLD — MORKOTH — MULE — MUMMY

MAMMOTH

FREQUENCY: *Common*
NO. APPEARING: *1-12*
ARMOR CLASS: *5*
MOVE: *12"*
HIT DICE: *13*
% IN LAIR: *Nil*
TREASURE TYPE: *Nil*
NO. OF ATTACKS: *5*
DAMAGE/ATTACK: *3-18/3-18/ 2-16/2-12/2-12*
SPECIAL ATTACKS: *Nil*
SPECIAL DEFENSES: *Nil*
MAGIC RESISTANCE: *Standard*
INTELLIGENCE: *Semi-*
ALIGNMENT: *Neutral*
SIZE: *L (10' to 14' tall)*
PSIONIC ABILITY: *Nil*
    Attack/Defense Modes: *Nil*

There are several varieties of mammoth, including the woolly and imperial — the latter sort being the largest. They inhabit climes ranging from subarctic to subtropical of the Pleistocene epoch. These massive herbivores are quite aggressive if threatened.

As with elephants (q.v.) and mastodons, the mammoth has 5 attack forms, but in general can apply no more than 2 versus a single opponent.

The tusks of the mammoth are 50% heavier than those of the elephant, and their value is proportionately higher.

MANTICORE

FREQUENCY: *Uncommon*
NO. APPEARING: *1-4*
ARMOR CLASS: *4*
MOVE: *12"/18"*
HIT DICE: *6 + 3*
% IN LAIR: *20%*
TREASURE TYPE: *E*
NO. OF ATTACKS: *3*
DAMAGE/ATTACK: *1-3/1-3/1-8*
SPECIAL ATTACKS: *Tail spikes*
SPECIAL DEFENSES: *Nil*
MAGIC RESISTANCE: *Standard*
INTELLIGENCE: *Low*
ALIGNMENT: *Lawful evil*
SIZE: *L*
PSIONIC ABILITY: *Nil*
    Attack/Defense Modes: *Nil*

Manticores prefer dismal lairs, so they are typically found in caves or underground. They range in all climes, although they enjoy warm places more than cold. The favorite prey of manticores is man, and they are usually encountered outside their lairs hunting for human victims.

A manticore attacks first by loosing a volley of 6 of its iron tail spikes (18' range as a light crossbow, 1-6 hit points damage per hit). They can fire four such volleys.

Description: The coloration of the manticore is that of its various parts — lion-colored body, bat-brown wings, human flesh head.

MASHER

FREQUENCY: *Uncommon*
NO. APPEARING: *2-8*
ARMOR CLASS: *7*

MOVE: *9"*
HIT DICE: *8*
% IN LAIR: *Nil*
TREASURE TYPE: *Nil*
NO. OF ATTACKS: *1*
DAMAGE/ATTACK: *5-20*
SPECIAL ATTACKS: *Nil*
SPECIAL DEFENSES: *Poison spines*
MAGIC RESISTANCE: *Standard*
INTELLIGENCE: *Non-*
ALIGNMENT: *Neutral*
SIZE: *L*
PSIONIC ABILITY: *Nil*
    Attack/Defense Modes: *Nil*

These worm-like fish move slowly along coral reefs, crushing and eating the coral growth. If surprised or threatened they are prone to attack in "self defense."

Mashers have a number of dorsal spines, 4' long, with poisonous secretions. An individual will have 4, 6, or 8. Unless fought from directly ahead or underneath, the masher is able to jut these spines so as to prevent attack or be stuck with a spine (save versus poison or be killed).

MASTODON

FREQUENCY: *Common*
NO. APPEARING: *1-12*
ARMOR CLASS: *6*
MOVE: *15"*
HIT DICE: *12*
% IN LAIR: *Nil*
TREASURE TYPE: *Nil*
NO. OF ATTACKS: *5*
DAMAGE/ATTACK: *2-16/2-16/ 2-12/2-12/2-12*
SPECIAL ATTACKS: *Nil*
SPECIAL DEFENSES: *Nil*
MAGIC RESISTANCE: *Standard*
INTELLIGENCE: *Semi-*
ALIGNMENT: *Neutral*
SIZE: *L (10' tall)*
PSIONIC ABILITY: *Nil*
    Attack/Defense Modes: *Nil*

Mastodons dwell in nearly any climate, from near arctic to tropical. These huge herbivores are distantly related to elephants, but their body is somewhat lower and longer. They are common on Pleistocene plains.

Although the mastodon has 5 attack modes (2 tusks, 1 trunk, 2 forefeet), they cannot employ more than 2 of them at one time against a single opponent. For details of attack limitations and other data see **ELEPHANT.**

Their tusks are of the same weight and value as those of elephants.

MEDUSA

FREQUENCY: *Rare*
NO, APPEARING: *1-3*
ARMOR CLASS: *5*
MOVE: *9"*
HIT DICE: *6*
% IN LAIR: *50%*
TREASURE TYPE: *P, Q (× 10), X, Y*
NO. OF ATTACKS: *1*
DAMAGE/ATTACK: *1-4*
SPECIAL ATTACKS: *Gaze turns to stone + poison*
SPECIAL DEFENSES: *Nil*
MAGIC RESISTANCE: *Standard*
INTELLIGENCE: *Very*
ALIGNMENT: *Lawful evil*
SIZE: *M*
PSIONIC ABILITY: *Nil*
    Attack/Defense Modes: *Nil*

Medusae are hateful humanoid creatures which dwell in dark caves or caverns, venturing forth on occasion to seek prey. They try to beguile humans to look into their eyes.

The gaze of a medusa's eyes will turn creatures within 3" to stone unless they make their saving throw versus petrifaction. If an opponent averts his eyes, the medusa rushes up so that its asp-like head growth can bite at the victim. The range of such attacks is but 1', and the victim bitten must save versus poison or die. If the medusa's gaze is reflected back, the creature will turn itself to stone! Medusae speak both their tongue and the common one. Medusae are able to see astral and ethereal creatures, and their petrifying gaze is as effective on those planes as it is on the material.

Description: The body of a medusa appears quite shapely and human. They typically wear human clothing. However, the face is of horrid visage, and its snakey hair writhes, so at a close distance (20') this gives the creature away. The glaring red-rimmed eyes of a medusa are visible clearly at 30'.

MEN

Normal men have from 1-6 hit points each. There are many types of men which are commonly encountered in the wilderness or in dungeons, always appearing in groups — smaller bands underground, larger outdoors is a good general rule. Each type will be detailed separately hereunder.

Note that there will always be higher level characters with any group of men encountered, the exact number being given under each separate heading.

All higher level fighters will usually be mounted on unbarded medium warhorses and have plate armor and shield. The same is true for clerics. For each level that these fighters, magic-users, and clerics have attained there is a 5% chance that they will have magical accouterments as shown below. Roll for each "yes," reroll if a cursed or otherwise undesirable item is indicated, but only one reroll is allowed, and if no usable item is indicated there is no item in the category.

	Fighter	Magic-user	Cleric	Thief
Armor	yes	no	yes	no
Shield	yes	no	yes	yes
Sword	yes	no	no	yes
Miscellaneous Weapon	yes	no	yes*	yes
Potion	yes	no	yes	yes
Scroll	no	yes	yes	no
Ring	no	yes	no	yes
Wand/Staff/Rod	no	yes	no*	no
Miscellaneous Magic	no	yes	yes	yes

*If no miscellaneous weapon, or one with an edge, roll again for possibility of a wand/staff/rod; if one is indicated, but it is not usable by a cleric, there is no such item possessed.

Example: A 6th level cleric is being checked. There is a 30% chance for the character to have magical armor, shield, miscellaneous weapon, potion, scroll, and a miscellaneous magic item. Rolling percentile dice for each category, the cleric scores positively in the shield, miscellaneous weapon and scroll classes. He gets a cursed shield first, but a reroll shows a +1 shield. For a miscellaneous weapon, the cleric gets magic arrows — not usable — so a roll on the wand/staff/rod table is called for, but the result shows an item not usable by him, so the category is dropped. Finally, a roll on the table for scrolls indicates the cleric has a *protection from undead* scroll.

High level leader-types will have the usual chance for psionic abilities.

Bandit *(Brigand)*

FREQUENCY: *Common*
NO. APPEARING: *20-200*
ARMOR CLASS: *See below*
MOVE: *See below*
HIT DICE: *1-6 Hit points*
% IN LAIR: *20%*
TREASURE TYPE: *Individuals M, A in lair*
NO. OF ATTACKS: *1*
DAMAGE/ATTACK: *By weapon type*
SPECIAL ATTACKS: *Leader types*
SPECIAL DEFENSES: *Standard*
MAGIC RESISTANCE: *Standard*
INTELLIGENCE: *Mean: average to very*
ALIGNMENT: *Neutral (chaotic evil)*
SIZE: *M*
PSIONIC ABILITY: *Leader types*
    Attack/Defense Modes: *Leader types*

Bandits roam every clime from temperate to subtropical. They travel in groups, generally led by high level fighters, magic-users and clerics. Those encountered in dungeons will be far fewer in number and often cooperating with thieves. For every 20 bandits encountered there will be an additional 3rd level fighter, for every 30 there will be an additional 4th level fighter, for every 40 there will be an additional 5th level fighter, and for every 50 there will be an additional 6th level fighter.

Bandits will always be led by an 8th, 9th, or 10th level fighter, with 6 guards of the 2nd level fighting ability and a lieutenant of 7th level. These 8 bandits are also in addition to the number indicated by the dice. To determine the level of the bandit leader use the following guide: if under 100 bandits are encountered the leader will be 8th level, if 100 to 150 the leader will be 9th level, and if 150 or more the leader will be 10th level.

For every 50 bandits there is a 25% chance that there will be a magic-user of 7th, 8th, 9th, or 10th level (roll a 4-sided die for level if one is with the group) in addition, i.e. if there are 200 bandits there will always be a magic-user.

For every 50 bandits there is a 15% chance that there will be a cleric of 5th or 6th level, with an assistant of 3rd or 4th level (dice only for the former) in addition.

Bandit lairs will be informal camps 80% of the time, but 10% will be cave complexes with a secret entrance, and 10% will be regular castles with 1-4 light catapults for defense. Bandits will have from 2-20 important prisoners in their lair, as well as 5-30 camp followers/slaves.

The mounting, armor, and arms of a force of bandits are:

medium horse, chainmail & shield, sword	10%
light horse, leather armor & shield, spear	10%
light horse, leather armor, light crossbow	10%
leather armor & shield, sword	40%
leather armor, pole arm	10%
leather armor, light crossbow	10%
leather armor, short bow	10%

Terrain will vary the percentage of mounted bandits. In hilly and mountainous terrain no more than 10% of the total would be horsed, while in open country 90% of the force would be horsed. They have normal chances for having psionically endowed leader-types with a party.

Brigands: Brigands are chaotic evil bandits. They conform to the characteristics of bandits in general. The brigands will have a cave complex lair 20% of the time and a castle 30% of the time. They will have only 1-10 important prisoners, but there will be 20-50 camp followers/slaves. They have high morale in combat, so they get a + 1 on reaction morale dice.

Example of Bandits (or Brigands):

Number encountered:	110
horsed	33
afoot	77
Additional high level fighters:	
3rd level	5
4th level	3
5th level	2
6th level	1
leader, 9th level	1
lieutenant, 7th level	1
guards, 2nd level	6
Total	130
chance for a magic-user	50%
chance for 2 clerics	30%

Berserker

FREQUENCY: Rare
NO. APPEARING: 10-100
ARMOR CLASS: 7
MOVE: 12''
HIT DICE: 2-7 Hit points
% IN LAIR: 10%
TREASURE TYPE: Individuals K, B
  in lair
NO. OF ATTACKS: 1 (or 2)
DAMAGE/ATTACK: By weapon
  type
SPECIAL ATTACKS: Leader types
SPECIAL DEFENSES: Leader types
MAGIC RESISTANCE: Standard
INTELLIGENCE: Mean: average to
  very
ALIGNMENT: Neutral
SIZE: M
PSIONIC ABILITY: Nil
  Attack/Defense Modes: Nil

Berserkers are bands of fighters who gather together to go out and seek battle. They scorn armor and engage in combat mad with battle lust. This lust enables them to strike twice, or once with a +2 to hit.

For every 10 berserkers encountered there will be a 1st level fighter in addition, for every 20 there will be a 2nd level, for every 30 there will be a 3rd, for every 40 there will be a 4th, and for every 50 there will be a 5th — all in addition to the number indicated by the dice.

Berserkers will be led by a war chief of 9th or 10th level and two subchieftains of 6th or 7th level — if 60 or less berserkers, the lower levels, if more than 60, the higher levels.

For every 10 berserkers encountered there is a 50% chance that there will be a berserk cleric of 7th level and 1-4 of his assistants of 3rd or 4th level.

Berserkers never check morale. If they decide that a fight would bring them honor (and possibly loot) they will attack.

Buccaneer (Pirate)

FREQUENCY: Uncommon
NO. APPEARING: 50-300
ARMOR CLASS: See below
MOVE: 12''
HIT DICE: 1-6 Hit points
% IN LAIR: 80% or 100%

TREASURE TYPE: Individuals K, W
  in lair
NO. OF ATTACKS: 1
DAMAGE/ATTACK: By weapon
  type
SPECIAL ATTACKS: Leader types
SPECIAL DEFENSES: Leader types
MAGIC RESISTANCE: Standard
INTELLIGENCE: Mean: average to
  very
ALIGNMENT: Neutral (chaotic
  evil)
SIZE: M
PSIONIC ABILITY: Leader types
  Attack/Defense Modes: Leader types

Buccaneers are found on the oceans, seas, large lakes, and broad rivers of the world. Their armor depends upon where they are located. Usually the encounter will be in the buccaneers' lair, which is their vessel(s). Only 20% of the time will they be encountered off of their ship(s) along some coast or shore.

For every 50 buccaneers encountered there will be a 3rd level fighter and for every 100 a 5th level fighter, all in addition to the number indicated by the dice.

They will have from 2-5 prisoners in their lair, these unfortunates being held for ransom.

Buccaneers will always be led by a captain of 8th or 10th level — 8th if fewer than 200 buccaneers. He will have a 6th or 7th level lieutenant and 4 mates of 4th level. These are all in addition to the regular buccaneers.

For every 50 buccaneers there is a 15% chance for a cleric of 12th, 13th, 14th, or 15th level and a 10% chance for a magic-user of 6th, 7th, or 8th level.

The armor and arms of a force of buccaneers are:

chainmail & shield, sword, hand axe	5%
chainmail & sword	5%
leather armor & shield, sword	10%
leather armor & spear	30%
leather armor & axe	20%
leather armor & heavy crossbow	10%
leather armor & light crossbow	20%

Note: All leaders and high level types in a force will wear chainmail rather than plate armor, and if magical armor is indicated it will be of the chain variety.

Pirate: Pirates are chaotic evil buccaneers who in all other respects conform to the characteristics of the latter type of men.

Caveman (Tribesman)

FREQUENCY: Rare
NO. APPEARING: 10-100 (120)
ARMOR CLASS: 8 (7)
MOVE: 12''
HIT DICE: 2 (1)
% IN LAIR: 40%
TREASURE TYPE: See below
NO. OF ATTACKS: 1
DAMAGE/ATTACK: By weapon type
SPECIAL ATTACKS: Nil
SPECIAL DEFENSES: Nil
MAGIC RESISTANCE: Standard
INTELLIGENCE: Low (to average)
ALIGNMENT: Neutral
SIZE: M
PSIONIC ABILITY: Nil
  Attack/Defense Modes: Nil

Cavemen are primitive, very fierce humans found in areas which are otherwise uninhabited by humans.

For every 10 cavemen there will be an additional 3rd level fighter. Cavemen will always be led by a 5th level fighter (chief) with 1-4 4th level subchiefs — all in addition to the number indicated by the dice. For every 10 cavemen encountered there is a 10% chance that they will have a 3rd level cleric with them (also a caveman, but possessing normal cleric spells).

Cavemen always lair in caves or caverns. There will be females and young equal to 100% and 50% respectively of the number of males encountered. There might be a chance that they will have ivory tusks, gold nuggets, or uncut gems — allow 5% chance for each per 10 cavemen, but if any one is indicated there will be no other treasures. Ivory is valued at 1,000 gold pieces per tusk (2 men to carry each), and there can be 2-12 tusks. Gold nuggets are the size of 5 gold pieces, and there can be 20-80 of them. Uncut gems are base 10 gold piece value, and there can be 1-100 of them.

Cavemen are armed as follows:

spear & stone axe	10%
stone axe	20%
club	50%
spear	20%

Treat stone axes as battle axes, clubs as morning stars. Note that due to their strength cavemen add +1 to damage rolls.

They tend to be frightened by the unknown, so subtract 1 from reaction dice in such morale checks.

Tribesman: Primitive tribesmen are typically found in tropical jungles or on islands. They use large shields. Their leaders conform to those of cavemen, but they have the following additional figures:

1 — 4th level cleric for every 10 tribesmen
1 — 6th level cleric for every 30 tribesmen
1 — 8th level head cleric (witchdoctor)

Tribesman clerics will be druidical in nature.

These men dwell in villages of grass, bamboo or mud huts. There is a 50% chance that the village lair will be protected by a log palisade. The village will contain females and young equal to 100% of the males encountered. There is a 75% chance that there will be 20-50 slaves. There is a 50% chance that there will be 2-12 captives (food!) held in a pen. Their treasure is exactly that of cavemen, but the tribesmen can possess all three types.

Tribesmen are armed as follows:

shield, spear & club	30%
shield & 2 spears	40%
shortbow & club	30%

Treat tribesmen's clubs as maces.

Dervish (Nomad)

FREQUENCY: Rare (Uncommon)
NO. APPEARING: 30-300
ARMOR CLASS: See below
MOVE: See below
HIT DICE: 1-6 Hit points
% IN LAIR: 5% (15%)
TREASURE TYPE: Individuals J (L),
    Z in lair
NO. OF ATTACKS: 1
DAMAGE/ATTACK: By weapon
    type
SPECIAL ATTACKS: Leader types
SPECIAL DEFENSES: Leader types
MAGIC RESISTANCE: Standard
INTELLIGENCE: Mean: average to
    very
ALIGNMENT: Lawful good
    (neutral)
SIZE: M
PSIONIC ABILITY: Leader types
    Attack/Defense Modes: Leader types

Dervishes are highly religious nomads (see below). They are encountered only in desert or steppes/plains areas.

For every 30 dervishes encountered there will be an additional 3rd level

fighter, for every 40 there will be a 4th level, for every 50 there will be a 5th level, and for every 60 there will be a 6th level.

Dervishes will be led by a cleric of 10th, 11th, or 12th level — 10th if under 125 in the party, 11th if under 250, 12th if 250 or more. The leader will have 2 assistant clerics of 4th, 5th, or 6th, 7th, or 8th level as his personal bodyguard. All these characters are in addition to the number of dervishes indicated by the dice.

For every 50 dervishes encountered there is a 15% chance that there will be a magic-user of 7th or 8th level and two assistants of 3rd or 4th level in addition to the other members of the group. If more than 200 dervishes are encountered the magic-users will be of the higher possible level.

Dervishes will have a walled fortress as a lair. There will be 200 to 300 dervishes there. The fortress will contain 1-4 each ballistae and light catapults and 1-2 heavy catapults as defenses.

The mounting, armor, and arms of a force of dervishes are:

medium warhorse, chainmail & shield, lance, sword	25%
medium warhorse, chainmail & shield, composite bow, sword	5%
light warhorse, leather armor & shield, lance, sword	50%
light warhorse, leather armor & shield, composite bow, sword	10%
light warhorse, leather armor & shield, light crossbow, mace	10%

Due to their fanatical nature, dervishes add 1 to their hit probability and damage dice. They never check morale in combat. Their leaders wear chainmail, so if magic armor is indicated, it will be of that variety.

Dervish leaders have normal chances for possession of psionic abilities.

Nomad: Nomads are bands of desert or steppes/plains dwellers who roam freely about herding and hunting. They surprise on a 1-4 due to their ability to use terrain to conceal themselves.

Nomads will have higher level fighters in addition to their indicated numbers as do dervishes. They have normal possibilities for psionic abilities.

The leader of a band of nomads will be a fighter of 8th, 9th, or 10th level — 8th level if under 150 nomads are in the group, 9th if 150-250, and 10th if 250 or more. The leader will have a subcommander of 6th, 7th, or 8th level, and 12 guards of 2nd level. All these characters are in addition to the number of nomads indicated by the dice.

For every 50 nomads encountered there is a 15% chance that there will be a cleric of 4th-7th level with the group. There is a like chance for a 5th-8th level magic-user. Regardless of the results of the above, there will always be 2 clerics of 3rd level and a 4th level magic-user with a band of nomads.

If nomads are encountered in their lair it is 90% likely to be an encampment of tents (or yurts and carts) at an oasis or stream. There will be females there equal in number to 200% of the males, and children equal to 100% of their number. There will be from 10-100 slaves. There will be 100-400 horses and double that number of herd animals (sheep, goats, camels, cattle and/or yaks). 10% of the time the lair will be a small walled city, with an additional 20-80 footmen armored with chain and shield and armed with spear and sword (50%) and composite bow and sword (50%). Other people and animals in the lair are commensurate with the number of men.

The mounting, armor, and arms of a force of nomads depends upon where they are encountered:

Desert Nomads:

medium warhorse, chainmail & shield, lance & sword	10%
medium warhorse, chainmail, light crossbow, sword	10%
light warhorse, leather armor & shield, lance, sword	50%
light warhorse, leather armor & shield, sword, 2 javelins	20%
light warhorse, leather armor, light crossbow, sword	10%

Steppes/Plaines:

medium warhorse, chainmail & shield, lance, sword	20%
medium warhorse, chainmail, composite bow, sword	10%
light warhorse, leather armor & shield, lance, sword	20%
light warhorse, leather armor, composite bow, sword	50%

Nomads will typically withdraw from a force which inflicts over 25% casualties upon them if the enemy appears to be able to continue stout resistance. Nomads will also feign retreat in order to lure an enemy into ambush. They are 75% likely to capture weaker groups, but they are 90% likely to parley with parties of near equal strength.

Merchant

FREQUENCY: *Common*
NO. APPEARING: *50-300*
ARMOR CLASS: *See below*
MOVE: *See below*
HIT DICE: *1-6 Hit points*
% IN LAIR: *0%*
TREASURE TYPE: *See below*
NO. OF ATTACKS: *See below*
DAMAGE/ATTACK: *By weapon type*
SPECIAL ATTACKS: *See below*
SPECIAL DEFENSES: *See below*
MAGIC RESISTANCE: *Standard*
INTELLIGENCE: *Mean: very to high*
ALIGNMENT: *Neutral*
SIZE: *M*
PSIONIC ABILITY: *See below*
    Attack/Defense Modes: *See below*

Merchants are, as the name implies, traders in goods and like merchandise. These traders travel in caravans — pack animals and/or wagons — from city to city in order to do business, so they are found nearly everywhere.

Only 10% of any band of merchants will actually be tradesmen. 10% will be drovers. The balance (80%) of the party will be mercenary guards.

The guards will be led by a fighter of 6th-11th level, with a lieutenant 1 level lower (5th-10th). These leaders will have 12 guards of 2nd level.

For every 50 persons in the merchant caravan there is a 10% chance for a magic-user of 6th-8th level. There is a 5% chance per 50 for a cleric of 5th-7th level. There is a 15% chance per 50 that there will be a thief of 8th-10th level with 1-4 lesser thieves (roll for the level of each, 3rd-7th).

All the leaders, guards, and special characters will be in addition to the numbers indicated by the dice.

The mercenaries guarding a caravan will be mounted, armored, and armed as follows:

heavy warhorse, plate armor & shield, lance, sword*	10%
medium warhorse, chainmail & shield, lance, sword	20%
medium warhorse, chainmail & shield, flail, mace	10%
light warhorse, scale mail, light crossbow, sword	10%
chainmail, pole arm, mace	10%
chainmail, heavy crossbow, mace	10%
ringmail & shield, spear, morning star	30%

*All 1st level fighters

All higher level fighters and clerics will have plate armor and shield.

A caravan of merchants will have various sorts of treasure. Merchants will individually have J, K, L, M, N, and Q treasures with them. The mercenaries will individually have type K, leaders type M. Somewhere in the caravan will be hidden the pay chest containing (100% certain) 2,000-4,000 gold pieces, 100-400 platinum pieces, and 4-16 base 100 gold piece gems. The merchandise will be worth from 10,000 to 60,000 gold pieces, being

carried on the pack animals, and/or wagons. It requires 10 pack beasts or 1 wagon for each 5,000 gold pieces worth of goods.

The merchants will always be mounted on very swift, light horses.

Pilgrim

FREQUENCY: *Uncommon*
NO. APPEARING: *10-100*
ARMOR CLASS: *See below*
MOVE: *See below*
HIT DICE: *1-6 Hit points*
% IN LAIR: *0%*
TREASURE TYPE: *See below*
NO. OF ATTACKS: *See below*
DAMAGE/ATTACK: *By weapon type*
SPECIAL ATTACKS: *See below*
SPECIAL DEFENSES: *See below*
MAGIC RESISTANCE: *Standard*
INTELLIGENCE: *Mean: average to very*
ALIGNMENT: *See below*
SIZE: *M*
PSIONIC ABILITY: *See below*
    Attack/Defense Modes: *See below*

Pilgrims are simply groups of individuals on their way to visit some place which is holy (or unholy) to them. They are thus found nearly everywhere.

A group of pilgrims will always have the following additional characters:

> 1-6 2nd level clerics
> 1-4 4th level clerics
> 1-2 6th level clerics
> 1 — 8th level cleric with a 3rd and 5th level assistant

There is a 25% chance that a 5th or 6th level monk will be with the party. For every 10 pilgrims there is a 10% chance that there will be 1-10 fighters of 1st-8th level. There is a like chance that there will be 1-6 thieves of 2nd-7th level. There is a 5% chance per 10 pilgrims that a magic-user of 6th-9th level is with the group. If the pilgrims are lawful good, fighters will be paladins. If the party is chaotic good the fighters will be rangers. If the party is neutral the clerics will be druids. If the pilgrims are lawful evil, all of the pilgrims will fight as berserkers, although they will be armed only with daggers. If the party is chaotic evil the thieves will be assassins of the level indicated.

A group of pilgrims is likely to be aligned as follows:

lawful good	35%
chaotic good	20%
neutral	10%
chaotic evil	15%
lawful evil	20%

All above average characters have normal chances for possession of psionic abilities.

Pilgrims are 75% likely to be afoot, 25% probability of being mounted — all will be either one or the other.

Pilgrims and monks will carry type J treasure. Fighters will carry types L and M, while clerics have types J, K, and M. Magic-users will have treasure types, L, N, and Q, thieves types J, N, and Q. There is a 5% chance that some high level member of the band of pilgrims is carrying a religious artifact. Any such artifact will be carefully hidden and well guarded by traps and/or magic devices.

MERMAN

FREQUENCY: *Uncommon*
NO. APPEARING: *20-200*
ARMOR CLASS: *7*
MOVE: *1″//18″*
HIT DICE: *1 + 1*
% IN LAIR: *25%*
TREASURE TYPE: *C, R*
NO. OF ATTACKS: *1*
DAMAGE/ATTACK: *By weapon type*
SPECIAL ATTACKS: *See below*
SPECIAL DEFENSES: *Nil*
MAGIC RESISTANCE: *Standard*
INTELLIGENCE: *Average to very*
ALIGNMENT: *Neutral*
SIZE: *M*
PSIONIC ABILITY: *Nil*
 Attack/Defense Modes: *Nil*

Mermen are found in the seas and oceans in the warm temperate and tropical areas. They range over areas harvesting the vegetation and hunting the fish the seas provide. Additionally, mermen actually herd certain fishes. They venture out of water only to sun themselves or to visit some coastal spot.

Mermen have regular undersea communities, generally a reef or cliff honeycombed with passages and rooms. Only 10% of the time will they construct a village of shells, rocks, and coral. This community will have areas where the merwomen and their young (100% and 100% of the total merman population respectively) live, netted pens where food fishes are kept, workshops, and so on. These communities will be guarded by from 3-18 of the larger-sized barracuda (q.v.), for mermen have learned to tame and use these fish.

The arms used by mermen are:

trident, dagger*	50%
crossbow, dagger	30%
net, javelin, dagger	20%

*20% of these mermen will have grapples and 50′ lines also.

On occasion mermen will attack surface vessels; to do so they must surface and grapple it. They are very accurate with these hooks and are 90% likely to hit. 10 mermen will then hold the line, and the ship will be slowed 1″ for every such grappling. Meanwhile, the other mermen will fire their crossbows and darts at exposed crewmen. Grappling hooks can be thrown up to 3″. If grappling hooks are loosened or cut, the mermen pulling on the line are not able to attack during the next melee round. A motionless ship will be held by the mermen in 4-16 melee rounds. The ship will then slowly sink and eventually be looted by the victors. During such an attempt the attacking mermen are exposed to missile fire from the vessel, and if flame is used against them the mermen take double damage.

Mermen speak their own language and 50% also speak locathah.

MIMIC

FREQUENCY: *Rare*
NO. APPEARING: *1*
ARMOR CLASS: *7*
MOVE: *3″*
HIT DICE: *7-10*
% IN LAIR: *Nil*
TREASURE TYPE: *Nil*
NO. OF ATTACKS: *1*
DAMAGE/ATTACK: *3-12*
SPECIAL ATTACKS: *Glue*
SPECIAL DEFENSES: *Camouflage*
MAGIC RESISTANCE: *Standard*
INTELLIGENCE: *Semi- to average*
ALIGNMENT: *Neutral*
SIZE: *L*
PSIONIC ABILITY: *Nil*
 Attack/Defense Modes: *Nil*

Mimics are subterranean creatures which cannot stand the light of the sun.

They are able to perfectly mimic stone or wood. There are two varieties of this creature, the large (9-10 dice), semi-intelligent carnivorous "killer mimic" and the slightly smaller, intelligent sort. While the former will attack anything which is nearby, the latter are generally friendly if offered food. All mimics move about constantly in their search of prey.

Mimics pose as stonework, door, chests, or any other substance or item they can imitate. When a creature touches the mimic, the latter lashes out with a pseudopod, delivering 3-12 points of damage per hit. Meanwhile, the mimic excretes a glue which holds fast whatever member the creature touched the mimic with.

The killer mimics do not speak, but the other breeds have their own language and can usually speak several other tongues such as common, orcish, etc. For consideration they will usually tell a party about what they have seen nearby.

MIND FLAYER

FREQUENCY: *Rare*
NO. APPEARING: *1-4*
ARMOR CLASS: *5*
MOVE: *12″*
HIT DICE: *8 + 4*
% IN LAIR: *50%*
TREASURE TYPE: *B, S, T, X*
NO. OF ATTACKS: *4*
DAMAGE/ATTACK: *2 each*
SPECIAL ATTACKS: *Mind blast*
SPECIAL DEFENSES: *Nil*
MAGIC RESISTANCE: *90%*
INTELLIGENCE: *Genius*
ALIGNMENT: *Lawful evil*
SIZE: *M*
PSIONIC ABILITY: *241-340*
 Attack/Defense Modes: *B/FGH*

Mind flayers are found only in subterranean places, as they detest sunlight. They are greatly evil and consider the bulk of humanity (and its kin) as cattle to feed upon.

The mind flayer's physical attack is by striking a victim with its four tentacles. If a tentacle hits it will reach the opponent's brain in 1-4 melee rounds and draw it forth, immediately killing the creature. The mind flayer then devours the brain. Its more feared attack mode, however, is the *mind blast* of psionic power. All within a 6″ directional cone of ½″ diameter at the point of emanation and 2″ diameter at extreme range are affected (psionic attack on non-psionic).

Mind flayers have the following psionic abilities: *levitation, domination, ESP, body equilibrium, astral projection, probability travel*. They perform at 7th level mastery.

If an encounter is going against a mind flayer it will immediately flee, seeking to save itself regardless of its fellows or its treasure.

These monsters speak only their own arcane language and several other weird tongues — purportedly those of terrible races of things which dwell in regions of the subterranean world far deeper than mankind has ever ventured. It is also rumored that these monsters have a city somewhere deep beneath the earth.

Description: The mind flayer's skin glistens with slime. Its skin color is a nauseous mauve, its tentacles being purplish black. A mind flayer's eyes are dead white, no pupil being evident. The three long fingers of each hand are reddish, but the hands are mauve.

MINOTAUR

FREQUENCY: *Rare*
NO. APPEARING: *1-8*
ARMOR CLASS: *6*
MOVE: *12''*
HIT DICE: *6 + 3*
% IN LAIR: *20%*
TREASURE TYPE: *C*
NO. OF ATTACKS: *2*
DAMAGE/ATTACK: *2-8 or 1-4/By weapon type*
SPECIAL ATTACKS: *Nil*
SPECIAL DEFENSES: *Surprised only on a 1*
MAGIC RESISTANCE: *Standard*
INTELLIGENCE: *Low*
ALIGNMENT: *Chaotic evil*
SIZE: *L*
PSIONIC ABILITY: *Nil*
    Attack/Defense Modes: *Nil*

Minotaurs are typically found only in labyrinthine places in the wilderness or underground. They are cruel, man-eaters, and although not particularly intelligent, they are cunning and have excellent senses. They are able to track prey by scent with 50% accuracy, and they will always pursue if it is in sight. They attack anything without fear, unless it is obviously beyond their ability to defeat.

In combat the minotaur can butt an opponent of 6' or more in height, or bite a shorter one, the former attack doing 2-8, the latter 1-4, points of damage. The creature also uses some form of weapon — usually a huge axe (treat as a halberd) or a flail (+2 on damage).

Minotaurs have their own language and are 25% likely to speak common as well.

MOLD

	Brown	Yellow
FREQUENCY:	Very rare	Uncommon
NO. APPEARING:	1 patch	1 patch
ARMOR CLASS:	9	9
MOVE:	0''	0''
HIT DICE:	—	—
% IN LAIR:	Nil	Nil
TREASURE TYPE:	Nil	Nil
NO. OF ATTACKS:	0	1
DAMAGE/ATTACK:	0	1-8
SPECIAL ATTACKS:	Freezing	Poison spores
SPECIAL DEFENSES:	See below	See below
MAGIC RESISTANCE:	See below	See below
INTELLIGENCE:	Non-	Non- (see below)
ALIGNMENT:	Neutral	Neutral
SIZE:	S to L	S to L
PSIONIC ABILITY:	Nil	Nil (see below)
Attack/Defense Modes:	Nil	Nil (see below)

Brown mold grows anywhere beneath the surface of the ground. It is light tan to golden brown in color. It cannot stand high concentrations of ultraviolet light, but it feeds on radiant energy of most other sorts. Where a patch of brown mold grows, the temperature will be below average. If a creature walks within 5' of the patch, the mold will begin absorbing its body heat — even from a basically cold blooded creature. Each melee round that a creature is within 5' of brown mold, the mold will drain heat equal to 1-8 hit points frost damage for every 10 degrees of body heat over 55 degrees the creature has. Worse still, this mold grows instantaneously from heat, so if a torch, flaming oil, or a fire ball is near the patch, it will be able to grow 2, 4, or 8 times its area from the heat fed to it. This growth will be so rapid that on the next melee round it will have spread and be draining any further heat in its new area of growth.

Brown mold is not fed by light spells or faerie fire. It is affected only by magical cold, and no other magical or non-magical attacks. Ice storms or walls of ice cause it to go dormant for 5-30 turns. A cold wand or white dragon breath will kill it. The growth does not harm creatures which use cold (white dragons, ice toads, or winter wolves.)

Yellow Mold: A more common underground fungus is yellow mold, which is pale yellow to a golden orange in color. Any creature which touches this mold is attacked by its enzymes. It also affects wood, albeit more slowly. It does no harm to metals or stone. If the substance is contacted roughly, there is a 50% chance per contact that the colony will release spores. These deadly spores shoot out in an asphyxiating cloud, 1'' by 1'' by 1'', originating from the center of impact. Any creature which is within this cloud will die, its lungs filled with yellow mold growth, unless it makes a saving throw versus poison. A *cure disease* and a *resurrection* are necessary within 24 hours to save such victims.

Yellow mold is affected only by fire based attacks — flaming oil, a fire elemental, etc. Continual light will cause it to become dormant for 2-12 turns, but thereafter the mold will grow over the light and obliterate it.

When formed into great colonies of at least 300 square feet in area this growth will form a collective intelligence about 1 time in 6. If this should happen the yellow mold will be aware mentally and psionically. It will attack by spore cloud if it senses the presence of other life forms (range of sensing will vary from 10' to 60') or psionically if such abilities are used within from 20' to 120' (random determination of sensing range). If it attacks psionically, it will await the approach of the life form and then loose an attack which is equal to the most powerful form of id insinuation. It cannot be counter-attacked psionically unless a cleric who has the power to telepathically communicate with plants is on hand, for he will be needed to channel such attacks into a form which will affect the vegetable intelligence of the mold colony. Otherwise, the yellow mold must be physically attacked and destroyed. The colony has sufficient power to make from 1 to 10 psionic attacks within as many turns, and after resting for 1-4 days it will thereafter be able to again attack in this manner.

MORKOTH

FREQUENCY: *Very rare*
NO. APPEARING: *1*
ARMOR CLASS: *3*
MOVE: *18''*
HIT DICE: *7*
% IN LAIR: *100%*
TREASURE TYPE: *G*
NO. OF ATTACKS: *1*
DAMAGE/ATTACK: *1-10*
SPECIAL ATTACKS: *Hypnosis*
SPECIAL DEFENSES: *Spell reflection*
MAGIC RESISTANCE: *See below*
INTELLIGENCE: *Exceptional*
ALIGNMENT: *Chaotic evil*
SIZE: *M*
PSIONIC ABILITY: *Nil*
    Attack/Defense Modes: *Nil*

The morkoth, or morlock, is a dim, shadowy monster often referred to as the "wraith of the deep." It is possibly humanoid, but reports vary. It inhabits dark, deep waters.

The lair of a morkoth is a series of spiraling tunnels, and at the nexus of these passages lurks the morkoth. Any creature passing over one of these tunnels is drawn towards it hypnotically, for the tunnels form a pattern which is *hypnotic*. When a victim is within the passages he approaches the morkoth without realizing it and will be *charmed* by a spell from the monster unless a saving throw at -4 on the die is made. The charmed victim will then be devoured at the morkoth's leisure. The tunnels of a morkoth are constructed so as to prevent large creatures from entering. There are typically 6 tunnels in a lair. Note that should any victim come closer than 6'', the hypnotic effect is broken.

The morkoth attacks by biting. A charmed creature will suffer this attack without knowledge, and thus enable the monster to consume it. Spell attacks of any sort are reflected by the morkoth, affecting the caster and possibly affecting others nearby also, if the spell is one with an area effect. However, if a *dispel magic* is cast simultaneously, the morkoth will be unable to reflect the spell and there is a 50% chance that the magic will affect the creature, although even then the morkoth is allowed a saving throw.

MULE

FREQUENCY: *Common*
NO. APPEARING: *1*
ARMOR CLASS: *7*
MOVE: *12''*
HIT DICE: *3*
% IN LAIR: *Nil*
TREASURE TYPE: *Nil*
NO. OF ATTACKS: *1 or 2*
DAMAGE/ATTACK: *1-2/1-6*
SPECIAL ATTACKS: *Nil*
SPECIAL DEFENSES: *Nil*
MAGIC RESISTANCE: *Standard*
INTELLIGENCE: *Semi-*
ALIGNMENT: *Neutral*
SIZE: *L*
PSIONIC ABILITY: *Nil*
     Attack/Defense Modes: *Nil*

Mules are generally sterile hybrids between horses and donkeys. They are strong and agile, thus able to negotiate dungeons well in most cases. Mules can be very stubborn and uncooperative at times, and they are likely to bite or kick their own handler if in a contrary mood. They are not panicked by fire, but strange smells may cause them to bolt away, or begin to bray loudly. A mule can carry 2000 gold pieces in weight at normal speed, 6000 at one-half speed.

MUMMY

FREQUENCY: *Rare*
NO. APPEARING: *2-8*
ARMOR CLASS: *3*
MOVE: *6*
HIT DICE: *6 + 3*
% IN LAIR: *80%*
TREASURE TYPE: *D*
NO. OF ATTACKS: *1*
DAMAGE/ATTACK: *1-12*
SPECIAL ATTACKS: *Fear*

SPECIAL DEFENSES: *See below*
MAGIC RESISTANCE: *See below*
INTELLIGENCE: *Low*
ALIGNMENT: *Lawful evil*
SIZE: *M*
PSIONIC ABILITY: *Nil*
     Attack/Defense Modes: *Nil*

Mummies are undead humans with existence on both the normal and the positive material planes. They are found near their tomb or in like burial places or ruins. They retain a semblance of life due to their evil, and they seek to destroy any living thing they encounter. Their unholy hatred of life and their weird un-life state gives them tremendous power, so that a blow from their arm smashes opponents for 1-12 hit points of damage. The scabrous touch of a mummy inflicts a rotting disease on any hit. The disease will be fatal in 1-6 months, and each month it progresses the diseased creature loses 2 points of charisma, permanently. It can be cured only by a magic spell, *cure disease*. The disease negates all *cure wound* spells. Infected creatures heal wounds at 10% of the normal rate.

The mere sight of a mummy within 6'' will cause such *fear* and *revulsion* in any creature, that unless a saving versus magic is successful, the victim will be *paralyzed* with fright for 1-4 melee rounds. Note that numbers will give courage, and for each creature above 6 to 1 mummy, the creatures add +1 to their saving throw. If humans confront a mummy, each will save at +2 on his dice.

Mummies can be harmed only by magical weapons, and even those do only one-half normal damage, dropping all fractions (5 becomes 2, 3 becomes 1, and 1 becomes 0 hit points of damage). *Sleep, charm, hold,* and *cold*-based spells have no effect upon them. Poison or paralysis do not harm them. A *raise dead* spell will turn the creature into a normal human (of 7th level fighting ability, naturally) unless the mummy saves versus magic. Mummies will suffer certain damage from fire, even flame of normal sort. A blow with a torch will cause 1-3 hit points of damage. A flask of burning oil will cause 1-8 hit points of damage on the first round it covers the mummy and twice that amount on the second melee round. Magical fires are at + 1 per die of damage. If holy water is splashed upon them they suffer 2-8 hit points of damage for every vial-full which strikes.

Any creature killed by a mummy rots and cannot be raised from death unless a *cure disease* and *raise dead* spell are used within 6 turns.

 NAGA — NEO-OTYUGH — NIGHT HAG — NIGHTMARE — NIXIE — NYMPH

NAGA

	Guardian	Spirit	Water
FREQUENCY:	Very rare	Rare	Uncommon
NO. APPEARING:	1-2	1-3	1-4
ARMOR CLASS:	3	4	5
MOVE:	15''	12''	9''//18''
HIT DICE:	11-12	9-10	7-8
% IN LAIR:	75%	60%	45%
TREASURE TYPE:	H	B, T, X	D
NO. OF ATTACKS:	2	1	1
DAMAGE/ATTACK:	1-6/2-8	1-3	1-4
SPECIAL ATTACKS:	See below	See below	See below
SPECIAL DEFENSES:	Nil	Nil	Nil
MAGIC RESISTANCE:	Standard	Standard	Standard
INTELLIGENCE:	Exceptional	High	Very
ALIGNMENT:	Lawful good	Chaotic evil	Neutral
SIZE:	L (20' long)	L (15' long)	M (10' long)
PSIONIC ABILITY:	Nil	Nil	Nil
Attack/Defense Modes:	Nil	Nil	Nil

Naga are snake-like creatures with good brains and magical abilities. They are encountered in warm climes in most cases.

Guardian Naga: Wise and good, guardian naga are found principally in sacred places, guarding treasure of lawful good minions, or as watchers over some evil. In addition to poisonous biting for 1-6 points of damage, and constricting for 2-8 points, a guardian naga can spit poison at an individual creature at up to 3'' range; and if the victim fails to make its saving throw versus poison the spittle will kill. Guardian naga also have

the ability to use clerical spells as if they were 6th level clerics, i.e. 2 — 1st, 2 — 2nd, 1 — 3rd, and 1 — 4th level clerical spells per day.

Guardian naga are covered in green-gold scales with silvery triangles along the back. Their eyes are golden.

Spirit Naga: Totally evil, spirit naga seek to do harm whenever and wherever possible. They prefer dwelling in ruined, dismal, or subterranean places. In addition to a poisonous bite for 1-3 hit points damage, these monsters can permanently *charm* (as a *charm* spell) any humanoid creature that meets a gaze of these monsters unless a saving throw versus paralyzation is made. Finally, spirit naga are able to use magical and clerical spells at 5th ability level of magic use and 4th level clerical ability, i.e. 4 — 1st, 2 — 2nd, and 1 — 3rd level magic-user and 2 — 1st and 1 — 2nd level cleric spells per day.

Spirit naga are black scaled with crimson bands. Their heads are bulbous and have a very human appearance, even to coloration and hair.

Water Naga: Found only in clear, fresh water, these creatures are curious but quite neutral in attitude. They seldom attack unless threatened or attacked first. As they generally inhabit places many feet beneath the surface of a pool, lake, or river, they are seldom disturbed in their lair. In addition to their poisonous bite for 1-4 points of damage, water naga are able to employ magic spells (excluding those which deal with fire) of 5th level ability, i.e., 4 — 1st, 2 — 2nd, and 2 — 3rd level magic-user spells per day.

Water naga are emerald green to turquoise in reticulated pattern with chocolate brown and pale jade green or dark gray and olive. Their eyes are pale green to bright amber.

NEO-OTYUGH

FREQUENCY: *Rare*
NO. APPEARING: *1*
ARMOR CLASS: *0*
MOVE: *6''*
HIT DICE: *9-12*
% IN LAIR: *Nil*
TREASURE TYPE: *See below*
NO. OF ATTACKS: *3*
DAMAGE/ATTACK: *2-12/2-12/1-3*
SPECIAL ATTACKS: *Disease*
SPECIAL DEFENSES: *Never surprised*
MAGIC RESISTANCE: *Standard*
INTELLIGENCE: *Average-very*
ALIGNMENT: *Neutral*
SIZE: *L*
PSIONIC ABILITY: *Nil*
    Attack/Defense Modes: *Nil*

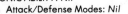

Neo-otyugh are a larger, more intelligent species of otyugh (qv). They conform to the general characteristics of otyugh, and are even more aggressive in their hunting of prey. Also, the neo-otyugh are slightly better at telepathic communication. Some specimens of these creatures reach 8' diameter and a height of 3' or more. The hide of a neo-otyugh is even tougher than that of an otyugh, although the appearance is similar.

NIGHT HAG

FREQUENCY: *Very rare*
NO. APPEARING: *1*
ARMOR CLASS: *9*
MOVE: *9''*
HIT DICE: *8*
% IN LAIR: *Nil*
TREASURE TYPE: *Nil*
NO. OF ATTACKS: *1*
DAMAGE/ATTACK: *2-12*
SPECIAL ATTACKS: *See below*
SPECIAL DEFENSES: *See below*
MAGIC RESISTANCE: *65%*
INTELLIGENCE: *Exceptional*
ALIGNMENT: *Neutral (evil)*
SIZE: *M*
PSIONIC ABILITY: *Nil*
    Attack/Defense Modes: *Nil*

The race of night hags rules the convoluted planes of Hades, and they are seldom encountered elsewhere. In their own region they are numerous, but they appear but singly on the material plane, and always in search of very evil persons to slay and bring to Hades to form another larvae — a valuable commodity to both demons and devils alike.

If a night hag finds a very selfishly evil person, she will cast a powerful *sleep* spell which affects even up to 12th level humans, unless a saving throw versus magic is successful. The night hag then strangles the sleeping victim. If the *sleep* spell fails, the hag will visit the victim nightly in ethereal state, intrude on the victim's dreams in order to cause him (or her) to become ethereal also, and then ride the victim until dawn. The night hag cannot be removed from the back by the victim, and each nightly ride permanently drains one point from the victim's constitution. When a 0 constitution is reached the victim is dead, and the night hag returns to Hades with the larval soul.

Night hags hate goodness, and they will attack any creature which is of good alignment as long as the possibilities of success appear favorable. Night hags are able to employ a *magic missile* spell 3 times per day, the missile causing 2-16 hit points of damage when it strikes. They can likewise use a *ray of enfeeblement* 3 times per day. They can become ethereal at will, as mentioned previously. Night hags also have the power to *know* a creature's *alignment* and *polymorph* themselves at will. If hard pressed, a night hag can attempt to *gate* in a demon of type I or a barbed devil (50%/50%). There is a 50% chance of the gate opening. The 'hag dislikes doing this, as she must then reward the demon or devil with a larva. They are totally invulnerable to *sleep, charm, fear, fire,* and *cold* based spells. It requires a silver, iron, or + 3 or better weapon to harm a night hag.

Night hags are able to astrally project their bodies, but in order to do so they must be in possession of a special periapt which each forges in Hades. If taken from a 'hag she can leave the plane she is in at the time of the loss. This periapt will cure diseases which the possessor contracts, and it gives a + 2 on all saving throws. However, in the hands of a good creature, the periapt decays 10% with each usage, eventually vanishing.

Description: The night hag is a hideous dark blue-violet color, with black hair and glowing red eyes. Her taloned hands and feet have nails of jet black.

NIGHTMARE

FREQUENCY: *Very rare*
NO. APPEARING: *1*
ARMOR CLASS: *-4*
MOVE: *15"/36"*
HIT DICE: *6 + 6*
% IN LAIR: *Nil*
TREASURE TYPE: *Nil*
NO. OF ATTACKS: *3*
DAMAGE/ATTACK: *2-8/4-10/4-10*
SPECIAL ATTACKS: *Nil*
SPECIAL DEFENSES: *See below*
MAGIC RESISTANCE: *Standard*
INTELLIGENCE: *High*
ALIGNMENT: *Neutral (evil)*
SIZE: *L*
PSIONIC ABILITY: *Nil*
    Attack/Defense Modes: *Nil*

Also known as "demon horses" and "hell horses," nightmares are creatures from the lower planes. They are ridden primarily by the more powerful demons and devils as well as by night hags. On occasion they serve as steeds for undead such as spectres, vampires and liches.

The nightmare attacks with its great fangs as well as its burning hooves. These creatures breathe out a smoking, hot cloud during combat, and it obscures vision by blinding the eyes and choking its opponent. Unless a saving throw is made the opponent attacks at -2 "to hit" and damage dice.

Nightmares can fly, become ethereal, and roam the astral plane. They hate material life and attack viciously, even without a rider to command them.

Description: The hell horse is gaunt and skeletal with a huge head, glowing red eyes, flaming orange nostrils, and hooves which burn like embers. The coat is dead black, and the creature's mane and tail are wild and rugged.

NIXIE

FREQUENCY: *Rare*
NO. APPEARING: *20-80*
ARMOR CLASS: *7*
MOVE: *6"//12"*
HIT DICE: *1-4 Hit points*
% IN LAIR: *95%*
TREASURE TYPE: *C, Q*
NO. OF ATTACKS: *1*
DAMAGE/ATTACK: *By weapon type*
SPECIAL ATTACKS: *Charm*
SPECIAL DEFENSES: *Nil*
MAGIC RESISTANCE: *25%*
INTELLIGENCE: *Very*
ALIGNMENT: *Neutral*
SIZE: *S (4' tall)*
PSIONIC ABILITY: *Nil*
    Attack/Defense Modes: *Nil*

Nixies are water sprites which inhabit lakes. They can, but seldom do, venture onto land. The nixies weave dwellings of living seaweed, so it is 95% unlikely that their lair will be noticed at any distance under 2". Furthermore, nixies will have giant fish to guard their lair — 1-2 gar (20%) or 2-5 pike (80%) — which obey simple commands given by the nixies. They can also summon 10-100 small fish.

Nixies delight in enslaving humans, and if one or more approach within 30' of a group of nixies, the latter will generate a powerful *charm* spell, one such spell for each 10 nixies, which requires the victim to save versus magic at -2 on the die roll. If a charmed person has a *dispel magic* spell cast upon him before entering the water, there is a 75% chance the charm will be broken, but once in the water the chance is only 10%. If a human is charmed by the nixies they will take the victim to their lair for 1 full year, but thereafter the charm wears off and the victim is allowed to go free. During any period of such enslavement, the nixies will keep a *water breathing* spell on the human captive. Each nixie has the power to cast a *water breathing* spell on any creature, or dispel it, once per day. It lasts 1 day. Nixies are armed with long daggers and darts (javelins). The latter

are used as spears under water, as missiles above. Each nixie carries one of each weapon. The javelins can be thrown 6" maximum (1" short range, 3" medium, etc.).

Although nixies are 25% magic resistant, they fear fire and very bright light. A flaming sword or a *light* spell will keep back the nixies. A *continual light* spell will keep them at bay until they can negate it by summoning small fish to crowd around the light and dim it.

Nixies speak their own language and the common tongue.

Description: Nixies appear to be very comely humanoids, with greenish skin, dark green hair and silver eyes. Their skin is lightly scaled and hands and feet are webbed.

NYMPH

FREQUENCY: *Very rare*
NO. APPEARING: *1-4*
ARMOR CLASS: *9*
MOVE: *12"*
HIT DICE: *3*
% IN LAIR: *100%*
TREASURE TYPE: *Q (× 10), X*
NO. OF ATTACKS: *0*
DAMAGE/ATTACK: *Nil*
SPECIAL ATTACKS: *See below*
SPECIAL DEFENSES: *See below*
MAGIC RESISTANCE: *50%*
INTELLIGENCE: *Exceptional*
ALIGNMENT: *Neutral (good)*
SIZE: *M*
PSIONIC ABILITY: *Nil*
    Attack/Defense Modes: *Nil*

These beautiful, ever-young appearing women inhabit the loveliest of wilderness places, grottos in the sea, clear lakes and streams, and crystalline caverns. They dislike any form of intrusion, and they have means to prevent it. Nymphs are able to *dimension door* once per day. A nymph is able to use druidical cleric spells at 7th ability level, i.e. 4 — 1st, 2 — 2nd, 2 — 3rd, and 1 — 4th level spell once per day. Looking at one will cause permanent blindness unless the onlookers save versus magic. If the nymph is nude or disrobes, an onlooker will die unless a saving throw versus magic is successful. There is a 10% chance that the nymph will be friendly if approached by a good creature without the latter first glimpsing the nymph, i.e. by calling or other prior notice. Similarly, if a nymph sees a human male with 18 charisma and good alignment before he sees her, it is 90% probable that the nymph will be favorably inclined towards the person.

Nymphs speak their own language and the common tongue.

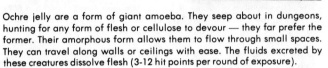
OCHRE JELLY — OCTOPUS, GIANT — OGRE — OGRE MAGE — ORC — OTTER, GIANT — OTYUGH — OWL, GIANT — OWLBEAR

OCHRE JELLY

FREQUENCY: *Uncommon*
NO. APPEARING: *1-3*
ARMOR CLASS: *8*
MOVE: *3''*
HIT DICE: *6*
% IN LAIR: *Nil*
TREASURE TYPE: *Nil*
NO. OF ATTACKS: *1*
DAMAGE/ATTACK: *3-12*
SPECIAL ATTACKS: *Nil*
SPECIAL DEFENSES: *See below*
MAGIC RESISTANCE: *Standard*
INTELLIGENCE: *Non-*
ALIGNMENT: *Neutral*
SIZE: *M*
PSIONIC ABILITY: *Nil*
　　Attack/Defense Modes: *Nil*

Ochre jelly are a form of giant amoeba. They seep about in dungeons, hunting for any form of flesh or cellulose to devour — they far prefer the former. Their amorphous form allows them to flow through small spaces. They can travel along walls or ceilings with ease. The fluids excreted by these creatures dissolve flesh (3-12 hit points per round of exposure).

Striking the ochre jelly with lightning bolts simply divides the creature into one or more smaller creatures, each doing one-half normal damage. Cold and fire based attacks have normal effect.

OCTOPUS, *Giant*

FREQUENCY: *Rare*
NO. APPEARING: *1-3*
ARMOR CLASS: *7*
MOVE: *3''//12''*
HIT DICE: *8*
% IN LAIR: *70%*
TREASURE TYPE: *R*
NO. OF ATTACKS: *7*
DAMAGE/ATTACK: *1-4 (× 6)/2-12*
SPECIAL ATTACKS: *Constriction*
SPECIAL DEFENSES: *See below*
MAGIC RESISTANCE: *Standard*
INTELLIGENCE: *Animal*
ALIGNMENT: *Neutral (evil)*
SIZE: *L*
PSIONIC ABILITY: *Nil*
　　Attack/Defense Modes: *Nil*

Giant octopi inhabit warm waters of medial to shallow depth. They lair in wrecked ships and undersea caves. They hunt at night, snatching and dining on any form of life which is vulnerable. They will readily attack swimmers or seize small vessels in order to eat the crew. These creatures are malicious and have a cunning bent. Several will cooperate to overwhelm a larger ship if opportunity presents itself. Vessels grabbed by giant octopi will lose way and come to a full stop in 3 turns.

A giant octopus will generally attack with 6 of its 8 tentacles, using 2 to anchor itself. Each tentacle striking does only 1-4 hit points of damage, but unless the member is loosened or severed, it will do twice initial damage (2-8 points) each melee round thereafter. The octopus also has a vicious beak which can bite nearby prey for 2-12 hit points.

Any creature will be struck only by 1 tentacle at a time unless it is larger than 8' or so tall/long. There is a 25% chance that a creature struck by a tentacle will have its upper limbs pinned, and a 25% chance that neither upper limb will be held. If both limbs are held the creature has no attack with them, if only 1 is pinned the creature attacks at -3 on "to hit" dice rolls, and if both are free the creature attacks only at -1. A tentacle grasps

with a grip equal to 18/20, and any creature with a strength equal to or greater than 18/20 can grasp the tentacle and negate its constriction; but this does not free it, and the octopus will immediately seek to drag the victim to its mouth to eat it. To break free, a tentacle must be severed. Each tentacle takes 8 hit points. This is in addition to the 8 dice the octopus itself has.

If 3 or more tentacles are severed it is 90% probable the octopus will retreat, blowing forth a cloud of black ink 4'' high by 6'' wide, by 6'' long. The octopus will then run to its lair or hide in some other nearby place, changing its color to blend with its surroundings. The ink cloud completely obscures the vision of any creature within it.

OGRE

FREQUENCY: *Common*
NO. APPEARING: *2-20*
ARMOR CLASS: *5*
MOVE: *9''*
HIT DICE: *4 + 1*
% IN LAIR: *20%*
TREASURE TYPE: *Individuals M (×* *10), Q, B, S in lair*
NO. OF ATTACKS: *1*
DAMAGE/ATTACK: *1-10 or by* *weapon*
SPECIAL ATTACKS: *Nil*
SPECIAL DEFENSES: *Nil*
MAGIC RESISTANCE: *Standard*
INTELLIGENCE: *Low*
ALIGNMENT: *Chaotic evil*
SIZE: *L (9'+ tall)*
PSIONIC ABILITY: *Nil*
　　Attack/Defense Modes: *Nil*

Ogres can be found in virtually any terrain, including subterranean places. They are ugly-tempered and voracious. Ogres are also fond of treasure, and they will sometimes be found serving as mercenaries in the ranks of orc tribes or evil clerics or joining with gnolls for a profitable raid. Ogres mingle freely with trolls and some giants, and they are at times enslaved by certain demons.

If 11 or more ogres are encountered, there will be one who is a leader (armor class 3, 30-33 hit points, attacking as a 7 hit dice creature and doing from 2-12 hit points damage/attack). If 16 or more are encountered there will be 2 such leaders plus 1 additional ogre, a chieftain with armor class 4, 34-37 hit points, and attacking as a 7 hit dice monster and doing 4-14 hit points damage/attack.

(If weapon type is used to determine damage/attack, give a standard bonus of +2 hit points to ogres and leaders/chieftains gain an additional +1/+2 bonus.)

If ogres are found in their lair there will be from 2-12 females who fight as normal ogres but do only 2-8 points of damage and take a maximum of 6 hit points per hit die. There will also be from 2-8 young who will fight as goblins. Ogres will take prisoners in order to use them as slaves (25%) or food (75%), so there is a 30% chance that an ogre lair will contain 2-8 slaves/prisoners. As they are very fond of halfling, dwarf, or elf flesh, there is only a 10% chance that such creatures will be found alive in an ogre lair.

Ogres speak their own language as well as that of chaotic evil, orcs, trolls, and stone giants.

Description: The hide of ogres varies from dull blackish-brown to dead yellow. Rare specimens are a sickly violet in color. Their warty bumps are often of different color — or at least darker than their hides. Hair is blackish-blue to dull dark green. Eyes are purple with white pupils. Teeth are black or orange, as are talons. Ogres wear any sort of skins or furs. They care for their arms and armor reasonably well. The life span of an ogre is not less than 90 years.

OGRE MAGE (Japanese Ogre)

FREQUENCY: *Very rare*
NO. APPEARING: *1-6*
ARMOR CLASS: *4*
MOVE: *9"/15"*
HIT DICE: *5 + 2*
% IN LAIR: *35%*
TREASURE TYPE: *G (magic), R, S*
NO. OF ATTACKS: *1*
DAMAGE/ATTACK: *1-12*
SPECIAL ATTACKS: *See below*
SPECIAL DEFENSES: *Nil*
MAGIC RESISTANCE: *Standard*
INTELLIGENCE: *Average to
    exceptional*
ALIGNMENT: *Lawful evil*
SIZE: *L(10½' tall)*
PSIONIC ABILITY: *Nil*
    Attack/Defense Modes: *Nil*

Japanese ogres, ogre magi, are not as rare elsewhere as they are in this part of the world. They normally seek uninhabited places in which to lair — typically in a fortified dwelling or some secure cavern complex below ground. From this location, the ogre magi will foray to capture treasure and humans for slaves and food.

If encountered in their lair, the ogre magi will always have a chief of great strength (+2 on each hit die, attacking and saving as a 9 hit dice monster) in addition to the others of his kind indicated by the die roll. There will be 2-12 slaves/prisoners in the lair.

Ogre magi are able to perform the following feats of magic: *fly* (for 12 turns), *become invisible, cause darkness* in a 1" radius, *polymorph* to human (or similar bipedal humanoid form from 4' to 12' size) form, and *regenerate* 1 hit point per melee round (lost members must be reattached to regenerate). Once per day they can also do any of the following: *charm person, sleep, assume gaseous form,* and create a *ray of cold* the same dimensions as that of a cold wand which does 8 — 8-sided dice of damage (unless the appropriate saving throw is made).

Japanese ogres speak their own language, that of normal ogres, the common tongue, and their alignment tongue.

Description: Ogre magi have light blue, light green, or pale brown skins. Their hair is typically of an opposite and darker color (blue-green, green-blue), except that brown skinned ogre magi have dark yellow hair. Their nails are black, and their teeth and tusks are very white. Horns are ivory colored. Their eyes are dark pupiled with white centers. Their apparel is typically colored in patterns familiar to their homeland.

ORC

FREQUENCY: *Common*
NO. APPEARING: *30-300*
ARMOR CLASS: *6*
MOVE: *9"*
HIT DICE: *1*
% IN LAIR: *35%*
TREASURE TYPE: *Individuals L; C,
    O, Q (× 10), S in lair*
NO. OF ATTACKS: *1*
DAMAGE/ATTACK: *1-8 or by
    weapon type*
SPECIAL ATTACKS: *Nil*
SPECIAL DEFENSES: *Nil*
MAGIC RESISTANCE: *Standard*
INTELLIGENCE: *Average (low)*
ALIGNMENT: *Lawful evil*
SIZE: *M (6'+ tall)*
PSIONIC ABILITY: *Nil*
    Attack/Defense Modes: *Nil*

Orc tribes are fiercely competitive, and when they meet it is 75% likely that they will fight each other unless a strong leader (such as a wizard, evil priest, evil lord) with sufficient force behind him is on hand to control the orcs. Being bullies, the stronger will always intimidate and dominate the weaker. (If goblins are near, for example, and the orcs are strong enough, they will happily bully them.) Orcs dwell in places where sunlight is dim or

non-existent, for they hate the light. In full daylight they must deduct 1 from their dice rolls to hit opponents, but they see well even in total darkness (infravision).

Known orc tribes include the following: Vile Rune, Bloody Head, Death Moon, Broken Bone, Evil Eye, Leprous Hand, Rotting Eye, Dripping Blade. If orcs from one of those tribes are encountered in an area, it is likely that all other orcs nearby will also be from this tribe.

For every 30 orcs encountered there will be a leader and 3 assistants. These orcs will have 8 hit points each (being the biggest/strongest/meanest in their group). If 150 or more orcs are encountered there will be the following additional figures with the band: a subchief and 3-18 guards, each having armor class 4, 11 hit points, and fighting as monsters with 2 hit dice (doing 2-7 hit points damage). If the orcs are not in their lair there is a 20% chance they will be escorting a train of 1-6 carts and 10-60 slave bearers bringing supplies and loot to their chief or to a stronger orc tribe. The carts will hold goods worth from 10 to 1,000 gold pieces, and each slave will bear goods worth from 5 to 30 gold pieces. If such a train is indicated, double the number of leaders and assistants, add 10 normal orcs for each cart in the train, and a subchief with 5-30 guards will always be in charge.

Orc lairs are underground 75% of the time, in an above ground village 25% of the time. There will always be the following additional orcs when the encounter is in the creatures' lair: a chief and 5-30 bodyguards (AC 4, 13-16 hit points, attack as monsters with 3 hit dice and do 2-8 hit points damage), females equal to 50% of the number of males, young equal to 100% of the number of males. If the lair is underground, there is a 50% chance that there will be from 2-5 ogres living with the orcs. If the lair is above ground it will be a rude village of wooden huts protected by a ditch, rampart, and log palisade. The village will have from 1-4 watch towers and single gate. There will be 1 catapult and 1 ballista for each 100 male orcs (round to the nearest hundred).

The weaponry of orcs is shown typically below:

sword & flail	5%
sword & spear	10%
axe & spear	10%
axe & pole arm	10%
axe & crossbow	10%
axe & bow	10%
sword & battleaxe	5%
spear	10%
axe	10%
polearm	20%

Leaders and above will always have two weapons. If a subchief is with a group the tribal standard will be present 40% of the time. The standard is always present when the tribal chief is. The standard will cause all orcs within 6" to fight more fiercely (+1 on hit dice and morale check dice).

Orcs are cruel and hate living things in general, but they particularly hate elves and will always attack them in preference to other creatures. They take slaves for work, food, and entertainment (torture, etc.) but not elves whom they kill immediately.

Orcs are accomplished tunnelers and miners. They note new or unusual constructions underground 35% of the time and spot sloping passages 25% of the time.

The majority of orcs speak goblin, hobgoblin, and ogre in addition to the languages of orcs and lawful evil.

Description: Orcs appear particularly disgusting because their coloration — brown or brownish green with a bluish sheen — highlights their pinkish snouts and ears. Their bristly hair is dark brown or black, sometimes with tan patches. Even their armor tends to be unattractive — dirty and often a bit rusty. Orcs favor unpleasant colors in general. Their garments are in tribal colors, as are shield devices or trim. Typical colors are blood red, rust red, mustard yellow, yellow green, moss green, greenish purple, and blackish brown. They live for 40 years.

Half-Orcs: As orcs will breed with anything, there are any number of unsavory mongrels with orcish blood, particularly orc-goblins, orc-hobgoblins, and orc-humans. Orcs cannot cross-breed with elves. Half-orcs tend to favor the orcish strain heavily, so such sorts are basically orcs although they can sometimes (10%) pass themselves off as true creatures of their other stock (goblins, hobgoblins, humans, etc.).

OTTER, *Giant*

FREQUENCY: *Rare*
NO. APPEARING: 2-5
ARMOR CLASS: 5
MOVE: 9''//18''
HIT DICE: 5
% IN LAIR: 10%
TREASURE TYPE: *Nil*
NO. OF ATTACKS: 1
DAMAGE/ATTACK: 3-18
SPECIAL ATTACKS: *Nil*
SPECIAL DEFENSES: *Nil*
MAGIC RESISTANCE: *Standard*
INTELLIGENCE: *Semi-*
ALIGNMENT: *Neutral*
SIZE: *L*
PSIONIC ABILITY: *Nil*
    Attack/Defense Modes: *Nil*

Giant otters dwell in lakes and rivers. These creatures are basically non-aggressive, but if threatened or cornered they can fight fiercely. These creatures love to play — sliding and tag are favorite pastimes. If such play is in progress when the otters are encountered, the creatures might panic horses, overturn wagons, accidentally break carts, etc. Even in the water similar danger exists with regard to boats and other small craft, for the otters may accidentally overturn them in playfulness.

If discovered in their lair, there will always be 5 giant otters — 2 adults and 3 young (40%-70% grown). The parent animals will always attack in this circumstance. The young will defend themselves.

The pelts of giant otter sell for from 1,000 to 4,000 gold pieces.

OTYUGH

FREQUENCY: *Uncommon*
NO. APPEARING: 1 (2)
ARMOR CLASS: 3
MOVE: 6''
HIT DICE: 6-8
% IN LAIR: *Nil*
TREASURE TYPE: *See below*
NO. OF ATTACKS: 3
DAMAGE/ATTACK: 1-8/1-8/2-5
SPECIAL ATTACKS: *Disease*
SPECIAL DEFENSES: *Never*
   surprised
MAGIC RESISTANCE: *Standard*
INTELLIGENCE: *Low-average*
ALIGNMENT: *Neutral*
SIZE: *M-L*
PSIONIC ABILITY: *Nil*
    Attack/Defense Modes: *Nil*

These weird monsters are omnivorous scavengers, not at all hesitant about adding a bit of fresh meat to their diet of dung, offal, and carrion. They hate direct sunlight or bright light, so they are found underground in most cases. Usually (90%) only a single individual is encountered, for otyugh typically live in partnership with other subterranean monsters. The otyugh will dwell in a truce state with other powerful monsters in order to scavenge droppings and other leavings. In most cases otyugh live in piles of dung and rubbish, and thrive there.

The otyugh has a sensory organ stalk and two tentacle arms which protrude from its hideous body. The eyes are always thrust above the offal the creature lairs under, and this prevents surprise. Its tentacles have sharp ridges and are used to deliver smashing blows to prey. The creature's mouth is sucker-like and filled with many teeth. If it bites any victim it is 90% likely to be infected by *disease* (typhus).

These monsters have no interest whatsoever in treasure as humans know it, but their partners may, occasionally making the guarding of treasure they value a condition of allowing otyugh to dwell in semi-symbiosis with them. Otyugh speak their own language and are semi-telepathic, thus often able to communicate with other life forms when the otyugh so desire.

(See also **NEO-OTYUGH.**)

OWL, *Giant*

FREQUENCY: *Rare*
NO. APPEARING: 2-5
ARMOR CLASS: 6
MOVE: 3''/18''
HIT DICE: 4
% IN LAIR: 5%
TREASURE TYPE: *Q* (× 5), *X*
NO. OF ATTACKS: 3
DAMAGE/ATTACK: 2-8/2-8/2-5
SPECIAL ATTACKS: *Surprise on a*
   1-5
SPECIAL DEFENSES: *Nil*
MAGIC RESISTANCE: *Standard*
INTELLIGENCE: *Very*
ALIGNMENT: *Neutral*
SIZE: *M*
PSIONIC ABILITY: *Nil*
    Attack/Defense Modes: *Nil*

Giant owls are rarely encountered as they inhabit only very wild areas. They are nocturnal predators and effective hunters. Giant owls speak their own language.

A giant owl strikes with its two sets of sharp talons and its strong beak. Its feathers allow it to fly with nearly absolute silence, thus it surprises on 1-5 (on a 6-sided die).

These creatures are intelligent and will sometimes befriend other creatures. If encountered in their lair there is a 20% chance that there will be 1-3 eggs (25%) or 1-3 hatchling owls, 20% to 70% grown. The parents will always attack any creature threatening the eggs/owlettes. Eggs sell for 1,000 gold pieces, young for 2,000 on the open market.

OWLBEAR

FREQUENCY: *Rare*
NO. APPEARING: 2-5
ARMOR CLASS: 5
MOVE: 12''
HIT DICE: 5 + 2
% IN LAIR: 30%
TREASURE TYPE: *C*
NO. OF ATTACKS: 3
DAMAGE/ATTACK: 1-6/1-6/2-12
SPECIAL ATTACKS: *Hug*
SPECIAL DEFENSES: *Nil*
MAGIC RESISTANCE: *Standard*
INTELLIGENCE: *Low*
ALIGNMENT: *Neutral*
SIZE: *L (8' tall)*
PSIONIC ABILITY: *Nil*
    Attack/Defense Modes: *Nil*

The horrible owlbear is probably the result of genetic experimentation by some insane wizard. These creatures inhabit the tangled forest regions of every temperate clime, as well as subterranean labyrinths. They are ravenous eaters, aggressive hunters, and evil tempered at all times. They attack prey on sight and will fight to the death.

The owlbear attacks with its great claws (two inches long on large males), its snapping beak, and then grasps a victim and squeezes and bites it to death. If it scores a paw hit of 18 or better with either of its forelimbs, the owlbear has dragged the victim to itself; and the opponent will take an additional 2-16 hit points damage from the hug, that melee round and every melee round thereafter until the owlbear is killed. (Note that if the armor class of an opponent is such that an 18 is insufficient to hit, the hug is *not* effective, and no damage is taken.)

If encountered in their lair there is a 25% chance that there will be 1-6 eggs (20%) or young (80%) in addition to the adults. Young owlbears will be 40% to 70% grown, and they will fight accordingly. Eggs are worth 2,000 gold pieces, young under 50% grown are worth 5,000, on the open market.

Description: Owlbears have brownish-black to yellow brown fur and feathers. The 1,300 to 1,500 pound males will be the darker colored. The beaks of these creatures are yellow to ivory. The eyes are red-rimmed and exceedingly terrible to behold.

PEGASUS — PERYTON — PIERCER — PIKE, GIANT — PIXIE — PORCUPINE, GIANT — PORTUGUESE MAN-O-WAR — PSEUDO-DRAGON — PURPLE WORM

PEGASUS

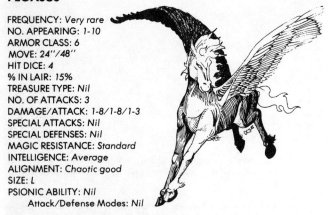

FREQUENCY: *Very rare*
NO. APPEARING: *1-10*
ARMOR CLASS: *6*
MOVE: *24''/48''*
HIT DICE: *4*
% IN LAIR: *15%*
TREASURE TYPE: *Nil*
NO. OF ATTACKS: *3*
DAMAGE/ATTACK: *1-8/1-8/1-3*
SPECIAL ATTACKS: *Nil*
SPECIAL DEFENSES: *Nil*
MAGIC RESISTANCE: *Standard*
INTELLIGENCE: *Average*
ALIGNMENT: *Chaotic good*
SIZE: *L*
PSIONIC ABILITY: *Nil*
    Attack/Defense Modes: *Nil*

Pegasi are found in remote places, for they are typically very shy and wild. These intelligent winged horses make the swiftest of steeds, and they are often sought for that reason. Pegasi will serve only good characters, but if they do so, they always serve unto death.

A pegasus fights with its two forehooves and its powerful teeth. A male specimen can carry weight equal to a medium warhorse (qv), a female equal to a light warhorse.

If encountered in their lair there will be 1 nest for every pair of pegasi. There is a 20% chance per nest that there will be 1-2 eggs (30%) or young animals (70%) of 20% to 50% maturity. The eggs are worth 3,000 gold pieces, the young 5,000, on the open market.

PERYTON

FREQUENCY: *Rare*
NO. APPEARING: *2-8*
ARMOR CLASS: *7*
MOVE: *12''/21''*
HIT DICE: *4*
% IN LAIR: *10%*
TREASURE TYPE: *B*
NO. OF ATTACKS: *1*
DAMAGE/ATTACK: *4-16*
SPECIAL ATTACKS: *+2 to hit*
SPECIAL DEFENSES: *+1 or better
  weapon to hit*
MAGIC RESISTANCE: *Standard*
INTELLIGENCE: *Average*
ALIGNMENT: *Chaotic evil*
SIZE: *M*
PSIONIC ABILITY: *Nil*
    Attack/Defense Modes: *Nil*

Perytons dwell in rocky hills or mountainous regions. They are omnivorous creatures of the weirdest appearance, likely the result of the same type of experimentation as brought about the owlbear.

The creature attacks with its sharp horns, having a +2 on "to hit" dice. Its claws are too weak to use. Each peryton attacks but a single creature, and when it is dead the peryton tears out the victim's heart with its teeth. The organ is necessary to the peryton to reproduce, and the creature immediately flies away in order to do so. Human hearts are the type most sought by perytons.

Normal weapons do not harm these creatures.

Perytons lair in caves high upon cliffs or in mountain peaks. They will sometimes take humans and similar creatures alive in order to hold them prisoner until needed as food and for reproduction needs.

Perytons speak their own language.

Description: The upper body and head of the peryton is blue-black, the creature's horns being jet black. The wing and back feathers are dark green, and the chest of the male peryton is light blue to medium blue, the females being drab.

PIERCER

FREQUENCY: *Uncommon*
NO. APPEARING: *3-18*
ARMOR CLASS: *3*
MOVE: *1''*
HIT DICE: *1-4*
% IN LAIR: *Nil*
TREASURE TYPE: *Nil*
NO. OF ATTACKS: *1*
DAMAGE/ATTACK: *1-6/2-12/3-18
  or 4-24*
SPECIAL ATTACKS: *95% likely to
  surprise*
SPECIAL DEFENSES: *Nil*
MAGIC RESISTANCE: *Standard*
INTELLIGENCE: *Non-*
ALIGNMENT: *Neutral*
SIZE: *S to M*
PSIONIC ABILITY: *Nil*
    Attack/Defense Modes: *Nil*

Piercers inhabit caves, caverns, and similar subterranean places. With their stoney outer casing these monsters are indistinguishable from stalactites found on cave roofs. They are attracted by noise and heat, and when a living creature passes beneath their position above they will drop upon it in order to kill and devour it. Larger varieties will be found with smaller ones.

The size of a piercer is equal to its hit dice, and there is an equal probability of a piercer being 1, 2, 3, or 4 dice in size. The largest piercer is about 6' long, 1' base diameter, and weights 500 pounds.

PIKE, *Giant*

FREQUENCY: *Rare*
NO. APPEARING: *1-8*
ARMOR CLASS: *5*
MOVE: *36''*
HIT DICE: *4*
% IN LAIR: *Nil*
TREASURE TYPE: *Nil*
NO. OF ATTACKS: *1*
DAMAGE/ATTACK: *4-16*
SPECIAL ATTACKS: *Surprise on a
  1-4*
SPECIAL DEFENSES: *Nil*
MAGIC RESISTANCE: *Standard*
INTELLIGENCE: *Non-*
ALIGNMENT: *Neutral*
SIZE: *L (9'-14' long)*
PSIONIC ABILITY: *Nil*
    Attack/Defense Modes: *Nil*

Giant pike inhabit large, deep lakes. They are aggressive predators and will not hesitate to attack any creature which is nearby when they are hungry. These creatures see well, and they move with great speed, surprising prey two-thirds of the time. Giant pike are often tamed by nixies.

PIXIE

FREQUENCY: Very rare
NO. APPEARING: 5-20
ARMOR CLASS: 5
MOVE: 6''/12''
HIT DICE: 1-4 Hit points
% IN LAIR: 5%
TREASURE TYPE: R, S, T, X
NO. OF ATTACKS: 1
DAMAGE/ATTACK: By weapon type
SPECIAL ATTACKS: See below
SPECIAL DEFENSES: See below
MAGIC RESISTANCE: 25%
INTELLIGENCE: Exceptional
ALIGNMENT: Neutral
SIZE: S (2½' tall)
PSIONIC ABILITY: Nil
    Attack/Defense Modes: Nil

Pixies dwell only in the most idyllic of woodlands. They are naturally invisible and are thus almost never noted even though some creature passes near their secluded home.

Pixies normally carry slim swords and fine bows similar to those of sprites (qv). Their swords are equal to daggers, but their arrows are more effective and are of three types. All have +4 chance to hit. The pixie war arrow inflicts 2-5 hit points of damage. Their second type causes *sleep* in a comatose state for 1-6 hours to any creature which fails to save versus magic when struck. The third sort which the pixies use causes no harm physically, but being struck causes a complete loss of memory which can only be restored by clerical *exorcism* unless the victim saves versus magic.

Pixies can become *visible* at will, *polymorph* themselves at will, *create illusions* with both audial and visual components which last without concentration until magically dispelled once per day each, and *know alignment*. Pixies can, by touch, *cause confusion* in any creature which fails its saving throw versus magic. Confusion is permanent unless a *remove curse* spell is applied. Once per day pixies are able to use *dispel magic* (at 8th level/ability), *dancing lights*, *ESP*, and 1 in 10 can use *Otto's Irresistable Dance* spells.

Because pixies are normally invisible, they gain the advantage of subtracting 4 from "to hit" dice rolls of all opponents unable to detect invisible objects. Similarly, pixies can attack while invisible.

Pixies are highly mischievous, and they will be prone to bother, harass, or fool creatures. They speak their own tongue, that of sprites, and common speech.

PORCUPINE, Giant

FREQUENCY: Uncommon
NO. APPEARING: 1-2
ARMOR CLASS: 5
MOVE: 6''
HIT DICE: 6
% IN LAIR: 0%
TREASURE TYPE: Nil
NO. OF ATTACKS: 1
DAMAGE/ATTACK: 2-8
SPECIAL ATTACKS: Shoot quills
SPECIAL DEFENSES: Quills
MAGIC RESISTANCE: Standard
INTELLIGENCE: Animal
ALIGNMENT: Neutral
SIZE: L
PSIONIC ABILITY: Nil
    Attack/Defense Modes: Nil

Giant porcupines are found primarily in wooded areas. They are stupid and non-aggressive, but if threatened they are able to defend themselves with ease. The giant porcupine can bite with some effect, but they will do this only in the most desperate defense (10% chance per melee round the creature is above 50% damaged). The main defense of the giant porcupine is its ability to shoot 1-8 quills from its tail, each quill doing 1-4 hit points of damage and having a range of 30'. As its quills are up to 3' long, any attack which comes within 6' of the creature will likewise suffer 1-4 quills in return from the porcupine's defensive movements. There is no practical limit to the number of quills the creature can use, as there are over 80 in its tail and over 300 on its body. The porcupine views any approach within 30' as a threat.

PORTUGUESE MAN-O-WAR, Giant

FREQUENCY: Uncommon
NO. APPEARING: 1-10
ARMOR CLASS: 9
MOVE: 1''
HIT DICE: 1-4
% IN LAIR: 0%
TREASURE TYPE: Nil
NO. OF ATTACKS: 1
DAMAGE/ATTACK: 1-10
SPECIAL ATTACKS: Paralyzation
SPECIAL DEFENSES: Transparent
MAGIC RESISTANCE: Standard
INTELLIGENCE: Non-
ALIGNMENT: Neutral
SIZE: S to L
PSIONIC ABILITY: Nil
    Attack/Defense Modes: Nil

Portuguese men-o-war float in warm sea waters, trailing their deadly tentacles below. Any creature which touches these appendages takes damage from their poison, and if a saving throw versus paralyzation is not made the victim is paralyzed and will be drawn up by the portuguese man-o-war's tentacles and devoured in 3-12 turns.

Each of these creatures has 10-40 tentacles. Their length is a factor of size. For each die the creature has, the tentacles have 10' of length. A one hit die portuguese man-o-war is 2½' in diameter and has 10 tentacles which are each 10' long. A two hit dice creature has 20 tentacles of 20' length, a three hit dice creature has 30 tentacles of 30' length and a four hit dice portuguese man-o-war is 10' in diameter and has 40 tentacles which trail downwards 40'. Each tentacle requires but a single hit point to sever, but this does not inflict damage on the creature, and tentacles will regenerate in several days. Only hits scored on the body of the creature kill it.

Portuguese men-o-war are transparent. It is 90% probable that they will be undetected unless the creature encountering them is able to detect invisible objects.

PSEUDO-DRAGON

FREQUENCY: Very rare
NO. APPEARING: 1
ARMOR CLASS: 2
MOVE: 6''/24''
HIT DICE: 2
% IN LAIR: 5%
TREASURE TYPE: Q (× 10)
NO. OF ATTACKS: 1
DAMAGE/ATTACK: 1-3
SPECIAL ATTACKS: Poison sting
SPECIAL DEFENSES: Chameleon power
MAGIC RESISTANCE: 35%
INTELLIGENCE: Average
ALIGNMENT: Neutral (good)
SIZE: S (1½' long)
PSIONIC ABILITY: Nil
    Attack/Defense Modes: Nil

Pseudo-dragons are found in any clime, save the coldest or hottest, when they are found at all. These creatures are rare indeed and highly sought after. They lair in great hollow trees or small caves.

The pseudo dragon can deliver a vicious bite with its small, dragon-like jaws, but its major weapon is its sting-equipped tail. This appendage is long and very flexible. The creature can move it with flashing speed, and strikes at +4 to its "to hit" dice. Any creature struck must save versus poison or go into a state of catalepsy which lasts for 1-6 days. During this time the victim appears dead and there is a 25% chance the creature will actually die.

Pseudo-dragons have a chameleon-like power, so that they can blend with any typical background and become 80% undetectable to creatures not able to see invisible objects. They can see invisible objects.

Magic resistance is an innate characteristic of pseudo-dragons, and they are able to transmit this resistance to a human (or humanoid) companion when the pseudo-dragon is touching the other creature.

A pseudo-dragon communicates by means of a limited form of telepathy. If the pseudo-dragon elects to become a companion of a human (or humanoid), it can also transmit what it sees and hears to its companion up to a distance of 24''.

Description: Pseudo-dragons appear exactly as miniature red dragons. However, their coloration is a basic red brown, and can be changed as noted.

PURPLE WORM

FREQUENCY: *Rare*
NO. APPEARING: *1-2*
ARMOR CLASS: *6*
MOVE: *9''*
HIT DICE: *15*
% IN LAIR: *30%*
TREASURE TYPE: *B, Q (× 5), X*
NO. OF ATTACKS: *1 and 1*
DAMAGE/ATTACK: *2-24/2-8*
SPECIAL ATTACKS: *See below*
SPECIAL DEFENSES: *Nil*
MAGIC RESISTANCE: *Standard*
INTELLIGENCE: *Non-*
ALIGNMENT: *Neutral*

SIZE: *L (50' long)*
PSIONIC ABILITY: *Nil*
    Attack/Defense Modes: *Nil*

Purple worms burrow deep beneath the ground in a constant search for food. They sense vibrations at 60' and move to attack. Generally only adult specimens, 8'-9' in diameter and 40'-50' long, are encountered. Young are 1' in diameter and about 5' when they hatch, a typical hatching being 10-20, each with 1 hit die +4 hit points. They return to their lairs to rest, and there they expel such indigestible waste as metal and mineral crystals.

A purple worm attacks by biting (2-24 points of damage), and any hit 20% over the required score (that is 4 or more over the required number) or a 100% (die roll of 20) score in any case indicates the creature has engulfed its victim. A mature purple worm can swallow, whole, a creature as large as 8' or so tall and up to 6' wide, or vice versa. Any creature swallowed will be dead in 6 melee rounds. The worm will digest its meal in 12 turns, and at that time the creature is totally gone and cannot be raised from the dead. Note, however, that a creature swallowed can try to cut its way *out* of the purple worm's stomach. The inner armor class of the 'worm is 9, but each round the creature is in the worm it subtracts 1 from the damage each of its attacks does. This subtraction is cumulative, so on the second melee round there is a -2, on the third a -3, etc.

Additionally, the purple worm has a poisonous stinger in its tail. This weapon is only used in rear defense, however, or if the 'worm is fighting large or numerous opponents in a very spacious area which will allow it freedom to use its stinger. The sting causes 2-8 hit points of damage when it hits, and if the victim fails its poison saving throw it is killed by the purple worm's poison.

Mottled Worm: The mottled worm is an aquatic variety of the purple worm. It inhabits shallow bottom muck but will surface for prey. It otherwise conforms to the characteristics of the purple variety.

 QUASIT

QUASIT

FREQUENCY: *Very rare*
NO. APPEARING: *1*
ARMOR CLASS: *2*
MOVE: *15''*
HIT DICE: *3*
% IN LAIR: *0%*
TREASURE TYPE: *Q (×3)*
NO. OF ATTACKS: *3*
DAMAGE/ATTACK: *1-2/1-2/1-4*
SPECIAL ATTACKS: *See attacks*
SPECIAL DEFENSES: *See below*
MAGIC RESISTANCE: *25%*
INTELLIGENCE: *Low*
ALIGNMENT: *Chaotic evil*
SIZE: *S*
PSIONIC ABILITY: *Nil*
    Attack/Defense Modes: *Nil*

While the quasit is rare on the material plane, they are not on the planes of Pandemonium and the Abyss. The quasit is a larva changed into a minor demon form to serve as familiar to a chaotic evil magic-user or cleric. A quasit is able to *polymorph* itself into the shape of any two of the following creatures, this power being given to it by its demon lord: giant centipede, bat, frog, or wolf.

The attack mode of an unpolymorphed quasit is by means of its claws and fangs. The wounds caused by its claws cause a burning itch which drain 1 from its opponent's dexterity each time it is wounded unless a saving throw versus poison is made. Dexterity loss remains for 2-12 melee rounds. The magical powers of a quasit are held by its polymorphed form also. All quasits *detect* both *good* and *magic.* They *regenerate* at 1 hit point per melee round. They can become *invisible* at will, and once per day they can send out a blast of *fear* in a 3'' radius. Only magical or cold iron weapons will harm these monsters. Cold, fire, and lightning do not affect them. For purposes of spell attack upon them, quasits are considered as 7 hit dice creatures.

Although intelligence is low, quasits are sly and cunning, and in certain situations they are able to call upon the thinking power of a demon lord.

Once the quasit becomes a familiar, it passes along to its "master" the following: telepathic communication which enables the character to use all senses (including infravision) of the familiar, even up to a mile away. The quasit's presence within 1'' of its "master" allows the latter the quasit's magic resistance (25%) and also enables regeneration at 1 hit point per melee round. When the quasit is within a mile of its "master," the latter gains an additional level of ability. If the quasit is farther away, the character loses 1 level, and if the quasit is killed, the loss to the character is 4 levels. Finally, in addition to its normal advice, the quasit is able to contact a lower plane once per week in order to help its "master" decide some course of action. This contact is like a *commune* spell, but 6 questions are allowed.

The major aim of a quasit is to enable its "master" to wreak greater and more chaotic evil. It also wishes to destroy lawful evil humans in order to steal their souls for the demons, as the quasit will be rewarded accordingly when (and if) it returns to the planes of the Abyss. At the time of its "master's" death the quasit must grab the soul and rush back to there, and if it has not been actively evil prior to that, its demon lord might change the quasit to a manes or larva or send it forth as a quasit again rather than making it into a type I or II demon.

RAKSHASA — RAM, GIANT — RAT, GIANT — RAY — REMORHAZ — RHINOCEROS — ROC — ROPER — ROT GRUB — RUST MONSTER

RAKSHASA

FREQUENCY: *Very rare to rare*
NO. APPEARING: *1-4*
ARMOR CLASS: *-4*
MOVE: *15''*
HIT DICE: *7*
% IN LAIR: *25%*
TREASURE TYPE: *F*
NO. OF ATTACKS: *3*
DAMAGE/ATTACK: *1-3/1-3/2-5*
SPECIAL ATTACKS: *See below*
SPECIAL DEFENSES: *See below*
MAGIC RESISTANCE: *See below*
INTELLIGENCE: *Very*
ALIGNMENT: *Lawful evil*
SIZE: *M*
PSIONIC ABILITY: *Nil*
　　Attack/Defense Modes: *Nil*

Known first in India, these evil spirits encased in flesh are spreading. They are fond of a diet of human meat, and as masters of illusion they can easily gain this end. Rakshasas are able to employ *ESP* and then *create the illusion* of what those who have encountered them deem friendly. They can then withhold attack until their prey can be taken off-guard. Although capable of using both magic user's spells (up to 3rd level) and cleric's spells (1st level), they are not affected by spells under the 8th level. Rakshasas cannot be harmed by non-magical weapons, magical weapons below + 3 do one-half damage, but hits by crossbow bolts *blessed* by a cleric kill them. If more than 1 rakshasa is encountered in its lair, the group will be a male and 1 or more females.

RAM, *Giant*

FREQUENCY: *Rare*
NO. APPEARING: *2-8*
ARMOR CLASS: *6*
MOVE: *15''*
HIT DICE: *4*
% IN LAIR: *Nil*
TREASURE TYPE: *Nil*
NO. OF ATTACKS: *1*
DAMAGE/ATTACK: *2-12*
SPECIAL ATTACKS: *Charge*
SPECIAL DEFENSES: *Nil*
MAGIC RESISTANCE: *Standard*
INTELLIGENCE: *Animal*
ALIGNMENT: *Neutral*
SIZE: *L (6' at shoulder)*
PSIONIC ABILITY: *Nil*
　　Attack/Defense Modes: *Nil*

Giant sheep are found only in hilly or mountainous regions. All full-grown specimens, male or female, will conform to the above statistics. Males (giant rams), however, will charge to attack, delivering a butt of double the damage parameters shown. These animals are not normally aggressive, but if they believe the flock is threatened they will defend it to the death.

A flock will consist of a ram, four ewes, and the balance will be lambs (roll percentile dice to determine size, halving the number rolled and adding it to 50%).

RAT, *Giant (Sumatran)*

FREQUENCY: *Common*
NO. APPEARING: *5-50*
ARMOR CLASS: *7*
MOVE: *12''//6''*
HIT DICE: *1-4 Hit points*
% IN LAIR: *10%*

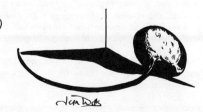

TREASURE TYPE: *C*
NO. OF ATTACKS: *1*
DAMAGE/ATTACK: *1-3*
SPECIAL ATTACKS: *Disease*
SPECIAL DEFENSES: *Nil*
MAGIC RESISTANCE: *Standard*
INTELLIGENCE: *Semi-*
ALIGNMENT: *Neutral (evil)*
SIZE: *S*
PSIONIC ABILITY: *Nil*
　　Attack/Defense Modes: *Nil*

Rats of all sorts are common, and the giant Sumatran sort are a plague in many places such as crypts and dungeons. Their burrows honeycomb many graveyards, where they seek to cheat ghouls of their prizes by tunneling to newly interred corpses.

Any creature bitten by a giant rat has a 5% chance per wound inflicted of contacting a *serious disease*. If such infection is indicated the victim is diseased unless a saving throw versus poison is successful.

Giant rats will avoid attacking strong parties unless commanded to fight by such creatures as wererats or vampires. They are fearful of fire and flee from it. Giant rats swim quite well, and they can attack in water as well.

RAY

	Manta	Pungi	Sting
FREQUENCY:	*Uncommon*	*Rare*	*Common*
NO. APPEARING:	*1*	*1-3*	*1-3*
ARMOR CLASS:	*6*	*7*	*7*
MOVE:	*18''*	*12''*	*9''*
HIT DICE:	*8-11*	*4*	*1*
% IN LAIR:	*0%*	*0%*	*0%*
TREASURE TYPE:	*J-N (×10), Q(×5), X*	*Nil*	*Nil*
NO. OF ATTACKS:	*1 and 1*	*1 to 12*	*1*
DAMAGE/ATTACK:	*3-12/2-20*	*1-4 each*	*1-3*
SPECIAL ATTACKS:	*See below*	*See below*	*See below*
SPECIAL DEFENSES:	*Nil*	*Nil*	*Nil*
MAGIC RESISTANCE:	*Standard*	*Standard*	*Standard*
INTELLIGENCE:	*Non-*	*Non-*	*Non-*
ALIGNMENT:	*Neutral*	*Neutral*	*Neutral*
SIZE:	*L*	*L*	*S*
PSIONIC ABILITY:	*Nil*	*Nil*	*Nil*
Attack/Defense Modes:	*Nil*	*Nil*	*Nil*

Manta Ray: These huge creatures "fly" through the warm ocean waters searching for prey. Small specimens have a tip-to-tip spread of 32', while the largest grow to some 44' across. They often rest on the floor of the sea, their coloration blending with the bottom, waiting for a victim to pass. The manta ray then attacks. It has a huge maw — the mouth size equal to one-quarter of its width — which can totally engulf most non-giant creatures in a single gulp. If the manta scores 10% (2 numbers) over its required "to hit" score, it has swallowed such prey as will fit in its mouth. Any creature swallowed will be dead in 6 melee rounds. The creature may attack the manta ray from inside, its armor class remains the same, and hits are at a cumulative -1 per melee round with regard to damage, i.e. -6 in the last melee round the swallowed creature can attack before being dead. In addition to its bite, the manta ray has a powerful tail spine. This weapon inflicts 2-20 points of damage upon any creature it strikes, and if the victim fails to make a saving throw against paralyzation it is stunned for 2-8 melee rounds from the force of the blow. The manta ray will strike with its tail spine only in situations where it is seriously threatened and the opponent to be struck must be at the rear quarter of the ray. The manta ray's stomach is the repository of indigestible items — such as the treasure types indicated.

Pungi Ray: Another of the tropical rays, the pungi is found only in relatively shallow bottoms. The creatures conceal themselves in the sand, with their terrible back spines protruding. These spines are greenish or brown, resembling plant growth so closely as to be 90% indistinguishable from normal seaweed. Pungi rays are some 15' across and 6' or so long. Their back spines are in an area of 3' by 4', with an average of 1 such spine per square foot, or 12 spines altogether. The spines vary from 1' to 2' in length. Any creature landing on a spine must save versus poison or be killed instantly. A footstep upon a pungi ray will equal 1 attack; if a human fell across a pungi ray he would suffer from 2-8 spine attacks. If a pungi ray is attacked it will try to escape by flight.

Sting Ray: These rays are seemingly harmless bottom feeders found in shallow tropical waters. However, they cover themselves with sand and are 90% invisible. If any creature steps upon them they lash up with their tail spine, inflicting 1-3 points of damage when they hit. Also, any such hit necessitates a saving throw versus poison, and if the victim fails its saving throw it is paralyzed for 5-20 turns and takes a like number of hit points of additional damage.

REMORHAZ

FREQUENCY: *Very rare*
NO. APPEARING: *1*
ARMOR CLASS: *Overall 0,*
    head 2, underside 4
MOVE: *12''*
HIT DICE: *7-14*
% IN LAIR: *20%*
TREASURE TYPE: *F*
NO. OF ATTACKS: *1*
DAMAGE/ATTACK: *6-36*
SPECIAL ATTACKS: *See below*
SPECIAL DEFENSES: *See below*
MAGIC RESISTANCE: *75%*
INTELLIGENCE: *Animal*
ALIGNMENT: *Neutral*
SIZE: *L (21' to 42' long)*
PSIONIC ABILITY: *Nil*
    Attack/Defense Modes: *Nil*

Remorhaz, sometimes known as polar worms, inhabit only the chill wastes. They are very aggressive predators. If encountered in its lair, a remorhaz is 25% likely to have a mate and 1-2 eggs there. The size of one of these creatures is determined by its hit dice: a 7 dice remorhaz is 21' long, an 8 dice creature 24' long, etc. Remorhaz eggs are valued at 5,000 gold pieces each.

In combat the remorhaz beats its small wings and rears the front quarter of its body. It then snaps itself forward, striking with blinding speed, and the largest-sized specimens are able to swallow prey whole in this manner. Any victim swallowed in this manner is instantly killed due to the intense heat in the monster's digestive system. Prey is swallowed whole on a score of 20. When aroused, the remorhaz secretes substances internally which cause its intestines to become very hot, and its back protrusions actually glow cherry-red with the excess heat. Any non-magical weapon striking the back of a remorhaz will melt from the heat, and any creature touched by these surfaces suffers 10-100 points of damage.

Description: The remorhaz has ice blue coloration everywhere except along its back where a streak of white sets off the large protrusions there. The creature's multi-faceted eyes are white.

RHINOCEROS

	Rhinoceros	Woolly Rhinoceros
FREQUENCY:	Common	Common
NO. APPEARING:	1-6	1-4
ARMOR CLASS:	6	5
MOVE:	12''	12''
HIT DICE:	8-9	10
% IN LAIR:	Nil	Nil
TREASURE TYPE:	Nil	Nil
NO. OF ATTACKS:	1	1
DAMAGE/ATTACK:	2-8/2-12	2-12
SPECIAL ATTACKS:	Charge	Charge
SPECIAL DEFENSES:	Nil	Nil
MAGIC RESISTANCE:	Standard	Standard
INTELLIGENCE:	Animal	Animal
ALIGNMENT:	Neutral	Neutral
SIZE:	L	L
PSIONIC ABILITY:	Nil	Nil
Attack/Defense Modes:	Nil	Nil

Rhinoceroses are aggressive herbivores, by and large. A few types are less aggressive and will run away if they feel threatened, but most will charge. They have poor eyesight but keen senses of hearing and smell. If more than one-half the possible number are encountered, 1 or 2 will be young (from 30% to 60% mature).

Single horned rhinoceroses do 2-8 hit points of damage and have 8 hit dice. Two-horned rhinos have 9 hit dice and do more damage when they hit (2-12 points). A charging rhino does double damage. They will trample any opponent which is low enough for this action. Trampling inflicts 2-8 hit points of damage for each forefoot which hits.

Woolly Rhinoceros: A large, very aggressive species of rhinoceros which roams the cold temperate and subarctic regions of the Pleistocene epoch, the woolly rhino conforms to the characteristics of its modern relatives.

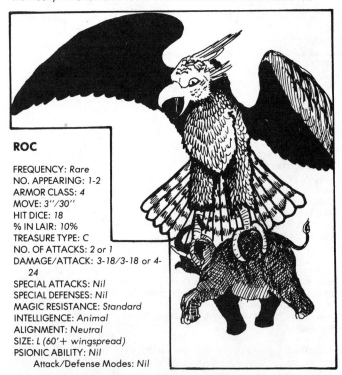

ROC

FREQUENCY: *Rare*
NO. APPEARING: *1-2*
ARMOR CLASS: *4*
MOVE: *3''/30''*
HIT DICE: *18*
% IN LAIR: *10%*
TREASURE TYPE: *C*
NO. OF ATTACKS: *2 or 1*
DAMAGE/ATTACK: *3-18/3-18 or 4-24*
SPECIAL ATTACKS: *Nil*
SPECIAL DEFENSES: *Nil*
MAGIC RESISTANCE: *Standard*
INTELLIGENCE: *Animal*
ALIGNMENT: *Neutral*
SIZE: *L (60'+ wingspread)*
PSIONIC ABILITY: *Nil*
    Attack/Defense Modes: *Nil*

Rocs are huge birds somewhat resembling eagles. They inhabit the highest mountains in warm regions. They prey upon large creatures such as cattle, horses, and elephants. The roc swoops down upon prey, seizes it in its powerful talons, and carries it off to its lair. If the creature resists, the roc will strike it with its beak, inflicting 4-24 points of damage per hit.

The lair of a roc will be a vast nest of trees, branches, and the like. There its treasure will be strewn about, for the creature does not value such . . . it is the residue of its victims.

Rocs are occasionally tamed and used by giants.

ROPER

FREQUENCY: *Rare*
NO. APPEARING: *1-3*
ARMOR CLASS: *0*
MOVE: *3"*
HIT DICE: *10-12*
% IN LAIR: *90%*
TREASURE TYPE: *See below*
NO. OF ATTACKS: *1*
DAMAGE/ATTACK: *5-20*
SPECIAL ATTACKS: *6
    poisonous strands*
SPECIAL DEFENSES: *See below*
MAGIC RESISTANCE: *80%*
INTELLIGENCE: *Exceptional*
ALIGNMENT: *Chaotic evil*
SIZE: *L*
PSIONIC ABILITY: *Nil*
    Attack/Defense Modes: *Nil*

Ropers inhabit subterranean caverns. They prey upon all forms of creatures, but humans are their favorite form of food. These monsters can stand upright in order to resemble a pillar or stalagmite or flatten themselves at full length upon the floor so as to look like nothing more than a hump. The roper has a gizzard-like organ which holds 3-18 platinum pieces and can contain 5-20 gems (35% chance).

The roper has six strands of strong, sticky rope-like excretion which it can shoot from 2"-5". A hit causes *weakness* (50% from strength in 1-3 melee rounds), and the roper then draws its prey into its toothy maw where it is quickly devoured. The chance for breaking a strand is the same for opening a door, but every round the roper will drag the victim 10' closer. They are unaffected by lightning, take half damage at most from cold, but are very susceptible to fire (-4 on saving throw).

Description: This yellowish gray monster appears to be a mass of foul, festering corruption. The roper is cigar-shaped, about 9' long, with a diameter of some 3'.

ROT GRUB

FREQUENCY: *Rare*
NO. APPEARING: *5-20*
ARMOR CLASS: *9*
MOVE: *1"*
HIT DICE: *1 Hit point*
% IN LAIR: *0%*
TREASURE TYPE: *Nil*
NO. OF ATTACKS: *0*
DAMAGE/ATTACK: *Nil*
SPECIAL ATTACKS: *See below*

SPECIAL DEFENSES: *Nil*
MAGIC RESISTANCE: *Standard*
INTELLIGENCE: *Non-*
ALIGNMENT: *Neutral*
SIZE: *S*
PSIONIC ABILITY: *Nil*
    Attack/Defense Modes: *Nil*

Rot grubs are occasionally found in heaps of offal or dung. They are rarely found in ceilings, walls, or floors. These small creatures will viciously burrow into any living flesh which touches them, for they greatly enjoy such fare to dine upon. The victim must immediately apply flame to the wound (1-6 hit points damage per application) or have a *cure disease* spell cast upon him. Otherwise, the rot grubs will burrow to the heart and kill their host in 1-3 turns.

RUST MONSTER

FREQUENCY: *Uncommon*
NO. APPEARING: *1-2*
ARMOR CLASS: *2*
MOVE: *18"*
HIT DICE: *5*
% IN LAIR: *10%*
TREASURE TYPE: *Q (× 10)*
NO. OF ATTACKS: *2*
DAMAGE/ATTACK: *Nil*
SPECIAL ATTACKS: *See below*
SPECIAL DEFENSES: *Nil*
MAGIC RESISTANCE: *Standard*
INTELLIGENCE: *Animal*
ALIGNMENT: *Neutral*
SIZE: *M*
PSIONIC ABILITY: *Nil*
    Attack/Defense Modes: *Nil*

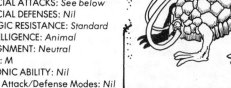

Rust monsters inhabit only dark subterranean places. They roam such places in search of their food — metals of all sorts, but principally ferrous based metals such as iron, steel, and steel alloys (such as mithral and adamantite arms and armor). If the rust monster touches the metal with its two antennae (roll "to hit" die) it rusts or corrodes the metal. Note that magically endowed items gain a saving throw, a 10% chance of not being affected for each plus, i.e. a +2 weapon or armor gains a 20% chance of being saved. Metal affected rusts or corrodes and immediately falls to pieces (which are easily eaten and digested by the creature). Weapons striking a rust monster are affected just as if the creature's antennae had touched them. Rust monsters can smell metal at 9" distance. They will stop for a melee round to devour such items as a handful of iron spikes or a mace if a fleeing party throws them away, but they will go after ferrous metal in preference to copper, silver, etc.

SAHUAGIN — SALAMANDER — SATYR — SCORPION, GIANT — SEA HAG — SEA HORSE, GIANT — SEA LION — SHADOW — SHAMBLING MOUND — SHARK — SHEDU — SHRIEKER — SKELETON — SKUNK, GIANT — SLITHERING TRACKER — SLUG, GIANT — SNAKE, GIANT — SPECTRE — SPHINX — SPIDER — SPRITE — SQUID, GIANT — STAG — STIRGE — STRANGLE WEED — SU-MONSTER — SYLPH

SAHUAGIN

FREQUENCY: *Uncommon*
NO. APPEARING: *20-80*
ARMOR CLASS: *5*
MOVE: *12"//24"*
HIT DICE: *2 + 2*
% IN LAIR: *25%*
TREASURE TYPE: *Individuals N; I,*
   O, P, Q (× 10), X, Y in lair
NO. OF ATTACKS: *1*
DAMAGE/ATTACK: *By weapon*
   type
SPECIAL ATTACKS: *See below*
SPECIAL DEFENSES: *See below*
MAGIC RESISTANCE: *Standard*
INTELLIGENCE: *High*
ALIGNMENT: *Lawful evil*
SIZE: *M (some L)*
PSIONIC ABILITY: *Nil*
   Attack/Defense Modes: *Nil*

The sahuagin, sometimes referred to as "seadevils" or "devil men of the deep," dwell in warm salt waters at depths of 100' to 1,500'. The legends about and history of these monsters will be dealt with later. Sahuagin are predatory in the extreme, and they pose a constant threat to all living things because they kill for sport and pleasure as well as for food. These creatures abhor fresh water. They dislike light, and bright light (such as that created by a light spell) is harmful to their eyes, as will be discussed hereafter. Sahuagin will venture ashore on dark, moonless nights to raid and plunder human villages. They hate even the evil ixitxachitl (q.v.) and only sharks are befriended by them.

The social structure of the sahuagin is based upon rule by a king who holds court in a vast undersea city deep beneath the waves. This overlord's domain is divided into 9 provinces, each ruled by a prince. Each of these nobles controls the small groups of sahuagin dwelling in his fief. This organization mirrors that of the plancs of Hell, for the sahuagin are devil worshippers.

A band of sahuagin will always be led by a chieftain. He will have 1 lieutenant for every 10 members of the group. The chieftain will have 4 hit dice +4 hit points, and his lieutenants will each have 3 hit dice +3 hit points. All are in addition to the group.

If sahuagin are encountered in their lair there will be the following additional sahuagin:

    1 baron (6 hit dice +6 hit points)
    9 guards (3 hit dice +3 hit points)
    30 — 120 females (2 hit dice)
    10-40 hatchlings (1 hit die)
    20 — 80 eggs

Also, there is a 10% chance per 10 male sahuagin that there will be a cleric (evil) and 1-4 assistant priestesses, for the religious life of these creatures is dominated by the females. If a cleric is with the group in the lair, she will be of 5th to 8th level ability, and her lesser clerics will be 3rd or 4th level.

There are always 2-8 sharks with sahuagin in their lair. Sahuagin are able to make these monsters obey simple one or two word commands.

Whenever a sahuagin lair is encountered there is a 5% chance that it will be the stronghold of a prince. The prince will have 8 hit dice +8 hit points, 9 guards of chieftain strength, and there will be 1 — 8th level sahuagin evil high priestess and 4 — 4th level underclerics. The numbers of males, females, hatchlings and eggs in a prince's lair is double the number rolled. There will be 4-24 sharks present at all times.

Sahuagin lairs are actual villages or towns, constructed of stone. The buildings are domed, and the seaweed and similar marine plants growing around and on these buildings make them hard to detect.

Although these creatures do not wear armor, their scaly hides are very tough and equal to armor class 5. Sahuagin wear a harness to carry their personal gear and weapons. A group of these creatures is typically armed as follows:

spear & dagger	30%
trident, net & dagger	50%
heavy crossbow & dagger	20%

Spears are used only as thrusting weapons. Nets are set with dozens of hooks which make escape from one virtually impossible for unarmored victims or creatures not able to grasp and tear with a strength of 16 or greater. Nets are replaced by 3 javelins when the band forays onto land. The crossbows fire a maximum of 30' underwater, normally above water. Nets are used to entrap victims. Tridents have three uses: to spear small prey, to pin prey trapped in nets, and to hold threatening opponents at bay.

Sahuagin are well-equipped to attack even without weapons, for they have long, sharp claws on their webbed hands which can inflict 1-2 hit points per attack, and they can use both simultaneously. Their powerful rear legs are likewise taloned, and if they kick an opponent with them they inflict 1-4 hit points damage with each hit from either foot. The sahuagin's mouth is filled with teeth and fangs, and if one successfully bites an opponent, from 1-4 points of damage will be inflicted. Thus it is possible for an unarmed sahuagin to attack 3 or 5 times in a melee round causing 1-2/1-2/1-4 and 1-4/1-4 if the legs can rake.

The eyes and ears of these monsters are particularly keen. Sahuagin can see 30" underwater at 100' depth. For each 100' of greater depth, their vision is reduced 1", i.e. at 500 they can see 26", at 1,000 they can see 21". Their ears are so sharp as to be able to detect the clinking of metal at 1 mile, or a boat oar splashing at the same distance. However, at 24" or less their ears cannot detect the sounds of swimming or similar noise, although the sahuagin can still hear metallic or other clanks, clicks, thuds, etc.

Sahuagin speak their own tongue, and some are evidently able to converse with the ixitxachitl in their own language.

Description: A typical sahuagin is blackish green on the back shading to green on the belly. The fins are black. The great staring eyes are deep, shining black. About 1 in 216 sahuagin is a mutation with 4 arms which are completely usable. These specimens are usually black shading to gray. Females are indistinguishable from males, except that they are slightly smaller. Hatchlings are light colored, but they darken and attain full growth approximately 1-2 months after hatching.

History and Legend: The sahuagin are chronicled because of their evil, having time and again raided the land, desolating whole coasts, and, of course, destroying passing ships continually. The exact origin of the sahuagin is unknown. It is suggested that they were created from a nation of particularly evil humans by the most powerful of lawful evil gods in order to preserve them when the deluge came upon the earth. The tritons, however, are purported to have stated that sahuagin are distantly related to the sea elves, claiming that the drow spawned the sahuagin.

Few persons have survived capture by the sahuagin, for prisoners are usually imprisoned, tortured, and eaten. Creatures taken alive are brought to the sahuagins' lair and confined in cells. Although sahuagin are able to stay out of water for up to 4 hours, there is no air in the confinement areas in the typical village, but in the towns of the nobles there are special quarters to maintain air-breathing creatures. The sahuagin will set aside a few prisoners to torture and provide sport — typically a fight to the death between two different creatures in an arena. The bulk of captives are simply killed and eaten. It is seldom that any prisoner escapes, although the sahuagin find sport in allowing captives to think that they have found freedom, only to be encircled by sadistic guards while a school of sharks come for the kill.

The sahuagin are cruel and brutal, the strongest always bullying the weaker. Any injured, disabled, or infirm specimen will be slain and eaten by these cannibalistic monsters. Even imperfect hatchlings are dealt with in this fashion. This strict law has developed a strong race, however, and any leader is always subject to challenge. Sahuagin never stop growing, although they grow slowly, and death comes to most before many years allow growth to large size. Leaders are the largest and strongest. It is reported that the 9 princes of the sahuagin are each of the 4-armed sort, as is the king. In any event, the loser of a challenge duel is always slain — in combat or afterwards. Duels are fought without weapons, only fang and claw being permitted.

The king is supposed to inhabit a city somewhere at the greatest depth sahuagin can exist. This place is supposedly built in an undersea canyon, with palaces and dwellings built along either face. There, fully 5,000 of these monsters dwell, not counting the king's retinue of queens, concubines, nobles, guards, etc. said to number 1,000 or more. The king of the sahuagin is reported as huge of size (10 hit dice +10 hit points) and of greatest evil. He is always accompanied by 9 noble guards (6 hit dice +6) and the evil high priestess of all sahuagin, with her train of 9 under-clerics.

SALAMANDER

FREQUENCY: *Rare*
NO. APPEARING: *2-5*
ARMOR CLASS: *5/3*
MOVE: *9"*
HIT DICE: *7 + 7*
% IN LAIR: *75%*
TREASURE TYPE: *F*
NO. OF ATTACKS: *2*
DAMAGE/ATTACK: *By weapon type/2-12*
SPECIAL ATTACKS: *Heat*
SPECIAL DEFENSES: *+1 or better weapon to hit*
MAGIC RESISTANCE: *Standard*
INTELLIGENCE: *High*
ALIGNMENT: *Chaotic evil*
SIZE: *M*
PSIONIC ABILITY: *Nil*
    Attack/Defense Modes: *Nil*

Salamanders are creatures of the elemental plane of fire. They come to the material plane occasionally for purposes known only to them. Salamanders hate cold, preferring temperatures of 300 degrees upwards, and they can abide lower temperatures only for a few hours. Their lair is typically at least 500 degrees temperature, and such treasure as is found there will be the sort to survive such heat.

The human-like upper body of a salamander has an armor class of 5, while the lower body is armor class 3.

A salamander typically attacks with a metal spear which inflicts damage of 1-6 hit points plus a like amount for its heat. At the same time it can lash out and coil around an opponent with its snake-like tail, constricting for 2-12 hit points damage plus causing an additional 1-6 points of damage from the heat of its body. While fire resistant creatures will not suffer heat damage, they will be subject to normal attack damage.

Salamanders can be affected only by magical weaponry or by creatures of a magical nature or with great strength. They are impervious to all fire-based attacks. *Sleep, charm,* and *hold* spells are ineffective against them. Cold based attacks cause an additional 1 point of damage per die of attack value.

Description: The head and torso of a salamander is copper-colored, with yellow, glowing eyes. The lower body is an orange shading to dull red at the tail end.

SATYR

FREQUENCY: *Uncommon*
NO. APPEARING: *2-8*
ARMOR CLASS: *5*
MOVE: *18"*
HIT DICE: *5*
% IN LAIR: *40%*
TREASURE TYPE: *I, S, X*
NO. OF ATTACKS: *1*
DAMAGE/ATTACK: *2-8*
SPECIAL ATTACKS: *See below*
SPECIAL DEFENSES: *See below*
MAGIC RESISTANCE: *50%*
INTELLIGENCE: *Very*
ALIGNMENT: *Neutral*
SIZE: *M*
PSIONIC ABILITY: *Nil*
    Attack/Defense Modes: *Nil*

Satyrs (or fauns) inhabit only sylvan woodlands. They are interested primarily only in sport — frolicking, piping, chasing wood nymphs, etc. They resent intrusion, however, and will drive away any creature which offends them. They can sometimes be lured/bribed with superior wine.

A satyr normally attacks by butting with its two sharp horns. They will occasionally (20%) make use of magical weapons. It is quite likely that a satyr will first play a tune on his pipes, an instrument only a satyr can properly employ. By means of these pipes the satyr can *charm, sleep,* or *cause fear* in all within a 6" hearing radius unless they save versus magic.

Only 1 satyr per band is likely to have pipes. If comely females are in the group the piping will be to charm, if the intruder is relatively inoffensive the piping will be to sleep (and choice items will be stolen from the sleeper), but if the party is powerful the piping will be to cause fear. Any creature which saves versus any form of piping is not affected by additional music from the same pipes.

Satyrs are very silent and have keen senses. They are surprised only on a 1, and they can blend with foliage so as to be 90% undetectable to creatures not able to see hidden or invisible things.

These creatures have their own tongue and are also able to speak elvish (understandable only to sylvan elves) and the common speech. Satyrs dwelling near centaurs are 80% likely to be friendly with the latter, cooperating with them and speaking their language.

Description: The skin of the upper body of a satyr is tan to light brown, its hair elsewhere being medium brown, reddish brown, or dark brown. Horns and hooves are black.

SCORPION, *Giant*

FREQUENCY: *Uncommon*
NO. APPEARING: *1-4*
ARMOR CLASS: *3*
MOVE: *15"*
HIT DICE: *5 + 5*
% IN LAIR: *50%*
TREASURE TYPE: *D*
NO. OF ATTACKS: *3*
DAMAGE/ATTACK: *1-10/1-10/1-4*
SPECIAL ATTACKS: *Poison sting*
SPECIAL DEFENSES: *Nil*
MAGIC RESISTANCE: *Standard*
INTELLIGENCE: *Non-*
ALIGNMENT: *Neutral*
SIZE: *M*
PSIONIC ABILITY: *Nil*
    Attack/Defense Modes: *Nil*

Giant scorpions are vicious predators which are likely to be found even in relatively cold places such as dungeons due to the adaptability of these mutations. They are likely to attack any creature which approaches. The monster seeks to grab prey with its huge pincers while its segmented tail lashes forward to sting its victim to death with poison. This latter attack inflicts 1-4 points of damage per hit and, if a poison saving throw fails, the victim dies immediately. The giant scorpion can fight up to 3 opponents at once. Note that the scorpion's poison kills it if it accidentally stings itself. Creatures killed are dragged to the scorpion's lair to be eaten.

SEA HAG

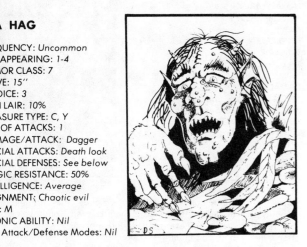

FREQUENCY: *Uncommon*
NO. APPEARING: *1-4*
ARMOR CLASS: *7*
MOVE: *15''*
HIT DICE: *3*
% IN LAIR: *10%*
TREASURE TYPE: *C, Y*
NO. OF ATTACKS: *1*
DAMAGE/ATTACK: *Dagger*
SPECIAL ATTACKS: *Death look*
SPECIAL DEFENSES: *See below*
MAGIC RESISTANCE: *50%*
INTELLIGENCE: *Average*
ALIGNMENT: *Chaotic evil*
SIZE: *M*
PSIONIC ABILITY: *Nil*
    Attack/Defense Modes: *Nil*

Sea hags inhabit thickly vegetated shallows in warm seas. A very rare variety dwells in fresh waters. They are reclusive and hate beauty, so their lairs are likely to be in very dismal, ugly places. The sea hag is so ghastly looking as to make a creature weak from *fright;* unless a saving throw versus magic is successful, the creature loses one-half of its strength for 1-6 turns. Worse still, the hag is able to cast a deadly glance up to 3'', and this look will kill any creature which fails its saving throw versus poison. A sea hag can employ this weapon but 3 times per day. Any victim of a sea hag is quickly devoured by the horrid victor.

SEA HORSE, *Giant*

FREQUENCY: *Common*
NO. APPEARING: *1-20*
ARMOR CLASS: *7*
MOVE: *21''*
HIT DICE: *2-4*
% IN LAIR: *0%*
TREASURE TYPE: *Nil*
NO. OF ATTACKS: *1*
DAMAGE/ATTACK: *1-4/2-5/2-8*
SPECIAL ATTACKS: *Nil*
SPECIAL DEFENSES: *Nil*
MAGIC RESISTANCE: *Standard*
INTELLIGENCE: *Semi-*
ALIGNMENT: *Neutral*
SIZE: *L*
PSIONIC ABILITY: *Nil*
    Attack/Defense Modes: *Nil*

Giant sea horses are herbivorous marine creatures found in all but the coldest of waters. They are naturally shy and avoid contact. They can, however, be trained to serve as steeds. In combat, the sea horse delivers a butt with its head. Size varies, the most common sort of sea horse being 2 hit dice; 30% are 3, and 10% are 4 hit dice in size. Occasionally aquatic elves and locathah will capture and train sea horses.

SEA LION

FREQUENCY: *Uncommon*
NO. APPEARING: *3-12*
ARMOR CLASS: *5/3*
MOVE: *18''*
HIT DICE: *6*
% IN LAIR: *20%*
TREASURE TYPE: *B*
NO. OF ATTACKS: *3*
DAMAGE/ATTACK: *1-6/1-6/2-12*
SPECIAL ATTACKS: *Nil*
SPECIAL DEFENSES: *Nil*
MAGIC RESISTANCE: *Standard*
INTELLIGENCE: *Semi-*
ALIGNMENT: *Neutral*
SIZE: *L*
PSIONIC ABILITY: *Nil*
    Attack/Defense Modes: *Nil*

Sea lions are fearsome carnivores which inhabit coastal marine waters. They hunt in packs and emit loud bellowing roars even underwater. Their maned heads are armor class 5, but their thick scales make the remainder of their body armor class 3. As they often drag prey to their lair, there is sometimes a residue of valuable items there. They attack with their clawed forelimbs and their jaws. Young sea lions can be tamed and trained for use in guarding and hunting.

SHADOW

FREQUENCY: *Rare*
NO. APPEARING: *2-20*
ARMOR CLASS: *7*
MOVE: *12''*
HIT DICE: *3 + 3*
% IN LAIR: *40%*
TREASURE TYPE: *F*
NO. OF ATTACKS: *1*
DAMAGE/ATTACK: *2-5*
SPECIAL ATTACKS: *Strength drain*
SPECIAL DEFENSES: *+1 or better*
    weapon to hit
MAGIC RESISTANCE: *See below*
INTELLIGENCE: *Low*
ALIGNMENT: *Chaotic evil*
SIZE: *M*
PSIONIC ABILITY: *Nil*
    Attack/Defense Modes: *Nil*

These horrible undead creatures are found amidst ancient ruins or deep beneath the ground. As they exist primarily on the negative material plane they drain strength by merely touching an opponent. They attack living things without hesitation in order to gain the life force of their prey. In addition to the 2-5 hit points of damage their chill touch causes, each hit also saps 1 point of the victim's strength. If a human opponent reaches 0 strength or hit points, the shadow drains his life force and he becomes a shadow. Note that strength returns to a creature 2-8 turns after being touched. Shadows are not affected by *sleep, charm* or *hold* spells. They are not subject to cold-based attacks. Shadows are 90% undetectable, as they appear to be nothing more than their name. If bright light is cast — such as from a *continual light* spell — they can be clearly seen.

SHAMBLING MOUND

FREQUENCY: *Rare*
NO. APPEARING: *1-3*
ARMOR CLASS: *0*
MOVE: *6''*
HIT DICE: *8-11*
% IN LAIR: *30%*
TREASURE TYPE: *B, T, X*
NO. OF ATTACKS: *2*
DAMAGE/ATTACK: *2-16/2-16*
SPECIAL ATTACKS: *Suffocation*
SPECIAL DEFENSES: *See below*
MAGIC RESISTANCE: *See below*
INTELLIGENCE: *Low*
ALIGNMENT: *Neutral*
SIZE: *L*
PSIONIC ABILITY: *Nil*
    Attack/Defense Modes: *Nil*

Shambling mounds, or "shamblers," are found in dismal marshes or certain wet subterranean places. They are omnivorous, feeding upon any living material (via their weird roots and tendrils). They attack fearlessly, clubbing with their limbs twice per melee round. If both of a shambler's clubbing attacks hit a single opponent, the victim is entangled and will be suffocated in the creature's slime in 2-8 melee rounds unless the creature is killed.

The brain of the shambler is located in its mid-portion, and its thick fibrous layers make it difficult to penetrate to its only vital area. In fact, most hits upon it do but little damage (thus armor class 0). As it is wet and slimy, fire has no effect, lightning causes it to grow (add 1 hit die), and cold does either one-half or no damage due to its vegetable constitution. All weapons score only one-half damage. It can flatten itself, so that crushing has small effect. Spells which affect plants are effective against shambling mounds, *plant control* and *charm plant* being good examples.

Description: Appearing as a heap of rotting vegetation, the shambler is actually an intelligent form of vegetable life. It is generally from 6' to 9' in height, with a girth of about 6' at its base and 2' at its summit.

SHARK

	Shark	Giant Shark (Megalodon)
FREQUENCY:	Common	Rare
NO. APPEARING:	3-12	1-3
ARMOR CLASS:	6	5
MOVE:	24''	18''
HIT DICE:	3-8	10-15
% IN LAIR:	0%	0%
TREASURE TYPE:	Nil	Nil
NO. OF ATTACKS:	1	1
DAMAGE/ATTACK:	2-5 or 2-8 or 3-12	4-16 or 5-20 or 6-24
SPECIAL ATTACKS:	Nil	See below
SPECIAL DEFENSES:	Nil	Nil
MAGIC RESISTANCE:	Standard	Standard
INTELLIGENCE:	Non-	Non-
ALIGNMENT:	Neutral	Neutral
SIZE:	M to L	L
PSIONIC ABILITY:	Nil	Nil
Attack/Defense Modes:	Nil	Nil

Sharks of all sorts roam the oceans and seas, constantly in motion and seeking food to satisfy their voracious appetites. The shark is a killing machine, attacking any recognizable food source at any time. Sharks are attracted by noise (pressure changes) from a mile or more, and they can smell blood from at least the same distance. Any creature which appears hurt is 90% likely to be attacked. A wounded creature will always be attacked, and this will cause all sharks nearby to go into a frenzy where they will attack any thing that remotely resembles food. They sieze prey, tearing off a mouthful if it is not bite-sized, and swim away to swallow it, only to return again for more. Sharks are particularly vulnerable to ramming attacks, such as dolphins deliver, for they rupture internal organs which allow the creatures to swim. Similarly, a motionless shark dies in 2-5 melee rounds.

Giant Shark (Megalodon): Giant white sharks and prehistoric species of sharks range in size from 20' to 50', the largest being the prehistoric sharks.

The only difference between these monsters and their smaller kin is the former's ability to swallow large objects whole — commensurate with the other factors which large size gives them. A creature swallowed whole has 6 melee rounds to free itself by attack. If it cuts its way out (reduces the shark to 0 hit points) within this time it will not be dead. Each attack from inside is at a cumulative -1 per round with regard to damage; thus attacks on the 1st round cause damage -1, those on the 2nd cause damage -2, etc.

SHEDU

FREQUENCY: *Rare*
NO. APPEARING: *2-8*
ARMOR CLASS: *4*
MOVE: *12''/24''*
HIT DICE: *9 + 9*
% IN LAIR: *25%*
TREASURE TYPE: *G*
NO. OF ATTACKS: *2*
DAMAGE/ATTACK: *1-6/1-6*
SPECIAL ATTACKS: *See below*
SPECIAL DEFENSES: *See below*
MAGIC RESISTANCE: *25%*
INTELLIGENCE: *Exceptional*
ALIGNMENT: *Lawful good*
SIZE: *L*
PSIONIC ABILITY: *70-100*
    Attack/Defense Modes: *All/all*

Shedu travel about the world seeking to further the ends of lawful good, helping allied creatures when in need. Although shedu can attack with their powerful front hooves, they are more likely to use their psionic abilities 3 major and 5 minior disciplines. All such abilities are performed at 9th level of mastery. Shedu can become ethereal at will, and they frequently travel the astral and ethereal planes. Shedu have their own language and know most human tongues; as they have a limited form of telephathy, shedu generally communicate by direct mind contact.

SHRIEKER

FREQUENCY: *Common*
NO. APPEARING: *2-8*
ARMOR CLASS: *7*
MOVE: *1''*
HIT DICE: *3*
% IN LAIR: *0%*
TREASURE TYPE: *Nil*
NO. OF ATTACKS: *0*
DAMAGE/ATTACK: *Nil*
SPECIAL ATTACKS: *Nil*
SPECIAL DEFENSES: *Noise*
MAGIC RESISTANCE: *Standard*
INTELLIGENCE: *Non-*
ALIGNMENT: *Neutral*
SIZE: *S to L*
PSIONIC ABILITY: *Nil*
    Attack/Defense Modes: *Nil*

Shriekers are normally quiet, mindless fungus which are ambulatory. They live in dark places beneath the ground. Light within 30' or movement within 10' will cause them to emit a piercing shriek which lasts for 1-3 melee rounds. This noise has a 50% chance of attracting wandering monsters each round thereafter. Purple worms and shambling mounds greatly prize shrieker as food.

SKELETON

FREQUENCY: *Rare*
NO. APPEARING: *3-30*
ARMOR CLASS: *7*
MOVE: *12''*
HIT DICE: *1*
% IN LAIR: *Nil*
TREASURE TYPE: *Nil*
NO. OF ATTACKS: *1*
DAMAGE/ATTACK: *1-6*

SPECIAL ATTACKS: *Nil*
SPECIAL DEFENSES: *See below*
MAGIC RESISTANCE: *See below*
INTELLIGENCE: *Non-*
ALIGNMENT: *Neutral*
SIZE: *M*
PSIONIC ABILITY: *Nil*
    Attack/Defense Modes: *Nil*

Skeletons are magically animated, undead monsters. They are enchanted by a powerful magic-user or cleric of evil alignment. The skeletons perform according to the command of their animator — the command being limited in scope to but a dozen or two words. They are found only in burial places or dungeons and similar forsaken places.

The skeleton strikes with some form of weapon, but regardless of the weapon type the damage caused by a hit will be 1-6 hit points.

Skeletons suffer only one-half damage from sharp and/or edged weapons (such as spears, daggers, swords). Blunt weapons such as clubs, maces, flails, etc. score normal damage. Fire scores normal damage. *Sleep, charm, hold* and *cold*-based spells do not affect skeletons. Holy water causes 2-8 hit points of damage on a skeleton for each vial which strikes it. Skeletons attack until destroyed.

SKUNK, *Giant*

FREQUENCY: *Uncommon*
NO. APPEARING: *1*
ARMOR CLASS: *7*
MOVE: *9"*
HIT DICE: *5*
% IN LAIR: *0%*
TREASURE TYPE: *Nil*
NO. OF ATTACKS: *1*
DAMAGE/ATTACK: *1-6*
SPECIAL ATTACKS: *Squirt musk*
SPECIAL DEFENSES: *Squirt musk*
MAGIC RESISTANCE: *Standard*
INTELLIGENCE: *Animal*
ALIGNMENT: *Neutral*
SIZE: *M*
PSIONIC ABILITY: *Nil*
    Attack/Defense Modes: *Nil*

Giant skunks are forest dwelling omnivores not adverse to raiding human camps for a bit of food. They will react to any serious threat by backing towards an opponent and if the other creature does not quickly get beyond 6", the skunk will loose a spray of vile musk quickly in a cloud 2" wide by 2" high by 6" long. If the opponent fails to save versus poison it will be blinded for 1-8 hours, and in any event the musk will cause the creature to retreat a full move and lose 50% of both strength and dexterity due to nausea for 2-8 turns. Furthermore, any creature touched by the skunk's musk will have a disgusting stench. Other creatures will shun it. All cloth material will rot and become useless, including magical garb which fails its saving throw. Creatures and non-cloth garments and equipment must be washed and aired for several days to be completely free of the stench.

SLITHERING TRACKER

FREQUENCY: *Rare*
NO. APPEARING: *1*
ARMOR CLASS: *5*
MOVE: *12"*
HIT DICE: *5*
% IN LAIR: *10%*
TREASURE TYPE: *C*
NO. OF ATTACKS: *0*
DAMAGE/ATTACK: *Nil*
SPECIAL ATTACKS: *Paralyzation*
SPECIAL DEFENSES: *Transparency*
MAGIC RESISTANCE: *Standard*
INTELLIGENCE: *Average*
ALIGNMENT: *Neutral*
SIZE: *S (2½' long)*
PSIONIC ABILITY: *Nil*
    Attack/Defense Modes: *Nil*

This monster is transparent and almost impossible to discover (5% chance of spotting). It inhabits dungeons and other dark places, and does not normally attack its prey immediately (10% chance of immediate attack). The tracker usually follows the chosen victim to the place where the victim sleeps, and only when its prey is asleep will it strike. Because of its semi-fluid body, the slithering tracker can flow through openings as small as a rat hole or a large crack under a door. Attack is by contact with the exposed flesh of its prey, and the secretions of the monster will paralyze the victim unless a saving throw versus paralyzation is made. Once the victim is immobilized the 'tracker will draw all the plasma from the body of its prey in 6 turns.

SLUG, *Giant*

FREQUENCY: *Uncommon*
NO. APPEARING: *1*
ARMOR CLASS: *8*
MOVE: *6"*
HIT DICE: *12*
% IN LAIR: *0%*
TREASURE TYPE: *Nil*
NO. OF ATTACKS: *1*
DAMAGE/ATTACK: *1-12*
SPECIAL ATTACKS: *Spit acid*
SPECIAL DEFENSES: *See below*
MAGIC RESISTANCE: *Standard*
INTELLIGENCE: *Non-*
ALIGNMENT: *Neutral*
SIZE: *L*
PSIONIC ABILITY: *Nil*
    Attack/Defense Modes: *Nil*

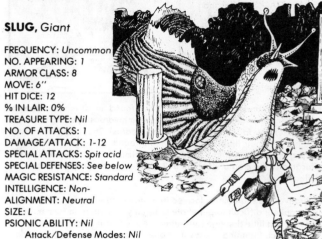

Giant slugs dwell away from light, preferring the depths of dungeons and similar places. Giant slugs are able to eat substances like wood or burrow through very hard earth using their rasp-like tongues. Although they are a great bulk, giant slugs are able to squeeze through very narrow or low openings, for they have no bones to prohibit such alteration of shape. Although able to bite with effect, the major weapon of these creatures is a highly corrosive acid saliva which they are able to spit with considerable accuracy at great distances. Normal range is 6", with a basic 50% chance of striking their target. For every 1" the range is lessened the base chance of hitting is increased 10%; ranges over 6" decrease the probability of hitting by 10%. Fortunately, the giant slug is always inaccurate on its first attack, and there is only a 10% chance of its hitting its target on the first spitting of acid; once the range is then determined, second and following attacks are at normal probabilities. As they are of great size, these creatures can sometimes be caught in a narrow corridor where they are unable to turn, and if they are then attacked from behind they can often be slain without loss to the attackers. Because of their size and structure, these beasts are not affected by blunt weapons, so they must be attacked by sharp-edged ones or magically. They have thick, rubbery hide, and their tremendous power allows them to break down doors with ease.

Description: Giant slugs are pale gray. Their underbelly is dead white.

SNAKE, *Giant*

	Amphisbaena	Constrictor	Poisonous	Sea	Spitting
FREQUENCY:	Very rare	Uncommon	Uncommon	Uncommon	Rare
NO. APPEARING:	1-3	1-2	1-6	1-8	1-4
ARMOR CLASS:	3	5	5	5	5
MOVE:	12"	9"	15"	12"	12"
HIT DICE:	6	6 + 1	4 + 2	8-10	4 + 2
% IN LAIR:	0%	0%	0%	0%	0%
TREASURE TYPE:	Nil	Nil	Nil	Nil	Nil
NO. OF ATTACKS:	2	2	1	2	1
DAMAGE/ATTACK:	1-3/1-3	1-4/2-8	1-3	1-6/3-18	1-3
SPECIAL ATTACKS:	Poison	Constriction	Poison	Constriction	See below
SPECIAL DEFENSES:	See below	Nil	Nil	Nil	Nil
MAGIC RESISTANCE:	Standard	Standard	Standard	Standard	Standard
INTELLIGENCE:	Animal	Animal	Animal	Animal	Animal
ALIGNMENT:	Neutral	Neutral	Neutral	Neutral	Neutral
SIZE:	M	L	L	L	M
PSIONIC ABILITY:	Nil	Nil	Nil	Nil	Nil
Attack/Defense Modes:	Nil	Nil	Nil	Nil	Nil

Giant snakes are likely to be found in any clime save the coldest. All are carnivorous.

Amphisbaena: These monsters have heads at both ends, and both heads are armed with poisonous fangs. The creature travels by grasping one of its necks and rolling like a hoop. It is able to attack with both heads, and victims failing to save versus poison when bitten die instantly. Cold-based attacks do not harm the amphisbaena.

Constrictor: These snakes usually drop coils from above, grab prey within their coils, deliver a bite, and then constrict causing 2-8 points of damage per melee round. If several strong creatures (such as 4 humans of 16 or greater strength) can grasp the creature at head and tail ends, they can uncoil it in 2-5 melee rounds. After eating, the snake sleeps for a period of several days.

Poisonous: Giant poisonous snakes need no lengthy explanation or description. Some varieties, however, are worth noting, as their poison is so strong that even if a saving throw is made the victim takes up to 3-18 hit points damage.

Sea: Found only in tropical waters, these marine creatures attack only when hungry (20% chance). They otherwise ignore other creatures unless molested. Sea snakes have a poisonous bite. The largest are able to coil about small vessels and crush them at a rate of 10% of total value per melee round of constriction.

Spitting: The spitting giant snake is a variety of the poisonous type which can emit a poisonous spittle, spraying it up to 3″ at any single creature. The victim must save versus poison. Naturally, the bite of these snakes is likewise poisonous. Giant spitting cobras are a typical example of the monster.

SPECTRE

FREQUENCY: *Rare*
NO. APPEARING: *1-6*
ARMOR CLASS: *2*
MOVE: *15″/30″*
HIT DICE: *7 + 3*
% IN LAIR: *20%*
TREASURE TYPE: *Q (× 3), X, Y*
NO. OF ATTACKS: *1*
DAMAGE/ATTACK: *1-8*
SPECIAL ATTACKS: *Energy drain*
SPECIAL DEFENSES: *+ 1 or better weapon to hit*
MAGIC RESISTANCE: *See below*
INTELLIGENCE: *High*
ALIGNMENT: *Lawful evil*
SIZE: *M*
PSIONIC ABILITY: *Nil*
Attack/Defense Modes: *Nil*

Spectres are very powerful undead humans whose primary existence is on the negative material plane. Spectres haunt the most desolate of places, tombs, and dungeons. They hate sunlight and living things. Daylight makes them powerless. Life makes them lament their unlife.

A spectre's chilling touch causes 1-8 hit points of damage and drains 2 life energy levels from an opponent, the latter due to the negative force of the spectre. Thus, an 11th level character, or an 11 hit dice creature, struck by a spectre would suffer 1-8 hit points of damage plus loss in level ability, hit dice, etc. Such loss is permanent, but characters can regain lost levels through continued acquisition of experience points, of course. Certain magic might restore lost levels as well.

Spectres are not affected by *sleep, charm, hold,* or *cold*-based spells. Poison or paralyzation do not harm spectres. Holy water causes a spectre to suffer 2-8 hit points of damage for every vial-full which hits it. A *raise dead* spell will destroy a spectre unless it makes its saving throw versus magic. Any human totally drained of life energy by a spectre becomes a half-strength spectre under the control of the spectre which drained him.

SPHINX

	Andro-	Crio-	Gyno-	Hieraco-
FREQUENCY:	*Very rare*	*Rare*	*Rare*	*Rare*
NO. APPEARING:	*1*	*1-4*	*1*	*1-6*
ARMOR CLASS:	*-2*	*0*	*-1*	*1*
MOVE:	*18″/30″*	*12″/24″*	*15″/24″*	*9″/36″*
HIT DICE:	*12*	*10*	*8*	*9*
% IN LAIR:	*60%*	*30%*	*15%*	*20%*
TREASURE TYPE:	*U*	*F*	*R, X*	*E*
NO. OF ATTACKS:	*2*	*3*	*2*	*3*
DAMAGE/ATTACK:	*2-12/2-12*	*2-8/2-8/3-18*	*2-8/2-8*	*2-8/2-8/1-10*
SPECIAL ATTACKS:	*See below*	*Nil*	*See below*	*Nil*
SPECIAL DEFENSES:	*Nil*	*Nil*	*Nil*	*Nil*
MAGIC RESISTANCE:	*Standard*	*Standard*	*Standard*	*Standard*
INTELLIGENCE:	*Exceptional*	*Average*	*Genius*	*Low*
ALIGNMENT:	*Chaotic good*	*Neutral*	*Neutral*	*Chaotic evil*
SIZE:	*L (8′ tall)*	*L (7½′ tall)*	*L (7′ tall)*	*L (7′ tall)*
PSIONIC ABILITY:	*Nil*	*Nil*	*Nil*	*Nil*
Attack/Defense Modes:	*Nil*	*Nil*	*Nil*	*Nil*

Sphinxes inhabit only warm climes. They are dissimilar with regard to species characteristics.

Andro-: The male, or andro-, sphinx is a very powerful and large creature. An androsphinx attacks with its two great paws in melee. It has the ability to use clerical spells as if it were a 6th level human cleric. They usually shun the company of gynosphinxes, for they resent the females' greater intelligence and neutral alignment. These creatures can speak all languages particular to sphinxes and the common tongue of mankind as well.

Thrice per day an androsphinx can emit a deafening roar which can be heard for several miles. The creature must be aroused and angry to utter the first, very angry to roar again, and infuriated to cut loose with the third. The first roar of an androsphinx causes all creatures within 36″ to save versus *fear* (as a wand) or flee in panic for 3 turns. The second roar is louder still, creatures within 20″ must save versus petrification or be *paralyzed* with fright for 1-4 melee rounds; and, in addition, creatures within 3″ of the androsphinx will be deafened for 2-12 melee rounds unless they are ogre-sized or larger (or have protected hearing organs). The third roar causes creatures within 24″ to save versus magic or lose 2-8 points of strength for a like number of melee rounds; and, in addition, any creature within a 3″ hemisphere of the androsphinx's mouth will be knocked over unless the creature is ogre-sized or larger. Creatures knocked over must save versus dragon breath or be *stunned* for 2-12 melee rounds. Creatures not knocked over will take 2-16 hit points of damage (unless they are lion or part lion). The force of the third roar will also affect stone within 3″, cracking it unless a saving throw versus petrification is made.

Crio-: The criosphinx is a ram-headed creature which is likely to be found in wooded areas. These creatures prize wealth and will usually seek to extort passersby — safe passage for a hefty bribe. In combat they attack with either their two forepaws or a great butt with their horned head. The criosphinx lusts after gynosphinxes, but the latter find them detestable. They speak their own tongue, that of andro/gynosphinxes, and can also speak with animals.

Gyno-: The gynosphinx is the female counterpart of the androsphinx. They are both knowledgeable and wise. As they are neutral, and prize gems and similar wealth, they will only help humans if they are paid — although they will sometimes accept payment in the form of riddles, poetry, prose, knowledge, or the location of an androsphinx. If payment is not made, the sphinx will not hesitate to devour the offender(s). A gynosphinx is able to use the following spells once per day: *detect magic, read magic, read languages, detect invisible, locate object, dispel magic, clairaudience, clairvoyance, remove curse, legend lore*. They can use each of the *symbols* once per week each. Gynosphinxes speak all the languages known to the males of their kind.

Hieraco-: The hawk-headed, or hieracosphinx, is evil and rapacious. They are found in hilly regions. They prey on warm blooded creatures by preference, humans being high on the list of favorite meals. They attack with forepaws and beak each melee round. Like other types of their race, they highly value treasure. It is not unknown for hieracosphinxes to serve as steeds for certain evil and powerful creatures.

SPIDER

	Giant	Huge	Large	Phase	Water, Giant
FREQUENCY:	Uncommon	Common	Common	Rare	Common
NO. APPEARING:	1-8	1-12	2-20	1-4	1-10
ARMOR CLASS:	4	6	8	7	5
MOVE:	3''*12''	18''	6''*15''	6''*15''	15''
HIT DICE:	4 + 4	2 + 2	1 + 1	5 + 5	3 + 3
% IN LAIR:	70%	50%	60%	75%	90%
TREASURE TYPE:	C	J-N, Q	J-N	E	J-N, Q
NO. OF ATTACKS:	1	1	1	1	1
DAMAGE/ATTACK:	2-8	1-6	1	1-6	1-4
SPECIAL ATTACKS:	See below	See below	Poison	See below	Poison
SPECIAL DEFENSES:	Nil	Nil	Nil	See below	Nil
MAGIC RESISTANCE:	Standard	Standard	Standard	Standard	Standard
INTELLIGENCE:	Low	Animal	Non-	Low	Semi-
ALIGNMENT:	Chaotic evil	Neutral	Neutral	Neutral	Neutral
SIZE:	L	M	S	L	M
PSIONIC ABILITY:	Nil	Nil	Nil	Nil	Nil
Attack/Defense Modes:	Nil	Nil	Nil	Nil	Nil

Spiders are found in all regions except those which are frigid, and legends tell of giant, fur-clad, white spiders inhabiting polar climes. All spiders are aggressive predators. Even if not hungry, they will attack creatures which disturb their web. They dwell both above and below ground.

Giant Spider: These monsters are web builders. They will construct their sticky traps horizontally or vertically so as to entrap any creature which touches the web. Some will lurk above a path in order to drop upon prey. The web is as tough and clinging as a web spell. Any creature with 18 or greater strength can break free in 1 melee round, a 17 strength requires 2 melee rounds, etc. Webs are quite inflammable. The bite of a giant spider is poisonous. A victim must save versus poison or be killed. A giant spider will flee from an encounter with a superior foe, typically hiding in some secret spot for safety.

Huge Spider: The typical huge spider is not a web builder but a roving hunter such as a wolf spider. It can leap 3'' upon prey and deliver its deadly bite. Others of this ilk build carefully hidden places of concealment and rush forth upon prey, i.e. trapdoor spiders of huge size. All saving throws versus the poison of huge spiders are at +1 on the dice. Note that these creatures surprise prey on a roll of 1-5 (out of 6).

Large Spider: These creatures scuttle and scurry about — on walls, ceilings, and floors, in and out of their webs, always searching for victims. They are 90% likely to attack any creature within 3''. Their poison is relatively weak in most cases, so saving throws are at +2.

Phase-Spider: Although these monsters appear to be nothing more than very great spiders, they are something quite beyond this. When attacking or being attacked the phase spider is able to shift out of phase with its surroundings, bringing itself back only when it is ready to deliver its poisonous bite. Victims must save at -2 on their poison saving throw. When out of phase they are impervious to nearly all forms of attack, although a *phase door* spell will cause one to remain in phase for 7 melee rounds. Oil of etherealness and armor of etherealness also put their wearers into the same phase as this monster when it shifts out of phase. Their webs are equal to those of giant spiders. Phase spiders will seek to evade encounters which are unfavorable.

Water, Giant, Spider: Fresh water dwellers, giant water spiders are found only in large lakes. They build great nests of air amidst underwater vegetation. These spiders are able to run along the bottom or up and down vegetable or mineral surfaces underwater. They snatch passing prey, deliver a poisonous bite, and bring the victim to their lair to be drained at leisure. The clever airlock allows free passage without loss of vital air. On occasion such water creatures as nixies will be on friendly terms with giant water spiders, for they are semi-intelligent and can be approached with offerings of food. Abandoned water spider lairs are excellent places of refuge for air-breathers.

A rare species of water spiders, twice the size of those discussed here, are found in salt water.

SPRITE

FREQUENCY: *Rare*
NO. APPEARING: *10-100*
ARMOR CLASS: *6*
MOVE: *9''/18''*
HIT DICE: *1*
% IN LAIR: *20%*
TREASURE TYPE: *C*
NO. OF ATTACKS: *1*
DAMAGE/ATTACK: *By weapon type*
SPECIAL ATTACKS: *See below*
SPECIAL DEFENSES: *See below*
MAGIC RESISTANCE: *Standard*
INTELLIGENCE: *Very*
ALIGNMENT: *Neutral (good)*
SIZE: *S (2' tall)*
PSIONIC ABILITY: *Nil*
    Attack/Defence Modes: *Nil*

Sprites dwell in meadows and wooded glens. They are very shy and reclusive, but they hate evil and ugliness of all sorts. They are armed with slim swords (equal to daggers) and small bows with but half the range and effect of a short bow. However, their arrows are coated with a special ointment which causes any creature struck to save versus poison or *sleep* for 1-6 hours in a comatose state. The sprites will then slay evil creatures or remove good ones to a place far from where they encountered the sprites. Note that sprites are 75% likely to be unnoticed by any creature, and they will attack only evil creatures unless molested first.

Sprites are able to *become invisible* at will, *detect good/evil* at a 5'' range, and move silently. When invisible they cause opponents to strike with a -4 on ''to hit'' dice.

Sprites speak their own language and the common tongue.

SQUID, *Giant*

FREQUENCY: *Rare*
NO. APPEARING: *1*
ARMOR CLASS: *7/3*
MOVE: *3''//18''*
HIT DICE: *12*
% IN LAIR: *40%*
TREASURE TYPE: *A*
NO. OF ATTACKS: *9*
DAMAGE/ATTACK: *1-6 (× 8)/5-20*
SPECIAL ATTACKS: *Constriction*
SPECIAL DEFENSES: *See below*
MAGIC RESISTANCE: *Standard*
INTELLIGENCE: *Non-*
ALIGNMENT: *Neutral*
SIZE: *L*
PSIONIC ABILITY: *Nil*
    Attack/Defence Modes: *Nil*

Giant squid inhabit deep waters, preferring depths of one-half mile or more. They are aggressive hunters, and they will occasionally surface to attack large prey — 10% chance to attack a ship passing over a giant squid. They fear only the hugest of sperm whales, for the latter hunt giant squids and kill them with ease.

A giant squid's body is protected by a hard shell, so its armor class is 3, but its tentacles and head are but armor class 7. The creature can jet backwards at great speed if it feels threatened.

When a giant squid attacks it will anchor itself — or stabilize itself — with two of its arms and attack with the other 8. Each tentacle does 1-6 hit points on the first melee round it hits, and thereafter it constricts the opponent for 2-12 points of damage per melee round. To prevent this the victim must sever the tentacle; there is no way to loosen its grasp short of severing the member or killing the squid. The great beak of a giant squid bites for 5-20 hit points of damage.

A creature grabbed by a giant squid is 25% likely to have both upper members pinned, 50% likely to have one pinned, and 25% likely to have both free. If both upper members are pinned, the victim is totally unable to attack with them, if one is held the victim will attack at -3, and if both

upper members are free the squid's opponent attacks at only -1 on ''to hit'' dice rolls. Only one tentacle will strike creatures of man-size at any one time. A squid's tentacle takes 10 hit points before being severed, and this is in addition to the 12 dice of damage a giant squid can take.

If 4 or more of a giant squid's arms are severed (or otherwise lost) the monster is 80% likely to squirt out a cloud of black ink 6'' high by 8'' long, and jet backwards to escape. The squid will always go to its lair in this case. The ink cloud completely obscures the vision of all within it.

The giant squid always seeks to drag its prey under water. A ship seized by a giant squid will not likely be dragged under, unless the vessel is small, but it will stop dead in the water in 1 turn due to the drag. If a ship is grabbed and held by 8 or more tentacles, it will take damage as if rammed, and ships with water in their holds are easily dragged down to squids' lairs.

STAG

	Stag	Stag, Giant
FREQUENCY:	Common	Rare
NO. APPEARING:	1-4	1-2
ARMOR CLASS:	7	7
MOVE:	24''	21''
HIT DICE:	3	5
% IN LAIR:	0%	0%
TREASURE TYPE:	Nil	Nil
NO. OF ATTACKS:	1 or 2	1 or 2
DAMAGE/ATTACK:	2-8 or 1-3/1-3	4-16 or 1-4/1-4
SPECIAL ATTACKS:	Nil	Nil
SPECIAL DEFENSES:	Nil	Nil
MAGIC RESISTANCE:	Standard	Standard
INTELLIGENCE:	Animal	Animal
ALIGNMENT:	Neutral	Neutral
SIZE:	L	L
PSIONIC ABILITY:	Nil	Nil
Attack/Defense Modes:	Nil	Nil

Stags are herbivores found in temperate forests and meadowlands. They are the aggressive males of a herd which numbers 4-8 times the number of stags encountered. These creatures will defend the herd against all but the most fearsome opponents. A stag can attack with its branching antlers or by lashing out with its sharp forehooves.

Giant Stag: These creatures are simply very large stags. They otherwise conform to the general characteristics of stags. A typical giant stag is 7' tall at the shoulder and weighs over 1,500 pounds.

STIRGE

FREQUENCY: *Uncommon*
NO. APPEARING: *3-30*
ARMOR CLASS: *8*
MOVE: *3''/18''*
HIT DICE: *1 + 1*
% IN LAIR: *60%*
TREASURE TYPE: *D*
NO. OF ATTACKS: *1*
DAMAGE/ATTACK: *1-3*
SPECIAL ATTACKS: *Drain blood*
SPECIAL DEFENSES: *Nil*
MAGIC RESISTANCE: *Standard*
INTELLIGENCE: *Animal*
ALIGNMENT: *Neutral*
SIZE: *S*
PSIONIC ABILITY: *Nil*
    Attack/Defense Modes: *Nil*

Stirges are found only in very dark, tangled forests or in subterranean lairs. They lay in wait for warm-blooded creatures, swoop down, and when their long, sharp proboscis is attached, the blood of the victim is drawn through to be eaten.

Stirges attack as if they were creatures with 4 hit dice rather than 1 + 1. The snakey proboscis of a stirge inflicts 1-3 hit points of damage when it hits. Each melee round after striking, until it has drained 12 hit points value in blood, the stirge drains blood equal to 1-4 hit points. Bloated with blood, a stirge draining 12 hit points worth will flap off to digest its repast. The only method to detach a stirge from its prey is to kill it.

Description: The feathers of a stirge are rusty red to red brown. Its eyes and feet are yellowish. The dangling proboscis of a stirge is pink at the tip, fading to gray at the base.

STRANGLE WEED

FREQUENCY: *Common*
NO. APPEARING: *3-12*
ARMOR CLASS: *6*
MOVE: *Nil*
HIT DICE: *2-4*
% IN LAIR: *100%*
TREASURE TYPE: *J-N, Q, C*
    (magic only)
NO. OF ATTACKS: *1*
DAMAGE/ATTACK: *See below*
SPECIAL ATTACKS: *See below*
SPECIAL DEFENSES: *Nil*
MAGIC RESISTANCE: *Standard*
INTELLIGENCE: *Animal*
ALIGNMENT: *Neutral*
SIZE: *S*
PSIONIC ABILITY: *Nil*
    Attack/Defense Modes: *Nil*

Strangle weed is an intelligent kelp found in relatively warm sea water. A bed of this carnivorous plant is indistinguishable from normal seaweed. The plant grows in an oval with 3-12 fronds in a patch of 3-12 square feet. The fronds vary from 7′ to 12′ long, and any creature within grasp of 1 or more fronds will be attacked. A hit by the strangle weed indicates the victim is entwined by the attacking frond. Each frond has a strength of 4-16 points. A victim compares its strength against the frond or fronds which have entwined it. The difference in the victim's favor is its chance of escaping, i.e., 1 equals 10%, 2 is 20%, etc. A negative difference, a balance in favor of the weed, indicates the victim has taken that number of points of crushing damage, i.e. a victim's strength of 18 compared to the 3 fronds holding it, 30, so the strangle weeds inflict 12 points of damage on their prey. Any creature entwined strikes at -2 on its "to hit" rolls. Treasure is found beneath the sand of the bed of the strangle weed — left by former victims.

SU-MONSTER

FREUENCY: *Uncommon*
NO. APPEARING: *1-12*
ARMOR CLASS: *6*
MOVE: *9″*
HIT DICE: *5 + 5*
% IN LAIR: *30%*
TREASURE TYPE: *C, Y*
NO. OF ATTACKS: *5*
DAMAGE/ATTACK: *1-4 (× 4)/2-8*
SPECIAL ATTACKS: *See below*
SPECIAL DEFENSES: *Nil*
MAGIC RESISTANCE: *Standard*
INTELLIGENCE: *Average*
ALIGNMENT: *Chaotic*
SIZE: *M*
PSIONIC ABILITY: *120*
    Attack/Defense Modes: *See below*

Su-monsters inhabit forsaken wilderness areas and subterranean lairs as well. They have prehensile tails which they use to swing from limb to limb or to hang upside down. From such a position they can attack with all four of their clawed feet as well as their jaws. All four feet are prehensile and armed with long and extremely sharp nails as well. Su-monsters are at home upright or hanging upside down — the latter being one of their favorite methods of lurking for prey. If more than 4 are encountered it is likely (50%) that the group will be a male, female, and young (determine growth state by rolling a 20-sided die for maturity, using 10% increment, and treating 10% as 20% and 100% as 30%). The female will fight at double value for six turns if the young are attacked, and the male will fight at double value for four turns if the female is attacked. Su-monsters have a latent psionic ability which enables them to deliver some form of psionic

attack once per day if psionic activity is being used within 12″ of them. Determine attack form by rolling a 6-sided die: 1-2 = *psychic crush,* 2-4 = *psionic blast,* 5-6 = *mind thrust.* Psionic defense is not necessary as the su-monster is not itself subject to psionic attack.

Description: The fur of a su-monster is dirty gray. The creature's tail and face are black, its paws are bloody red.

SYLPH

FREQUENCY: *Very rare*
NO. APPEARING: *1*
ARMOR CLASS: *9*
MOVE: *12″/36″*
HIT DICE: *3*
% IN LAIR: *10%*
TREASURE TYPE: *Q (× 10), X*
NO. OF ATTACKS: *0*
DAMAGE/ATTACK: *Nil*
SPECIAL ATTACKS: *See below*
SPECIAL DEFENSES: *See below*
MAGIC RESISTANCE: *50%*
INTELLIGENCE: *Exceptional*
ALIGNMENT: *Neutral (good)*
SIZE: *M*
PSIONIC ABILITY: *Nil*
    Attack/Defense Modes: *Nil*

Sylphs are very beautiful creatures similar to nymphs. The sylphs, however, dwell primarily in aerial places. They are fond of flitting about, and it is not likely that they will be encountered near the place where they dwell.

Sylphs sometimes (20%) befriend creatures of good alignment, aiding them in some way. A sylph has magical ability of 7th level (4 —1st level spells, 3 — 2nd, 2 — 3rd, and 1 —4th once per day) in addition to the abilities of *invisibility* at will and *conjuring* an *air elemental* once per week.

Sylphs speak their own and the common tongue.

THOUGHT EATER — TICK, GIANT — TIGER — TITAN — TITANOTHERE — TOAD, GIANT — TRAPPER — TREANT — TRITON — TROGLODYTE — TROLL — TURTLE, GIANT

THOUGHT EATER

FREQUENCY: *Rare*
NO. APPEARING: *1-3*
ARMOR CLASS: 9
MOVE: 6''
HIT DICE: 3
% IN LAIR: 0%
TREASURE TYPE: *Nil*
NO. OF ATTACKS: 0
DAMAGE/ATTACK: *Nil*
SPECIAL ATTACKS: *See below*
SPECIAL DEFENSES: *See below*
MAGIC RESISTANCE: *See below*
INTELLIGENCE: *Non-*
ALIGNMENT: *Neutral*
SIZE: *S*
PSIONIC ABILITY: *Nil*
    Attack/Defense Modes: *Nil*

Thought eaters are dwellers in the ether. Their senses, however, extend into the physical plane, and any psionic or psionic-related energy use in either area will attract their attention (range of ability or magic equals attraction range). The thought eater appears to be something like a sickly gray, skeletal-bodied, enormous headed platypus to those who are able to observe it. Its webbed paws allow it to swim through the ether. It can be attacked only by ethereal creatures. Its only desire is to feed on the mental energy of prey it is attracted to, and if it comes within 6'' of any creature in the ethereal or physical planes it will be able to absorb any psionic or spell energy they attempt to use; at a range of 1'' the thought eater is able to begin feeding on the actual thoughts of even non-psionic creatures. Each thought eater is able to consume from 101-200 psionic energy points before becoming sated. Convert magical energy to psionic points on a basis of 5 points per spell level, and actual thought consumption converts to 1 intelligence point equalling 10 psionic energy points. Note that if it feeds on thoughts the creature loses intelligence permanently. At intelligence 0 the creature is dead, 1 equals mindlessness, 2 idiocy, 3 imbecility, and an intelligence of 4 is equivalent to a low-grade moron. Mental defenses, including a *mind blank* spell, and magical devices against psionic and psionic related powers thwart attacks of these horrid things.

TICK, *Giant*

FREQUENCY: *Rare*
NO. APPEARING: *3-12*
ARMOR CLASS: 3
MOVE: 3''
HIT DICE: 2-4
% IN LAIR: 0%
TREASURE TYPE: *Nil*
NO. OF ATTACKS: 1
DAMAGE/ATTACK: 1-4
SPECIAL ATTACKS: *Blood drain*
SPECIAL DEFENSES: *Nil*
MAGIC RESISTANCE: *Standard*
INTELLIGENCE: *Non-*
ALIGNMENT: *Neutral*
SIZE: *S*
PSIONIC ABILITY: *Nil*
    Attack/Defense Modes: *Nil*

Giant ticks are found in forests and occasionally in caves or caverns as well. These insects seek to drop upon prey, insert their hollow mouthtube, and suck blood from the victim. A hit by a giant tick scores 1-4 points of damage and indicates the monster has attached itself. Each melee round thereafter it will drain 1-6 hit points of blood, until reaching satiation at a blood drain equal to its hit points, when it drops off. A giant tick must be killed, severely burned, or immersed in water to detach it prior to satiation. Any creature bitten has a 50% chance of contacting a fatal disease from the tick. The disease will be fatal in 2-8 days unless a *cure disease* spell is cast upon the victim.

TIGER

	Tiger	Sabre-Tooth (Smilodon)
FREQUENCY:	Uncommon	Rare
NO. APPEARING:	1-4	1-2
ARMOR CLASS:	6	6
MOVE:	12''	12''
HIT DICE:	5 + 5	7 + 2
% IN LAIR:	5%	10%
TREASURE TYPE:	Nil	Nil
NO. OF ATTACKS:	3	3
DAMAGE/ATTACK:	2-5/2-5/1-10	2-5/2-5/2-12
SPECIAL ATTACKS:	Rear claws for 2-8/2-8	Rear claws for 2-8/2-8
SPECIAL DEFENSES:	Surprised only on a 1	Surprised only on a 1
MAGIC RESISTANCE:	Standard	Standard
INTELLIGENCE:	Semi-	Animal
ALIGNMENT:	Neutral	Neutral
SIZE:	L	L
PSIONIC ABILITY:	Nil	Nil
Attack/Defense Modes:	Nil	Nil

Tigers range from subarctic to tropical areas, for they are highly adaptable and superb hunters. They often hunt in pairs or family groups. They climb well, and can leap 10' upwards and 30' to 50' ahead in attack. If encountered in their lair there is a 25% chance that there will be 1-3 cubs there, these young having no effective attacks, and are from 30% to 60% mature. When they score 2 forepaw hits in one melee round, tigers also get 2 additional rear claw attacks each at 2-8 hit points damage that round.

Sabre-Tooth Tiger: The most aggressive and fearsome predator of the Pleistocene epoch, these giants are seldom encountered elsewhere. They range only in warm regions but otherwise conform to the characteristics of normal tigers. Their six inch long fangs inflict terrible wounds, and the size of these teeth, along with the power of the sabre-tooth tiger's jaws, give the creature a +2 on "to hit" dice.

TITAN

FREQUENCY: *Very rare*
NO. APPEARING: *1-2 (10%)*
ARMOR CLASS: *2 to -3*
MOVE: *21'' or 15''*
HIT DICE: *17-22*
% IN LAIR: *10%*
TREASURE TYPE: *E, Q (× 10), R*
NO. OF ATTACKS: *1*
DAMAGE/ATTACK: *7-42/8-48*
SPECIAL ATTACKS: *See below*
SPECIAL DEFENSES: *See below*
MAGIC RESISTANCE: *60%*
INTELLIGENCE: *Genius to*
    supra-genius
ALIGNMENT: *Chaotic good*
SIZE: *L (18'+ tall)*
PSIONIC ABILITY: *101 to 200*
    Attack/Defense Modes: *B, C, D, E/Special*

Titans normally dwell on a plane somewhere above the material, but occasionally they will visit the latter plane for various periods of time. Those dwelling on the Prime Material Plane for an extended period will acquire treasure as indicated above.

To determine the armor class and hit dice of any given titan simply roll a 6-sided die: 1 = armor class 2 and 17 hit dice; 2 = 1 and 18; 3 = 0 and 19; 4 = -1 and 20; 5 = -2 and 21; and 6 = -3 and 22. Titans with only 17 or 18 hit dice move at 21''. Those with 21 or 22 hit dice do 8-48 hit points of damage/attack.

Titans can become *invisible* at will. They can also *levitate* and/or *become* ethereal twice per day. All titans are able to employ both magic-user and clerical spells of 4th, 5th, 6th or even 7th level. To determine how many levels of spell use in each category a given titan possesses, simply roll a 4-sided die and add the result to 3. For each level of spell use, the titan can use 2 spells of each category, so the minimum number of magic spells possible for any titan is 8, and the same applies to clerical spells — 2 of 1st level, 2 of 2nd level, 2 of 3rd level, and 2 of 4th level. (If specific titans are not prepared, simply determine which spells are known by any given titan at the time of encounter by random selection from the spell tables.) The protection from evil spell of titans is of twice normal strength with respect to lawful evil beings.

All titans possess 8 or more psionic abilities of the type possible for clerics. Roll two 6-sided dice and add the resulting number to a base of 6 to determine the total number of abilities. (Ignore the ability of levitation.) To determine psionic strength add the score rolled on percentile dice to a base of 100. They use all abilities at seventh mastery level. Psionic attacks have no affect on titans.

In addition to their own language, titans are able to speak the six dialects of the races of giants. All titans are also conversant in the common tongue as well as that of chaotic good.

Because of their particular predisposition, titans deal with storm giants on highly amicable terms. It is 20% probable that a storm giant will be with any single titan encountered.

Description: Titans appear very much as humans do, but they are all very muscular, handsome, and wear no facial hair. Their dress and armor appears Grecian.

TITANOTHERE

FREQUENCY: Uncommon
NO. APPEARING: 1-12
ARMOR CLASS: 6
MOVE: 12''
HIT DICE: 12
% IN LAIR: Nil
TREASURE TYPE: Nil
NO. OF ATTACKS: 1
DAMAGE/ATTACK: 2-16
SPECIAL ATTACKS: Charge & trample
SPECIAL DEFENSES: Nil
MAGIC RESISTANCE: Standard
INTELLIGENCE: Animal
ALIGNMENT: Neutral
SIZE: L (8')
PSIONIC ABILITY: Nil
    Attack/Defense Modes: Nil

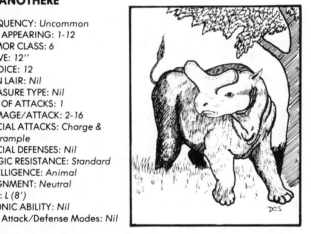

These huge and fearless plant-eaters roam the temperate plains of the Pleistocene era in herds. If more than 6 are encountered 1-4 of those numbering over one-half the possible total will be young, from 10% to 80% grown.

If any creature threatens the herd, the largest animals (males) will charge. If the charge strikes home, damage inflicted is double the amount shown on the dice (4-32). Titanotheres will trample (2-12 per foot) any opponent low enough for them to step upon.

TOAD, Giant

	Giant Toad	Ice Toad	Poisonous Toad
FREQUENCY:	Common	Rare	Uncommon
NO. APPEARING:	1-12	1-4	1-8
ARMOR CLASS:	6	4	7
MOVE:	6'' + 6'' hop	9''	6'' + 6'' hop
HIT DICE:	2 + 4	5	2
% IN LAIR:	0%	40%	0%
TREASURE TYPE:	Nil	C	Nil
NO. OF ATTACKS:	1	1	1
DAMAGE/ATTACK:	2-8	3-12	2-5
SPECIAL ATTACKS:	See below	See below	See below
SPECIAL DEFENSES:	Nil	Nil	Nil
MAGIC RESISTANCE:	Standard	Standard	Standard
INTELLIGENCE:	Animal	Average	Animal
ALIGNMENT:	Neutral	Neutral	Neutral
SIZE:	M	L	M
PSIONIC ABILITY:	Nil	Nil	Nil
Attack/Defense Modes:	Nil	Nil	Nil

Giant toads are found in most regions. Although their smaller cousins are beneficial insect eaters, the large toads are prone to devour any creature which appears edible. All toads are capable of hopping their movement distance. This hop clears objects up to one-third the linear distance in height, and it requires but a single melee round to accomplish, and they can attack in mid-air or at the end of their leap.

Ice Toad: These creatures are found in cold climes or far beneath the surface of the ground. In addition to their typical abilities these monsters are able to radiate cold in a 1'' radius from their body.

All non-cold using creatures within 1'' of the ice toad suffer 3-18 points of damage. The toad can do this but once every other melee round. The ice toads have their own weird language.

Poisonous Toad: The poisonous type of giant toad is indistinguishable from non-poisonous toads. Their bite necessitates a saving throw versus poison, or the victim will die immediately.

TRAPPER

FREQUENCY: Rare
NO. APPEARING: 1
ARMOR CLASS: 3
MOVE: 3''
HIT DICE: 12
% IN LAIR: 85%
TREASURE TYPE: G
NO. OF ATTACKS: 4+
DAMAGE/ATTACK: See below
SPECIAL ATTACKS: See below
SPECIAL DEFENSES: Standard
MAGIC RESISTANCE: Standard
INTELLIGENCE: Highly
ALIGNMENT: Neutral
SIZE: L
PSIONIC ABILITY: Nil
    Attack/Defense Modes: Nil

Trappers are clever monsters found only in caves, caverns, and other dark places. They prefer a subterranean habitation to all others. They shape their flat bodies to conform to the floor surface of their abode. Being of a consistency almost as hard as stone, trappers are nearly impossible to detect (95%) by any normal means. Usually a trapper will wait until its prey is near its center (where it often creates a protuberance which resembles a chest or box) and then suddenly closes itself upon the unsuspecting victims. The trapper then crushes them doing a base damage of 4 plus the armor class of the victim per turn of crushing. Those entrapped are unable to use weapons, for the great musculature of the trapper prevents it. Prey will be smothered in 6 melee rounds regardless of the damage sustained. It must be killed or faced with certain death to make it free its prey. Its treasure is kept beneath it. Trappers are resistant to fire and cold (half or no damage).

Description: Trappers are amorphous in form, so they are able to shape themselves to the form of the floors of the places they choose to await prey. A typical trapper is able to cover an area of up to 400 square feet, and giant specimens can cover as much as 600 square feet. The trapper also has the advantage of being able to alter its coloration to blend with the color of the floor or ground upon which it rests.

TREANT

FREQUENCY: *Rare*
NO. APPEARING: *1-20*
ARMOR CLASS: *0*
MOVE: *12"*
HIT DICE: *7-12*
% IN LAIR: *10%*
TREASURE TYPE: *Q (× 5), S*
NO. OF ATTACKS: *2*
DAMAGE/ATTACK: *2-16/3-18/4-24*
 (See below)
SPECIAL ATTACKS: *See below*
SPECIAL DEFENSES: *Never*
 surprised
MAGIC RESISTANCE: *Standard*
INTELLIGENCE: *Very*
ALIGNMENT: *Chaotic good*
SIZE: *L*
PSIONIC ABILITY: *Nil*
 Attack/Defense Modes: *Nil*

Treants are strangely related to humans and trees, combining features of both species. They dwell in woods and forests and are basically indistinguishable from trees. They hate evil things or unrestrained use of fire. If need arises treants can actually cause trees to come to life, move 3" per turn, and attack as a full-grown treant (2 attacks for 4-24 hit points of damage/attack). Aroused treants must be within 6" of a normal tree to cause it to move, and an individual treant can cause only one or two normal trees to move and attack as stipulated.

Because of their body and skin structures, treants have a very superior armor class rating. However, against fire they lose this superiority. Attacks based on fire are at a + 4 on "to hit" dice; treants save against such attacks at a -4, and fire damage dice are + 1 hit point.

Treants of small size (12'-15' tall) have 7 or 8 hit dice and do 2-16 hit points of damage/attack, middle-sized treants (16'-19') have 9-10 hit dice and attack damage of 3-18, and those of large size (20'-23'+) have 11-12 hit dice and do 4-24 points of damage. Treants and treant-controlled trees cause 1 point of structural damage on fortifications (this is for both attacks possible to any given treant or treant-controlled tree), regardless of the size of the treant attacking.

A treant lair will typically be a vast cave screened by many plants and trees. Treants resent greatly uninvited entrance into such a place.

TRITON

FREQUENCY: *Rare*
NO. APPEARING: *10-60*
ARMOR CLASS: *5*
MOVE: *15"*
HIT DICE: *3*
% IN LAIR: *25%*
TREASURE TYPE: *C, R, S, T, X*
NO. OF ATTACKS: *1*
DAMAGE/ATTACK: *By weapon type*
SPECIAL ATTACKS: *See below*
SPECIAL DEFENSES: *See below*
MAGIC RESISTANCE: *90%*
INTELLIGENCE: *High and up*
ALIGNMENT: *Neutral (good)*
SIZE: *M*
PSIONIC ABILITY: *See below*
 Attack/Defense Modes: *See below*

Tritons are rumored to be creatures from the elemental plane of water which have been planted on the material plane for some purpose presently unknown to man. They are sea dwellers, inhabiting warmer waters principally but equally able to live at shallow or great depths. They seldom venture forth upon dry land.

For every 10 tritons in a group encountered there will be an exceptional

one in addition, this triton having 4-6 hit dice. For every 20 tritons encountered there will be an exceptional triton with 7-8 hit dice. The leader of any group of tritons numbering 50 or more will have 9 hit dice. For every 10 tritons in a group there is a 10% chance that they will have with them 1-4 of their kind with magical ability of from 1st-6th level.

It is 90% likely that the tritons encountered will be mounted upon hippocampi (65%) or giant sea horses (35%).

If tritons are encountered in their lair there will always be the following additional figures:

> 60 males
> 6 exceptional males of 4-6 hit dice
> 3 exceptional males of 7-8 hit dice
> 1 magic-user of 7th-10th level
> 1 cleric of 8th-11th level
> 4 clerics of 2nd-5th level
> Females equal to 100% of males
> Young equal to 100% of males

There is also a 75% chance that there will be 2-12 sea lions as pets and guards. The triton lair will be an undersea castle (80%) or a sculpted cavern (20%).

Only male tritons will engage in combat, as a general rule. They will wear armor of scales which increases their protection to class 4. Mounted tritons bear long spears (lances) or tridents. The typical arms of a group of tritons are:

heavy crossbow & dagger	30%
sword & dagger	10%
spear & dagger	20%
trident & dagger	40%

Triton leaders will bear conch shell horns which will calm rough waters when blown a special way. These instruments are typically used as signal devices. The horns will, when blown properly, summon 5-20 hippocampi, 5-30 giant sea horses, or 1-10 sea lions. The conch shell horns can also cause marine creatures with animal intelligence or less to flee in panic — the creatures saving versus magic with a -5 on their "to hit" dice rolls — for 3-18 turns.

It is possible that psionically endowed tritons will be in any given group. 1 triton in 10 has a 5% chance of having psionic abilities of the sort applicable to magic-users. If a psionic individual is indicated, roll a 12-sided die for the number of abilities by random selection. Attack and defense modes are commensurate with potential, abilities, etc.

Tritons have their own language. They can also speak the tongue of sea elves and that of the locathah.

Description: Tritons have silvery skin which fades into silvery blue scales on their lower limbs. Their hair is deep blue or blue-green.

History: Tritons are known to serve the god, Triton, and little else is known about their purpose on the material plane. They have fought fierce wars with the sahuagin and skirmish continually with ixitxachitl, koalinths, and lacedons. They are generally well disposed towards humans who do not mean harm to the triton society.

TROGLODYTE

FREQUENCY: *Common*
NO. APPEARING: *10-100*
ARMOR CLASS: *5*
MOVE: *12″*
HIT DICE: *2*
% IN LAIR: *15%*
TREASURE TYPE: *A*
NO. OF ATTACKS: *3 or 1*
DAMAGE/ATTACK: *1-3/1-3/2-5 or*
   by weapon type
SPECIAL ATTACKS: *Revulsion odor*
SPECIAL DEFENSES: *See below*
MAGIC RESISTANCE: *Standard*
INTELLIGENCE: *Low*
ALIGNMENT: *Chaotic evil*
SIZE: *M*
PSIONIC ABILITY: *Nil*
   Attack/Defense Modes: *Nil*

Troglodytes are a race of reptilian humanoids who dwell in subterranean places. They loathe humans, and their aim is to slaughter all whom they encounter. Troglodytes have excellent infravision (90′).

For every 10 troglodytes encountered there will be 1 leader-type with 3 hit dice. For every 20 there will be an additional 2 leader types with 4 hit dice each. If 60 or more are encountered there will be a troglodyte chieftain with 6 hit dice, and 2-8 guards of 3 hit dice each.

The lair of a tribe of troglodytes is typically a large cave or cavern with small chambers adjoining it in which the individual units live. A lair will contain females equal to 100% of the males. Females fight as 1 + 1 hit dice monsters. There will also be hatchlings and eggs, but these are of no importance.

Troglodytes can attack with claws and teeth, but 50% of them use weapons of some type. The armed half of a group encountered will have:

javelin (2)	25%
battle axe (stone)	10%
morning star (stone)	10%
sword	5%

Their javelins are great vaned darts which have a +3 chance to hit when used by troglodytes and cause 2-8 hit points damage. They shun armor.

When aroused for battle, troglodytes emit a secretion which smells extremely disgusting to humans — including dwarves, elves, gnomes, half-elves and halflings. Those humans failing their saving throw versus poison are affected by revulsion so as to lose 1 point of strength per melee round for 1-6 rounds, cumulative. Loss of strength lasts 10 melee rounds after it has taken final effect.

Troglodytes have a chameleon-like power, so they can change their skin coloration to shades of gray, brown or green. They thus surprise on a 1-4 unless they are angry and excreting their stench. They use this coloration to hide when an encounter goes against them.

TROLL

FREQUENCY: *Uncommon*
NO. APPEARING: *1-12*
ARMOR CLASS: *4*
MOVE: *12″*
HIT DICE: *6 + 6*
% IN LAIR: *40%*
TREASURE TYPE: *D*
NO. OF ATTACKS: *3*
DAMAGE/ATTACK: *5-8/5-8/2-12*
SPECIAL ATTACKS: *See below*
SPECIAL DEFENSES: *Regeneration*
MAGIC RESISTANCE: *Standard*
INTELLIGENCE: *Low*
ALIGNMENT: *Chaotic evil*
SIZE: *L (9′ + tall)*
PSIONIC ABILITY: *Nil*
   Attack/Defense Modes: *Nil*

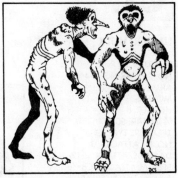

Trolls are horrid carnivores found in nearly every clime. They are feared by most creatures, as a troll knows no fear and attacks unceasingly. Their sense of smell is very acute, their infravision is superior (90′), and their strength is very great.

A troll attacks with its clawed forelimbs and its great teeth. A troll is able to fight 3 different opponents at once. 3 melee rounds after being damaged, a troll will begin to *regenerate*. Regeneration repairs damage at 3 hit points per round; this regeneration includes the rebonding of severed members. The loathsome members of a troll have the ability to fight on even if severed from the body; a hand can claw or strangle, the head bite, etc. Total dismemberment will not slay a troll, for its parts will slither and scuttle together, rejoin, and the troll will arise whole and ready to continue combat. To kill a troll, the monster must be burned or immersed in acid, any separate pieces being treated in the same fashion or they create a whole again in 3-18 melee rounds.

Description: Troll hide is a nauseating moss green, mottled green and gray, or putrid gray. The writhing hair-like growth upon a troll's head is greenish black or iron gray. The eyes of a troll are dull black.

TURTLE

	Sea, Giant	Snapping, Giant
FREQUENCY:	*Uncommon*	*Uncommon*
NO. APPEARING:	*1-3*	*1-4*
ARMOR CLASS:	*2/5*	*0/5*
MOVE:	*1″//15″*	*3″//2″*
HIT DICE:	*15*	*10*
% IN LAIR:	*0%*	*0%*
TREASURE TYPE:	*Nil*	*Nil*
NO. OF ATTACKS:	*1*	*1*
DAMAGE/ATTACK:	*4-16*	*6-24*
SPECIAL ATTACKS:	*Nil*	*See below*
SPECIAL DEFENSES:	*See below*	*See below*
MAGIC RESISTANCE:	*Standard*	*Standard*
INTELLIGENCE:	*Non-*	*Non-*
ALIGNMENT:	*Neutral*	*Neutral*
SIZE:	*L*	*L*
PSIONIC ABILITY:	*Nil*	*Nil*
Attack/Defense Modes:	*Nil*	*Nil*

Turtle, Sea, Giant: These basically non-aggressive marine creatures will fight fiercely if annoyed or threatened. If they surface beneath a small craft there is a possibility of upsetting the vessel, i.e. 90% for a long boat, 10% for a typical long ship. The head and flippers of the creature are armor class 5, but they can be withdrawn to make these areas armor class 3.

Turtle, Snapping, Giant: Feared greatly for their voracious appetite and aggressiveness, giant snapping turtles are found in lakes and large rivers. They lurk near shore or on the bottom, as they do not swim quickly. They remain motionless, thus surprising on 1-4 (out of 6), and then shoot forth their long neck (up to 10′ long) to grab their prey. The head and limbs of these monsters are armor class 5, but they can be withdrawn to offer armor class 2.

UMBER HULK — UNICORN

UMBER HULK

FREQUENCY: *Rare*
NO. APPEARING: *1-4*
ARMOR CLASS: *2*
MOVE: *6'' (1''-6'')*
HIT DICE: *8 + 8*
% IN LAIR: *30%*
TREASURE TYPE: *G*
NO. OF ATTACKS: *3*
DAMAGE/ATTACK: *3-12/3-12/2-10*
SPECIAL ATTACKS: *Confusion*
SPECIAL DEFENSES: *Nil*
MAGIC RESISTANCE: *Standard*
INTELLIGENCE: *Average*
ALIGNMENT: *Chaotic evil*
SIZE: *L (8' tall, 5' wide)*
PSIONIC ABILITY: *Nil*
   Attack/Defense Modes: *Nil*

Umber hulks are subterranean predators. Their iron-like claws enable them to burrow through solid stone at 1'' per turn and through loam at fully 6 times that rate. Their prey includes young purple worms, anhkheg, and similar monsters. However, the favorite prey of umber hulks are humans. They attack with claws and their powerful mandibles. Worse still, any intelligent creature which views the umber hulk's four eyes squarely must save versus magic or be confused for 3-12 melee rounds. These creatures have their own language.

Description: Umber hulks are black, shading to yellowish gray on the front. Their head is gray on top, and the mandibles are ivory colored. Because of their dark color they can easily be mistaken for some humanoid creature at 40' or more distance.

UNICORN

FREQUENCY: *Rare*
NO. APPEARING: *2-5*
ARMOR CLASS: *2*
MOVE: *24''*
HIT DICE: *4 + 4*
% IN LAIR: *5%*
TREASURE TYPE: *X*
NO. OF ATTACKS: *3*
DAMAGE/ATTACK: *1-6/1-6/1-12*
SPECIAL ATTACKS: *Charge*
SPECIAL DEFENSES: *See below*
MAGIC RESISTANCE: *See below*
INTELLIGENCE: *Average*
ALIGNMENT: *Chaotic good*
SIZE: *L*
PSIONIC ABILITY: *Nil*
   Attack/Defense Modes: *Nill*

Unicorns dwell only in temperate woodlands, away from human habitation. These fierce but good creatures shun contact with all creatures except sprites, dryads and the like. Elven and human maids of pure heart and good alignment may sometimes (25%) tame unicorns for use as steeds, and such are faithful, obedient mounts. Unicorns lair in open dells, their warded treasure kept in a nearby hollow tree, rocky niche, etc.

When a unicorn charges into combat it does not strike with its two front hooves, but its horn strikes for double damage (2-24). Because the unicorn is magical, its horn gains a bonus of +2 on ''to hit'' dice, and possession of a unicorn horn is a sovereign remedy against all forms of poison, gas included. Naturally, the unicorn is not subject to poison. A unicorn always senses the approach of an enemy at 24'' distance. They move very silently and surprise opponents on a 1-5. Once per day unicorns are able to use a *teleportation* spell of limited distance — a *dimension door* — to appear up to 36'' away from their former position. They may so teleport with a rider on their back.

Unicorns make all saving throws as if they were magic-users of the 11th level. They cannot be *charmed* or *held* by magic. Death spells do not affect them. They speak their own language.

VAMPIRE

VAMPIRE

FREQUENCY: *Rare*
NO. APPEARING: *1-4*
ARMOR CLASS: *1*
MOVE: *12"/18"*
HIT DICE: *8 + 3*
% IN LAIR: *25%*
TREASURE TYPE: *F*
NO. OF ATTACKS: *1*
DAMAGE/ATTACK: *5-10*
SPECIAL ATTACKS: *Energy drain*
SPECIAL DEFENSES: *+1 or better weapon to hit*
MAGIC RESISTANCE: *See below*
INTELLIGENCE: *Exceptional*
ALIGNMENT: *Chaotic evil*
SIZE: *M*
PSIONIC ABILITY: *Nil*
    Attack/Defense Modes: *Nil*

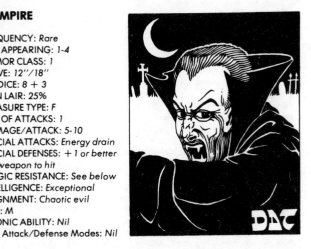

The most dreaded of the chaotic evil undead is the night-prowling vampire. These creatures must rest in a coffin or similar receptacle during hours of sunlight unless far beneath the surface of the ground, and in the latter case they must occasionally return to such rest, for their power is restored by contact with soil from their grave. Like all undead, vampires exist in two planes at once — in this case the material and negative material. Vampires have 18/76 strength.

If a vampire scores a hit upon an opponent, its powerful blow causes 5-10 points of damage, and its powerful negative force drains 2 life energy levels from the victim, complete with corresponding losses in hit dice, ability level, attack level, etc.

Vampires are affected only by magical weapons. They regenerate damage at 3 hit points per melee round. If brought to 0 hit points by combat, the vampire is not killed, but it is forced into *gaseous form*. It must then return to its coffin within 12 turns, rest 8 hours, and reform a corporeal body.

Sleep, charm, and *hold* spells do not affect vampires. Neither do poison or paralysis. Vampires take only one-half damage from spells based on cold or electricity.

A vampire can assume *gaseous form* at will. Likewise, a vampire can

shape change into a large bat whenever desired — thus the flying movement shown for this monster. If it gazes into a person's eyes, the vampire will have the effect of *charming,* with the victim subtracting 2 from the saving throw versus magic. Charmed persons behave as if they had been successfully struck with a *charm person* spell. All vampires also have the ability to *summon* creatures to aid them; in subterranean surroundings usually 10 to 100 rats or bats (the latter only confusing and obscuring opponents' vision, not physically attacking), and in wilderness surroundings typically 3-18 wolves. These creatures come within 2-12 melee rounds.

Vampires recoil from strong garlic, the face of a mirror, or a cross (or several other holy symbols of lawful good) if any of these objects are presented boldly. Note, however, that none of these devices harm or drive the monster off. They do cause a vampire to hesitate 1 to 4 rounds before attacking in the case of garlic; a mirror or holy symbol will cause a vampire to position itself so that the object is not between the vampire and its intended victim — or the vampire will have one of its creatures remove the device whose power is keeping it at bay. It must be stressed that lawful good holy symbols such as the cross are sovereign against vampires of all sorts, regardless of the religious background of the vampire in its human existence.

A vampire can be slain by the following methods: exposure to direct sunlight kills the creature in 1 turn, and it becomes powerless immediately. A vampire immersed in running water for 3 melee rounds is killed. The vampire loses one-third of its hit points per round of immersion. If a wooden stake is driven through a vampire's heart it is killed, but only for so long as the stake remains; to finish this task the vampire's head must also be cut off and its mouth filled with holy wafers.

Holy water splashed upon a vampire causes 2-7 hit points of damage per vial-full which strikes the monster.

Any human or humanoid drained of all life energy by a vampire becomes an appropriately strengthed vampire under control of its slayer. This transformation takes place 1 day after the creature is buried, but if and only if the creature is buried. Thus it is possible to have a vampiric thief, cleric (chaotic evil in vampire form, of course), etc. If the vampire which slew the creature is itself killed, the vampires created by it become free-willed monsters.

Vampires of the eastern world are invisible. This gives them all appropriate consideration for invisibility, including a -2 on "to hit" dice rolls for opponents not able to see invisible objects. These vampires cannot *charm,* however, nor do they have power to assume *gaseous form* at will.

WASP, GIANT — WATER WEIRD — WEASEL, GIANT — WHALE — WIGHT — WILL-O-WISP — WIND WALKER — WOLF — WOLVERINE — WRAITH — WYVERN

WASP, *Giant*

FREQUENCY: *Rare*
NO. APPEARING: *1-20*
ARMOR CLASS: *4*
MOVE: *6"/21"*
HIT DICE: *4*
% IN LAIR: *25%*
TREASURE TYPE: *Q (× 20)*
NO. OF ATTACKS: *2*
DAMAGE/ATTACK: *2-8/1-4*
SPECIAL ATTACKS: *Poison*
SPECIAL DEFENSES: *Nil*
MAGIC RESISTANCE: *Standard*
INTELLIGENCE: *Non-*
ALIGNMENT: *Neutral*
SIZE: *M*
PSIONIC ABILITY: *Nil*
    Attack/Defense Modes: *Nil*

Giant wasps are feared because they continually hunt for prey — both to

devour and to place in a paralyzed state with their eggs. Other giant insects are most often victims, but even humans are not immune. Certain wasps build mud cases for their eggs, but those which build paper nests are the ones which are most feared, for their lair will contain 21-40 adult wasps. A giant wasp attacks with both its powerful jaws and its poisonous sting. It can use the latter weapon repeatedly. Any victim of a sting must save versus poison or become paralyzed permanently, with death occurring in 2-5 days unless a *neutralize poison* spell or antidote is applied. (Victims are typically eaten by the wasp larvae in the 2-5 day period.) Wasp wings are very vulnerable to fire, and they will immediately be burned off if within the radius of a *fire ball* or even exposed to hot flame. This does not injure the wasp, but it makes the creature flightless.

WATER WEIRD

FREQUENCY: *Very rare*
NO. APPEARING: *1-3*
ARMOR CLASS: *4*
MOVE: *12"*
HIT DICE: *3 + 3*
% IN LAIR: *50%*
TREASURE TYPE: *I, O, P, Y*
NO. OF ATTACKS: *0*
DAMAGE/ATTACK: *Nil*
SPECIAL ATTACKS: *Drowning*
SPECIAL DEFENSES: *See below*
MAGIC RESISTANCE: *Standard*
INTELLIGENCE: *Very*
ALIGNMENT: *Chaotic evil*
SIZE: *L (10'+ long)*
PSIONIC ABILITY: *Nil*
    Attack/Defense Modes: *Nil*

The water weird are a life form originating in the elemental plane of water. They attack all living things, feeding from their essences in some unknown manner. The creature forms in two melee rounds from the water, appearing as a serpent, and lashes out, striking as a 6 hit dice monster. Any creature struck will be dragged into the water unless it saves versus paralyzation. Sharp weapons cause but 1 hit point of damage; blunt ones cause normal damage when striking these monsters. Damage equal to its total hit points disrupts the water weird; it reforms again in 2 melee rounds. Cold spells slow it, *fire-based* spells do half or no damage, but a *purify water* spell actually kills. All other attacks simply do not harm or disrupt the creature. A water weird can take over a water elemental on a dice score of 11 or better on a 20-sided die.

WEASEL, *Giant*

FREQUENCY: *Rare*
NO. APPEARING: *1-8*
ARMOR CLASS: *6*
MOVE: *15"*
HIT DICE: *3 + 3*
% IN LAIR: *15%*
TREASURE TYPE: *Nil*
NO. OF ATTACKS: *1*
DAMAGE/ATTACK: *2-12*
SPECIAL ATTACKS: *Drain blood*
SPECIAL DEFENSES: *Nil*
MAGIC RESISTANCE: *Standard*
INTELLIGENCE: *Animal*
ALIGNMENT: *Neutral*
SIZE: *M*
PSIONIC ABILITY: *Nil*
    Atttack/Defense Modes: *Nil*

Giant weasels are very vicious and hunt prey aggressively. They will attack until destroyed. They favor woodlands but also roam subterranean places in hunting.

In addition to its bite, a giant weasel drains blood, for on the melee round after it successfully bites an opponent, it does not release its jaws, but instead the giant weasel sucks the blood from the victim at a rate of 2-12 hit points of damage per melee round.

If taken before half-grown, and carefully trained, giant weasels can sometimes (25%) be used as hunting animals and guards. When encountered in their lair, there will always be 4 or more giant weasels — 2 parents and young from 10% to 80% mature. The young also attack, doing damage appropriate to their development.

Weasel pelts sell for 1,000 to 6,000 gold pieces.

WHALE

FREQUENCY: *Common*
NO. APPEARING: *1-8*
ARMOR CLASS: *4*
MOVE: *18" to 24"*
HIT DICE: *12 to 36*
% IN LAIR: *0%*
TREASURE TYPE: *See below*
NO. OF ATTACKS: *1 or 1*
DAMAGE/ATTACK: *5-20 to 15-60 or*
   1-8 to 5-40
SPECIAL ATTACKS: *Tail*
SPECIAL DEFENSES: *Nil*
MAGIC RESISTANCE: *Standard*
INTELLIGENCE: *Low*
ALIGNMENT: *Neutral*
SIZE: *L*
PSIONIC ABILITY: *Nil*
    Attack/Defense Modes: *Nil*

Whales great and small (for whales) populate the oceans. Many are plant-eaters, but a few are carnivores. The latter will occasionally attack humans (killer whales will always do so), and all forms of whales are very dangerous if molested. The carnivorous whales attack by biting (5-20 to 15-60, depending on size). Other whales use their great flukes to smash opponents (1-8 to 5-40, based on size). Whales at the surface can smash with their tails, causing damage equal to half their number of hit dice to any creature struck. Carnivorous whales will swallow prey whole, the huge (36 hit dice) sperm whale being able to swallow a long boat and its crew whole and alive. (While it is not too difficult to then escape, digestive juices will cause 1 point of damage per turn, and if the whale disgorges the prey swallowed alive due to their irritation of its stomach, there is a 50% chance this will be done at considerable depth.)

The stomach of a carnivorous whale can contain treasure. A 1% per hit die chance is allowed for each coin type, gems, jewelry, and magic items. The number of coins is 1,000-3,000 per type. Gems and jewelry will number from 1-20 each. 1-4 magic items can be contained. Sick whales give forth ambergris, a stinking mess which is worth 1,000 to 20,000 gold pieces in a large city. A whale carcass can be sold in a port for 100 gold pieces per hit die of size.

WIGHT

FREQUENCY: *Uncommon*
NO. APPEARING: *2-16*
ARMOR CLASS: *5*
MOVE: *12"*
HIT DICE: *4 + 3*
% IN LAIR: *70%*
TREASURE TYPE: *B*
NO. OF ATTACKS: *1*
DAMAGE/ATTACK: *1-4*
SPECIAL ATTACKS: *Energy drain*
SPECIAL DEFENSES: *Silver or magic weapons to hit*
MAGIC RESISTANCE: *See below*
INTELLIGENCE: *Average*
ALIGNMENT: *Lawful evil*
SIZE: *M*
PSIONIC ABILITY: *Nil*
    Attack/Defense Modes: *Nil*

The term wight has lost its old meaning of a person and come to stand for those undead humans who typically inhabit barrow mounds or catacombs. These creatures are most evil and hateful, seeking to destroy any life form they encounter. Wights shun bright lights and hate sunlight.

Because these monsters exist simultaneously on the normal and negative planes of the material plane, they are affected only by silver or magical weapons. This existence allows them to drain life energy levels — one such level each time they score a hit on an opponent. The creature so hit loses the hit points of damage scored (1-4) plus one experience level and all the bonuses derived from that level, i.e. hit dice, class bonuses, thief abilities, spell levels, etc. A 9th level magic user struck by a wight loses 1-4 hit points and he becomes an 8th level magic user; he has the spells and the hit points of an 8th level magic user, and he melees as an 8th level character of his class.

Wights are not affected by *sleep, charm, hold,* or *cold*-based spells. Neither poison nor paralyzation harms wights. Holy water causes 2-8 hit points of damage for every vial-full which strikes. A *raise dead* spell will destroy a wight. Any human totally drained of life energy by a wight will become a half-strength wight under control of its slayer.

WILL-O-(THE)-WISP

FREQUENCY: *Uncommon*
NO. APPEARING: *1 (or 1-3)*
ARMOR CLASS: *-8*
MOVE: *18"*
HIT DICE: *9*
% IN LAIR: *5%*
TREASURE TYPE: *Z*
NO. OF ATTACKS: *1*
DAMAGE/ATTACK: *2-16*
SPECIAL ATTACKS: *See below*
SPECIAL DEFENSES: *See below*
MAGIC RESISTANCE: *See below*
INTELLIGENCE: *Exceptional*
ALIGNMENT: *Chaotic evil*
SIZE: *S*
PSIONIC ABILITY: *Nil*
    Attack/Defense Modes: *Nil*

Will-o-wisps commonly haunt deserted, dangerous places such as bogs, fens, swamps, or catacombs where mires, quicksand, pit traps and the like are plentiful. A victim trapped by these hazards feeds the will-o-wisp as it expires, for the thing feeds upon the fleeing life force. Thus, will-o-wisps seek to lure prey to their doom. 10% of the time 1-3 are encountered, and in these cases the creatures' lair will be nearby 90% of the time. The creature can attack, however, any hit causing 2-16 points of electrical damage to the opponent.

A will-o-wisp is able to grow bright or very dim in order to confuse prey. It can move slowly or flit about. It can blank out its glow entirely for 2-8 melee rounds if it does not attack, and at that time it can be detected only by creatures able to see invisible objects.

While any weapon will harm a will-o-wisp, most spells do not affect it. The only spells which can affect the creature are *protection from evil, magic missile* and *maze*. If brought to 5 or fewer remaining hit points a will-o-wisp will reveal its lair and give over its treasure.

Description: A will-o-wisp is a glowing sphere, looking like a lantern, torch or even a *dancing lights* spell effect. In combat they glow blue, violet or pale green.

WIND WALKER

FREQUENCY: *Rare*
NO. APPEARING: *1-3*
ARMOR CLASS: *7*
MOVE: *15"/30"*
HIT DICE: *6 + 3*
% IN LAIR: *20%*
TREASURE TYPE: *C, R*
NO. OF ATTACKS: *See below*
DAMAGE/ATTACK: *3-18*
SPECIAL ATTACKS: *See below*
SPECIAL DEFENSES: *See below*
MAGIC RESISTANCE: *See below*
INTELLIGENCE: *Very*
ALIGNMENT: *Neutral*
SIZE: *L*
PSIONIC ABILITY: *Nil*
    Attack/Defense Modes: *Nil*

Wind walkers are creatures from the elemental plane of air, and on the material plane prefer to live high in mountains or in great caverns very far below the surface. Their approach is detectable at from 10"-30" as a whistling, howling or roaring depending on the number coming. These monsters are telepathic and can detect thoughts within 10"-30" (as they work in series to boost range).

They attack by wind force, each wind walker causing 3-18 points of damage per turn to all creatures within 1" of them who are hit.

Being ethereal, wind walkers can be fought only by such creatures as djinn, efreet, invisible stalkers, or aerial servants, or affected by spells such as *control weather* (unless save is made versus magic, the monster dies), *slow* (affects monster like a fire ball), and *ice storm* (drives them away for 1-4 melee rounds). *Haste* does one-half damage to wind

walkers, but it also doubles the amount of damage done by the wind walkers. Magical barriers will stop them, but wind walkers will otherwise pursue for 2-5 melee rounds minimum. They are subject to attack by *telepathy*. Wind walkers are sometimes forced into servitude by storm giants (for obvious reasons).

WOLF

	Wolf	Wolf, Dire (Worg)	Wolf, Winter
FREQUENCY:	Common	Rare	Very rare
NO. APPEARING:	2-20	3-12	2-8
ARMOR CLASS:	7	6	5
MOVE:	18"	18"	18"
HIT DICE:	2 + 2	3 + 3 (4 + 4)	6
% IN LAIR:	10%	10%	10%
TREASURE TYPE:	Nil	Nil	I
NO. OF ATTACKS:	1	1	1
DAMAGE/ATTACK:	2-5	2-8	2-8
SPECIAL ATTACKS:	Nil	Nil	Frost
SPECIAL DEFENSES:	Nil	Nil	Nil
MAGIC RESISTANCE:	Standard	Standard	Standard
INTELLIGENCE:	Semi-	Semi- (low)	Average
ALIGNMENT:	Neutral	Neutral (evil)	Neutral (evil)
SIZE:	S	M (L)	L
PSIONIC ABILITY:	Nil	Nil	Nil
Attack/Defense Modes:	Nil	Nil	Nil

Wolf: These carnivores are found in wild forests from the arctic to the temperate zones. They always hunt in packs and if hungry (75%) they will not hesitate to follow and attack prey, always seeking to strike at an unguarded moment. Their howling is 50% likely to panic herbivores which are not being held by humans and calmed. They love horsemeat. If encountered in their lair there is a 30% chance that there will be 1-4 cubs per pair of adult wolves. Cubs do not fight and can be trained as war dogs or hunting beasts.

Wolf, Dire: This variety of wolf is simply a huge specimen typical of the Pleistocene Epoch. They conform to the characteristics of normal wolves. **(Worgs):** Evil natured, neo-dire wolves are known as worgs. These creatures have a language and are often found in co-operation with goblins in order to gain prey or to simply enjoy killing. They are as large as ponies and can be ridden. They otherwise conform to the characteristics of wolves.

Wolf, Winter: The winter wolf is a horrid carnivore which inhabits only chill regions. It is of great size and foul disposition. Winter wolves can use their savage jaws or howl forth a blast of frost which will coat any creature within 1" of their muzzle. This frost causes 6-24 hit points damage — half that amount if a saving throw versus dragon breath is successful. The winter wolf is able to use the howling frost but once per 10 melee rounds. Cold-based attacks do not harm them, but fire-based attacks cause +1 per die of damage normally caused. They have their own language and can also converse with worgs. The coat of the winter wolf is glistening white or silvery, and its eyes are very pale blue or silvery. The pelt of the creature is valued at 5,000 gold pieces.

WOLVERINE

	Wolverine	Wolverine, Giant
FREQUENCY:	Uncommon	Rare
NO. APPEARING:	1	1
ARMOR CLASS:	5	4
MOVE:	12"	15"
HIT DICE:	3	4 + 4
% IN LAIR:	15%	15%
TREASURE TYPE:	Nil	Nil
NO. OF ATTACKS:	3	3
DAMAGE/ATTACK:	1-4/1-4/2-5	2-5/2-5/2-8
SPECIAL ATTACKS:	Musk	Musk
SPECIAL DEFENSES:	Nil	Nil
MAGIC RESISTANCE:	Standard	Standard
INTELLIGENCE:	Semi-	Semi-
ALIGNMENT:	Neutral (evil)	Neutral (evil)
SIZE:	S	M
PSIONIC ABILITY:	Nil	Nil
Attack/Defense Modes:	Nil	Nil

Wolverines inhabit only colder regions (which is fortunate for mankind, for these animals are horrible). They are vicious, hateful, destructive carnivores who kill for the sheer love of ending another creature's life. Bears and wolves respect these creatures' ferocity. Their speed is partially responsible for their high armor class, and their ferocity in combat makes their attacks have a +4 on ''to hit'' dice rolls: A wolverine can squirt its disgusting musk at any opponent at its rear. The musk is equivalent to that of a skunk (q.v.). A wolverine will purposefully destroy food or human goods of any sort by spraying musk upon the unwanted items. Although only semi-intelligent in most things, in hunting and combat the creature is exceptionally intelligent.

WRAITH

FREQUENCY: *Uncommon*
NO. APPEARING: *2-12*
ARMOR CLASS: *4*
MOVE: *12''/24''*
HIT DICE: *5 + 3*
% IN LAIR: *25%*
TREASURE TYPE: *E*
NO. OF ATTACKS: *1*
DAMAGE/ATTACK: *1-6*
SPECIAL ATTACKS: *Energy drain*
SPECIAL DEFENSES: *Silver or magic weapons to hit*
MAGIC RESISTANCE: *See below*
INTELLIGENCE: *Very*
ALIGNMENT: *Lawful evil*
SIZE: *M*
PSIONIC ABILITY: *Nil*
    Attack/Defense Modes: *Nil*

Wraiths are undead, similar in nature to wights, but they exist more strongly on the negative material plane. They are found only in dark and gloomy places, for they have no power in full sunlight.

In addition to the chilling effect of its touch (1-6 hit points damage), a wraith drains on life energy at the rate of 1 per hit, just as a wight does. Similarly, the wraith can be struck only with silver weapons (which cause only one-half damage) or weapons which are magically enchanted (which score full damage).

XORN

XORN

FREQUENCY: *Very rare*
NO. APPEARING: *1-4*
ARMOR CLASS: *-2*
MOVE: *9''*
HIT DICE: *7 + 7*
% IN LAIR: *40%*
TREASURE TYPE: *O, P, Q (× 5), X, Y*
NO. OF ATTACKS: *4*
DAMAGE/ATTACK: *1-3 (×3), 6-24*
SPECIAL ATTACKS: *Surprise on a 1-5*
SPECIAL DEFENSES: *See below*
MAGIC RESISTANCE: *Standard*
INTELLIGENCE: *Average*
ALIGNMENT: *Neutral*
SIZE: *M (5' tall)*
PSIONIC ABILITY: *Nil*
    Attack/Defense Modes: *Nil*

The xorn are a race of creatures found on the elemental plane of earth, but on rare occasions they will abide on the material plane for a time. When so doing, they seek deep subterranean places. Xorn feed on certain rare minerals which are the subject of their quest on the material plane.

The jaws of xorn are very powerful, and as the creature blends with stone

Wraiths are unaffected by *sleep, charm, hold,* or *cold*-based spells. Poison or paralysis are likewise ineffective, but holy water splashed upon a wraith will cause 2-8 hit points of damage for each vial full which hits. A *raise dead* spell will slay a wraith. If a wraith drains all life energy levels from a human (including dwarves, elves, gnomes, half-elves, or even halflings) the victim becomes a half-strength wraith under the control of the wraith which drained the victim.

WYVERN

FREQUENCY: *Uncommon*
NO. APPEARING: *1-6*
ARMOR CLASS: *3*
MOVE: *6''/24''*
HIT DICE: *7 + 7*
% IN LAIR: *30%*
TREASURE TYPE: *E*
NO. OF ATTACKS: *2*
DAMAGE/ATTACK: *2-16/1-6*
SPECIAL ATTACKS: *Poison*
SPECIAL DEFENSES: *Nil*
MAGIC RESISTANCE: *Standard*
INTELLIGENCE: *Low*
ALIGNMENT: *Neutral (evil)*
SIZE: *L (35' long)*
PSIONIC ABILITY: *Nil*
    Attack/Defense Modes: *Nil*

Wyverns are distantly related to dragons. These monsters also inhabit places favored by dragons — tangled forests, great caverns, and the like. They are rather stupid, but very aggressive, and wyverns will always attack.

The wyvern bites (2-16) and lashes with its sting-equipped tail at one or two opponents. Any creature struck by this tail must save versus poison or die. Even if the victim makes its saving throw, it takes 1-6 points of damage. Note that the tail is very long and mobile, easily striking over the back of the wyvern to hit an opponent before its front.

Description: Wyverns are dark brown to gray. Their eyes are orange or red.

— both in color and conformation and as a physical capability — it is very likely to surprise any other creature. The xorn is likely to demand such metals as copper, silver, etc. to snack upon, and if a passing creature refuses, the xorn is 90% likely to try to take the metal by force, for it can smell such at 20' distance.

These creatures are not harmed by *fire* or *cold*-based spells. Electrical attacks, such as lightning bolts, do either one-half or no damage, depending on the saving throw. They are flung back 3'' and stunned one melee round by a *move earth* spell, a *stone to flesh* or *rock to mud* spell will lower their armor class to 8 for 1 melee round (and the xorn cannot attack during that time as they must adjust their molecules), and a *passwall* spell delivers 11-20 hit points of damage to the creatures.

If a combat is going against a xorn, it will stop fighting, adjust its molecular structure, and pass through the nearest stone (usually the floor) to escape. This requires one melee round, and thereafter the xorn can progress at normal movement through solid stone, earth, or similar substances. If it is struck by a *phase door* spell when in this state a xorn is killed.

YETI

FREQUENCY: *Very rare*
NO. APPEARING: *1-6*
ARMOR CLASS: *6*
MOVE: *15''*
HIT DICE: *4 + 4*
% IN LAIR: *10%*
TREASURE TYPE: *D*
NO. OF ATTACKS: *2*
DAMAGE/ATTACK: *1-6/1-6*
SPECIAL ATTACKS: *See below*
SPECIAL DEFENSES: *Impervious to cold*
MAGIC RESISTANCE: *Standard*
INTELLIGENCE: *Average*
ALIGNMENT: *Neutral*
SIZE: *L (8' tall)*
PSIONIC ABILITY: *Nil*
    Attack/Defense Modes: *Nil*

Inhabiting only regions of icy cold, yeti are seldom encountered by warm-blooded mankind. Those who do have the misfortune to stumble upon these monsters seldom live to tell the tale, for yeti are very fond of human flesh.

Yeti attacks with two clawing strikes, and if any one of these attacks succeeds with a die score of 20 the yeti has grabbed and squeezed his opponent for 2-16 points of additional damage from the chill of the creature. Worse still, if the creature surprised an opponent, a saving throw versus paralyzation must be made, or the victim has looked into the creature's eyes and is rigid with fright for 3 melee rounds and can be automatically struck twice and squeezed by the yeti.

Yeti are nearly invisible until within 10' to 30' of their prey. (For each level above 1st add 5% chance of spotting a yeti at normal distance, i.e. a 2nd level character has a 5% chance of spotting one.)

Because of their adaption to cold, yeti are very susceptible to fire, and attacks employing such heat do 50% greater damage.

If found in their lair there is a 30% chance that there are 1-3 females there also, and a 15% chance of an additional 2-5 young if females are present.

Description: These bulky, 300+ pound, creatures are covered in long white fur. Their eyes are pale blue or almost colorless. Their claws and teeth are ivory white.

ZOMBIE

FREQUENCY: *Rare*
NO. APPEARING: *3-24*
ARMOR CLASS: *8*
MOVE: *6''*
HIT DICE: *2*
% IN LAIR: *Nil*
TREASURE TYPE: *Nil*
NO. OF ATTACKS: *1*
DAMAGE/ATTACK: *1-8*
SPECIAL ATTACKS: *Nil*
SPECIAL DEFENSES: *Nil*
MAGIC RESISTANCE: *See below*
INTELLIGENCE: *Non-*
ALIGNMENT: *Neutral*
SIZE: *M*
PSIONIC ABILITY: *Nil*
    Attack/Defense Modes: *Nil*

Zombies are magically animated corpses, undead creatures under the command of the evil magic-users or clerics who animated them. These creatures follow commands — as spoken on the spot or as given previously — of limited length and complication (a dozen words or so). Zombies are typically found near graveyards, in dungeons, and in similar charnel places.

Zombies are slow, always striking last, but always doing 1-8 hit points of damage when they hit. They always fight until destroyed and nothing short of a cleric can turn them back.

Sleep, charm, hold and *cold*-based spells do not affect zombies. Holy water vials score 2-8 hit points of damage for each one which strikes.

APPENDIX

TREASURE TYPES

Treasure Type	1,000's of Copper	1,000's of Silver	1,000's of Electrum	1,000's of Gold	100's of Platinum	Gems	Jewelry	Maps or Magic
A	1-6 :25%	1-6 :30%	1-6 :35%	1-10:40%	1-4 :25%	4-40 :60%	3-30:50%	Any 3: 30%
B	1-8 :50%	1-6 :25%	1-4 :25%	1-3 :25%	nil	1-8 :30%	1-4 :20%	Sword, armor, or misc. weapon: 10%
C	1-12:20%	1-6 :30%	1-4 :10%	nil	nil	1-6 :25%	1-3 :20%	Any 2: 10%
D	1-8 :10%	1-12 :15%	1-8 :15%	1-6 :50%	nil	1-10 :30%	1-6 :25%	Any 2 plus 1 potion: 15%
E	1-10: 5%	1-12 :25%	1-6 :25%	1-8 :25%	nil	1-12 :15%	1-8 :10%	Any 3 plus 1 scroll: 25%
F	nil	1-20 :10%	1-12:15%	1-10:40%	1-8 :35%	3-30 :20%	1-10:10%	Any 3 except swords or misc. weapons, plus 1 potion & 1 scroll: 30%
G	nil	nil	nil	10-40:50%	1-20:50%	5-20 :30%	1-10:25%	Any 4 plus 1 scroll: 35%
H	5-30:25%	1-100:40%	10-40:40%	10-60:55%	5-50:25%	1-100:50%	10-40:50%	Any 4 plus 1 potion & 1 scroll: 15%
I	nil	nil	nil	nil	3-18:30%	2-20 :55%	1-12:50%	Any 1: 15%
J	3-24 pieces per individual	nil	nil	nil	nil	nil	nil	nil
K	nil	3-18 pieces per individual	nil	nil	nil	nil	nil	nil
L	nil	nil	2-12 pieces per individual	nil	nil	nil	nil	nil
M	nil	nil	nil	2-8 pieces per individual	nil	nil	nil	nil
N	nil	nil	nil	nil	1-6 pieces per individual	nil	nil	nil
O	1-4 :25%	1-3 :20%	nil	nil	nil	nil	nil	nil
P	nil	1-6 :30%	1-2 :25%	nil	nil	nil	nil	nil
Q	nil	nil	nil	nil	nil	1-4 :50%	nil	nil
R	nil	nil	nil	2-8 :40%	10-60:50%	4-32 :55%	1-12:45%	nil
S	nil	nil	nil	nil	nil	nil	nil	2-8 potions: 40%
T	nil	nil	nil	nil	nil	nil	nil	1-4 scrolls: 50%
U	nil	nil	nil	nil	nil	10-80 :90%	5-30:80%	1 of each magic excluding potions & scrolls: 70%
V	nil	nil	nil	nil	nil	nil	nil	2 of each magic excluding potions & scrolls: 85%
W	nil	nil	nil	5-30:60%	1-8 :15%	10-80 :60%	5-40:50%	1 map: 55%
X	nil	nil	nil	nil	nil	nil	nil	1 misc. magic plus 1 potion: 60%
Y	nil	nil	nil	2-12:70%	nil	nil	nil	nil
Z	1-3 :20%	1-4 :25%	1-4 :25%	1-4 :30%	1-6 :30%	10-60 :55%	5-30:50%	Any 3 magic: 50%

INDEX OF MAJOR LISTINGS

E

F

G

H

I

J

K

L

M

N

O

P

DCS

TSR, Inc.
PRODUCTS OF YOUR IMAGINATION